IMPOSTRESS

IMPOSTRESS

The Dishonest Adventures of Sarah Wilson

R. J. CLARKE

The History Press

Cover illustration: Eleonora Gustafa Bonde af Björnö, Jakob Björk
(Finnish National Gallery/Wikimedia Commons)

First published 2019

The History Press
The Mill, Brimscombe Port
Stroud, Gloucestershire, GL5 2QG
www.thehistorypress.co.uk

British Library Cataloguing in Publication Data.
A catalogue record for this book is available from the British Library.

ISBN 978 0 7509 8992 3

Typesetting and origination by The History Press
Printed and bound in Great Britain by TJ International Ltd

CONTENTS

PRELUDE

Frensham

This story begins where the first newspaper account of our heroine begins: in a poor and dangerous area of desolate moorland, wild heaths and dark woods on the Surrey–Hampshire border close to the Devil's Punchbowl, the haunt of footpads and highwaymen waiting to waylay travellers where the London-to-Portsmouth road crossed those uninhabited wastes.

This was where a sailor travelling along the Portsmouth road was murdered by three men who, 'with their knives mangled his body in several parts, much too shocking to relate, and then nearly severed his head from his body'. As an indication of how lawless this isolated area was, on the very same day that murder took place, there was another entirely separate incident just 2 miles up the road. Two men attacked a lone traveller, threw him to the ground, stuffed his mouth with sand and robbed him of half a guinea.[1] The three men who murdered the sailor were caught, found guilty and executed. Their bodies were hung in chains on Gibbet Hill close to where the murder was committed, their rotting corpses serving as a warning to others.[2]

Smugglers passed through here on their way to London from the south coast. The wildness of the terrain, with its hills and hollows, rendered it uninviting to strangers and ideal for concealing contraband.[3] William Cobbett described it as 'certainly the most villainous spot that God had ever made.'[4] When Arthur Conan Doyle moved into the area many years later, after Hindhead had become fashionable, he used the local landscape as the inspiration for his book *The Hound of the Baskervilles*.

Thomas Boxall lived with his wife, Flora, and their son, also named Thomas, about a mile from the Devil's Punchbowl down a rough sandy track on the heathland in an area called Witmore (now Whitmore) in the south of the hamlet of Churt in the parish of Frensham.[5] They supplemented their small income from grazing cattle on the poor vegetation by selling brooms that they made from the birch and purple heather that grew nearby.

It was late autumn 1764 when a most surprising visitor arrived at Thomas Boxall's door. Instead of the rough countryfolk he might have expected to come knocking, his visitor was a young woman in her late teens or early twenties. She was petite and slender. Her jet-black hair contrasted with her pale complexion. The only thing that marred the beauty of her face was a speck or blemish in her right eye.

She was unaccompanied and appeared to have wandered off the main Portsmouth Road, lost and alone. She asked Thomas whether there was anywhere that offered accommodation. There was nowhere nearby, and as it was the time of the year when it got dark early and the nights grew cold, Thomas considered it unsafe to let a young woman wander alone in the dark, so he decided to offer her shelter for that night.

As they sat by the fire the young lady told him her name was Sarah Willsbrowson. She said she was the daughter of a nobleman. She had been forced from her father's house by ill-treatment and needed a temporary place to stay. This sad story so affected the farmer that he agreed that she could stay longer than the one night if she wished.

The Boxalls grew to enjoy Sarah's company. She appeared to be a very pleasant and well-spoken young lady. During the course of one of their fireside chats she let slip that she had a fortune of £90,000 that she would be able to get her hands on once she had spoken to the person in London who was holding it on her behalf.

Thomas's son, at 17, was slightly younger than Sarah, and it seemed that they were growing increasingly fond of each other – although whether his fondness was further aroused by the information about her fortune is unclear. However, one day Sarah told Thomas the elder that the best return she had in her power for the favours she had received in his household would be for her to marry his son if that was agreeable to them both. Both Thomases were overjoyed at the proposal. They arranged for the wedding to be held at St Mary's church in Frensham village.

The banns were read on three successive Sundays. As no one declared that they knew of any cause or just impediment why they should not be joined together in holy matrimony, Thomas Boxall and Sarah Charlotte Lewsearn Willsbrowson, both of the parish of Frensham, were married at St Mary's on 17 December 1764. Thomas and Sarah signed their names in the wedding register, although Sarah missed out the 'ow' in Willsbrowson and had to add the 'ow' above the line. Thomas's father acted as witness and signed his name with an X.

In line with the practice at the time, the ceremony took place in the morning. As the news of Thomas's good fortune spread round the neighbourhood, a great crowd of villagers would have been waiting outside the church door, curious to see his bride and ready to throw handfuls of grain over the couple to wish them a fruitful union. It is likely that they used the wedding as an excuse for revelry, with a wedding breakfast, a fiddle player, dancing and sports.

Some days after the wedding, Sarah told her father-in-law that she had great interest at court, and if he could raise money to 'equip them in a genteel manner' she could procure a colonel's commission for her husband and at the same time she would be able to claim her fortune.

Old Thomas mortgaged his little estate for £100. Thomas and Sarah used some of the money to buy some fashionable clothes, probably from Farnham. Once they bought all that they needed for their journey to London, Thomas and Sarah took the rest of the money and set off, accompanied by three of Thomas's friends.

They arrived at the Bear Inn in the Borough on Christmas Eve, where they lived for about ten days 'in an expensive manner'. Each morning Sarah went out in a coach saying that she was going to the St James's end of town, where she was making the arrangements to retrieve her fortune and obtain Thomas's commission. Each evening when she returned she presumably gave some explanation about why she had to wait a little while further until her money could be released and why there was a delay in the arrangements to get Thomas's commission. In the evenings Sarah charmed the company; she was 'not only very sprightly and engaging in conversation, but sung and played the guitar to perfection'.

Whether Sarah went out one day just as the money was running out and never returned, or whether Thomas and his friends discovered by other means that she was an imposter and challenged her with the accusation, the consequence was that Sarah disappeared and Thomas never saw his bride again.

Penniless and in debt to the innkeeper, Thomas and his friends had to sell their horses to pay the bills they and Sarah had racked up. On Saturday 5 January 1765 the four lads left London to walk back to Frensham, with Thomas facing the painful task of explaining to his father what had happened to his money.

According to Sabine Baring-Gould in an 1898 newspaper article entitled *The Besom Maker*, old Thomas threw good money after bad when he fell into the hands of a lawyer from Portsmouth who undertook to see Sarah prosecuted and the money returned. The only benefit they received was that lawyer apparently managed to establish that Sarah had been married before. Therefore Thomas's marriage to Sarah was invalid, so he was free to marry again.[6]

When Alderman John Hewitt, a Coventry magistrate, examined Sarah in 1766 he noted that, in addition to her marriage certificate from Frensham, she had a certificate of another marriage in Whitechapel, where she used the surname Wilbraham.[7] However, there is no known record of a marriage for a woman named Wilbraham in the St Mary Whitechapel parish registers. The document that Hewitt saw might have been a forgery. Even so, Thomas's marriage would still have been invalid as his bride, Sarah Willsbrowson, was a fictional character whom Sarah had invented.

Thomas did get married again (see Appendix 1). He started courting a girl in the next village: Anne Over from Headley. In 1776 Thomas and Anne had their banns read three times in All Saints church, Headley, and no impediment was alleged. However, for some reason they did not go through with the marriage. Whether this was because Anne found it difficult to come to terms with Thomas's previous relationship with Sarah, or whether there was some antipathy between Anne and Flora, Thomas's mother, is not known. Nonetheless, by 1779 Anne had moved to Frensham where she gave birth to an illegitimate daughter, also named Anne. Thomas was the father. Little Anne died when she was less than a month old.

Later that year Flora died; she was buried on 14 November. Three weeks later Thomas and Anne had their banns read again, but this time in St Mary's church, Frensham. After the banns had been read for three successive weeks, Thomas and Anne were married on 20 December 1779. It was as if they had been waiting for Flora to die.

There is no indication of whether old Thomas Boxall managed to retain his estate. Census records show that the Boxalls who were living in Frensham parish in Queen Victoria's time were mainly broom makers or agricultural labourers, some of whom were living in huts off the Portsmouth Road. Baring-Gould indicated that Thomas lost his freehold, and that his descendants were some of the broom makers who were then squatting in the Devil's Punchbowl.[8]

Baring-Gould said that Thomas and Sarah's story had not been forgotten. It lived on in a ballad, which began:

A cobbler there was, and he lived in a stall,
But Charlotte, my nymph, had no lodging at all;
And at a broom-squire's, in pitiful plight,
Did pray and beseech for a lodging one night.
She asked for admittance her story to tell,
Of all her misfortunes, and what her befell,
Of her parentage high; but so great was her grief,
She'd never a comfort to give her relief.

Baring-Gould said the song continued 'through many stanzas devoid of merit', but the remaining verses have proven elusive.

After Sarah abandoned her 'husband' at the Bear Inn, there is a gap in her history through most of 1765 until towards the end of the year, apart from an episode in Westmorland (now Cumbria). However, the newspaper account of her Frensham adventure said that she had 'for near two years past obtained money, by imposing on the compassion and credulity of different persons in town and country'.[9] The papers Alderman Hewitt found on her in June 1766 showed that, by that date, Sarah had wandered through 'most of the Northern Counties; likewise Gloucestershire, Wiltshire, Somersetshire, Berkshire, Monmouthshire, Staffordshire, and Worcestershire'.[10]

We do not know what adventures Sarah had before she turned up in Frensham, or what she got up to during most of 1765. A later newspaper report said:

> It seems this woman has, for some time past, been travelling through almost all parts of the Kingdom, assuming various titles and characters, at different times and places: she has presented herself to be of high birth and distinction [...] making promises of providing, by means of her weight and interest, for the families of [...] the lower class of people; unto those of higher rank in life she has represented herself to be in the greatest distress, abandoned and deserted by her parents and friends of considerable family [...] always varying the account of herself as she chanced to pick up intelligence of characters and connections of those she intended to deceive and impose upon.[11]

A WANDERER IN ENGLAND

Sarah cuts a recklessly romantic figure. Reckless, because of the disregard for her own safety. Travelling alone on foot was a brave thing to do at a time when the newspapers reported instances of women being robbed on the highway, and in some cases being raped and murdered. Reckless also because of the potential dangers for a young woman knocking on strangers' doors, and the ever-present danger of being caught and punished for her dishonest activities. But, despite (or possibly *because* of) her dishonesty, there is something romantic about Sarah – a lonesome traveller living on her wits to obtain free board and lodging, money and clothing; travelling by coach or carrier's waggon when she managed to dupe some unwary victim into giving her money, otherwise tramping the rough roads of eighteenth-century England wondering where she would be sleeping that night.

Another female adventuress of the eighteenth century, Charlotte Charke, who lived from hand to mouth as a strolling player, travelled around the country by all manner of means. When she had no money, she had to walk unless she could get a lift for some part of her journey by 'mounting up into a Hay-Cart, or a timely Waggon.'[1] On one occasion, she and a companion, being penniless, set off on foot from Devizes, and 'after a most deplorable, half-starving Journey through intricate Roads and terrible Showers of Rain, in three Days Time, we arrived at *Rumsey*, having parted from our last Three Halfpence to ride five Miles in a Waggon, to the great Relief of our o'er-tired Legs.'[2]

At the time when Sarah was wandering around England, the country was undergoing what became known as 'turnpike mania'. Between 1690 and 1750, only about 150 turnpike trusts had been created, mainly covering the radial roads from London and sections of the great post roads. Between 1751 and 1772 there was a massive burst of speculative activity. During those twenty-one years a further 389 trusts were added, covering some 11,500 miles of road. This was partly the result of a period of low interest rates, which meant that those with money could get a better rate of return by investing in a turnpike than by lending to the government. It was also due to the increasing number of coach and waggon services, which meant that the old arrangements for maintaining the major highways were becoming increasingly untenable.

The existence of a turnpike trust did not necessarily mean that there was an immediate improvement to the roads under its control. There was a period of construction, and before the great road builders of the early nineteenth century came along, individual surveyors had differing ideas about how best to maintain a highway, with mixed results.

Those highways not covered by turnpike trusts were still subject to sixteenth-century legislation. The Highways Act of 1555 placed the burden of the upkeep of the highways on individual parishes. Each parish had to appoint two surveyors of the highways and each householder had to work under the supervision of the surveyors for eight hours a day for four days a year (or pay someone else to do the work), repairing and maintaining those highways within the parish boundaries that ran to market towns. Roads that did not lead directly to market towns were not covered by the act. An act of 1562 extended the period of labour to six days a year, and the better-off inhabitants were obliged to provide carts and draught animals. This system was known as 'statute labour'.

Statute labour was deeply unpopular and of limited effectiveness; parishioners had no interest in maintaining a road from which they received no benefit. A correspondent to the *Gentleman's Magazine* in 1767 complained that:

> Teams and labourers coming out for statute work, are generally idle, careless, and under no commands [...] They make a holiday of it, lounge about, and trifle away their time. As they are in no danger of being turned out of their work, they stand in no awe of the surveyor.[3]

During the course of her adventures Sarah travelled great distances. Each journey took her over some roads that had been turnpiked and others that were still maintained by the local parish. In general, the roads were bumpy, rutted and full of potholes. When the potholes grew too deep, it was the practice to throw large stones or rocks in them. In dry weather, the roads became dusty and every time a horse or a coach went by, it raised a great cloud of choking dust. In wet weather the roads became sticky, treacherous swamps, and in the winter they were impassable for wheeled vehicles and slow, filthy and tedious for horse riders and pedestrians.

Before the hedge building that followed the various Enclosure Acts, the minor roads of England were often no more than well-trodden paths across open fields where it was easy for the unwary traveller to get lost. The writer Arthur Young, who travelled all over England at about the same time as Sarah, described one road as 'going over a common with roads pointing nine ways at once, but no direction-post'. The major roads were furrowed with deep ruts caused by the wheels of heavy carriers' waggons, and these ruts were full of water in wet weather. On one journey, Arthur Young complained that he was 'near being swallowed up in a slough'. On the turnpike between Preston and Wigan, Young measured ruts in the road that were 4ft deep.[4]

In 1727 Jonathan Swift remarked 'in how few hours, with a swift horse or a strong gale, a man may come among a people as unknown to him as the Antipodes'. By the time Sarah was travelling across England, little had changed. The accents and dialect words spoken by a person in one part of the country would still have been scarcely intelligible to a person living in another. When Sarah met people in her travels who had rarely ventured beyond their parish boundaries, she probably had difficulty trying to make out what they were saying, and what those local words meant.

At some stage during the course of her travels in 1765, Sarah called on Robert Hudson, a lawyer, at his home in the small market town of Brough in Westmorland, on the road from London to Carlisle. Sarah introduced herself as Viscountess Lady Wilbrihammon. It seems that Robert and his family were so honoured to have such a distinguished visitor that they entertained her as their guest for several days. She told them that she was an acquaintance of Lord Albemarle and would be able to procure a lieutenancy in the army for Robert's son-in-law[5] (Lord Albemarle, the great-grandson of Charles II, was lieutenant-general of the 3rd Regiment of Dragoons).

In the eighteenth century, commissions in the armed forces and offices in government were effectively private property, given as patronage and offered for sale. Most commissions in the army were obtained by purchase, and could be re-sold. As far as civil appointments were concerned, the offices were in the gift of the Crown or prime ministers and others acting on behalf of the Crown. Once an office had been granted, usually in return for political favours, it could be sold or bequeathed to heirs when the office holder died. All the offices provided an income for the office holder, either through fees – as in the case of the keepers of the London jails, who purchased their offices in the expectation of making a profit from charging fees from the prisoners – or from a share of revenues, as in the case of tax collectors. Where the office was too onerous, or where the office holder had managed to obtain several appointments, he could pay a deputy to do the work at a fraction of the remuneration he was receiving. Many of the offices were simply sinecures to which no significant duties were attached.

The sale of offices was so established that it even featured in newspaper advertisements. An advertiser in *The Times* was selling 'A Genteel Place under Government' that did 'not require much attendance', which came with a salary of £100 a year.[6] Another advertisement offered between 1,000 and 2,500 guineas to 'any Lady or Gentleman who will establish the Advertiser in a permanent Place of adequate Salary in any of the Public Offices under government'.[7]

These arrangements gave scope for imposters like Sarah to pretend to be in a position to be able to appoint a person to a lucrative post, or arrange for such appointment to be made in return for cash. In 1773 a person calling herself the Honourable Elizabeth Harriet Grieve appeared at the Public Office in Bow Street and was committed to Newgate to await her trial for defrauding a number of people by pretending to obtain various government posts for them.

Mrs Grieve appeared to be in a position to have those places at her disposal. She said she was the first cousin to the prime minister, Lord North; second cousin to the Duke of Grafton; and closely related to Lady Fitzroy.[8] She added verisimilitude to those claims by bribing Lord North's servants to let her park her coach outside his door for hours at a time. Even more convincing was the common sight of the coach belonging to the up-and-coming politician, Charles James Fox, outside her own door. She had befriended Fox, who was financially desperate as a result of incurring gambling debts; she told him that a Miss Phipps, an heiress with a fortune of £90,000 from the West Indies, was anxious to meet him, and 'was very desirous of a matrimonial connection'.

Mrs Grieve told Fox that a marriage could easily be arranged, but not yet, as Miss Phipps was still on her way from the Caribbean. Just as they were about to meet, their meeting was further delayed by Miss Phipps catching smallpox. Then there was yet another delay because Mrs Grieve told Fox that Miss Phipps preferred men with light-coloured hair, so he must powder his eyebrows.[9] When the story of Fox and the imaginary heiress broke, it gave rise to two satirical poems: 'Female Artifice; or, Charles F-x Outwitted', published in February 1774; and 'An Heroic and Elegiac Epistle from Mrs Grieve in Newgate, to Mr C- F-', which was printed in the March 1774 issue of the *Westminster Magazine*.

It turned out that Mrs Grieve's victims included the following:

William Kidwell, who paid her £30 on pretence of obtaining for him the appointment of Clerk of the Dry Stores in the Victualling Office;

William Kent of Streatley in Berkshire, who charged her with defrauding him of £30 in cash and a conditional bond for £230 on pretence of procuring the office of a Coast Waiter. Kent left his business in Berkshire and moved his wife and three children to London in anticipation of starting his new career;

Elizabeth Cooper, who charged her with defrauding her husband of £62 on a similar pretence 'in Consequence of which he died of a broken Heart'.[10]

Another of her victims was a Mr Greenleaf, a Quaker of Ipswich, who said he gave her £50 and a bond for £1,350 which was to be the consideration money for being appointed as a Commissioner of the Stamp Duties. According to the newspapers: 'The Impudence of this Woman was astonishing. She gave as a Reason why she did not procure him the Place, that he had three Bastards by his Servant Girl, and had been expelled [from] the Meeting-House to which he belonged.'[11]

At her trial on 27 October 1774, Mrs Grieve was found guilty of fraud and sentenced to be transported for seven years.[12] At eight o'clock in the morning, on 29 November 1774, she walked from Newgate to Blackfriars Bridge with her fellow convicts, including a Miss Roach, who was transported for receiving a watch from the highwayman Sixteen String Jack. She was put on board a lighter to travel down to Blackwall as the start of her journey across the Atlantic. She sailed to America on the *Thornton* convict ship, a vessel we will encounter later in this story.[13]

We know that Sarah was in London towards the end of 1765. It may be that Robert Hudson paid for her to travel to London, ostensibly to obtain the lieutenancy, possibly by the stagecoach that left the White Lion at Kendal. The coach took two nights and three days to complete the journey from Kendal and cost £3 7*s* for an inside seat.[14] Adding the cost of refreshments and other expenses on the road, the overall cost of the trip to London would not have been far short of £5.

It was not uncommon for women to travel alone by stagecoach. Parson Woodforde sometimes found that one of his fellow passengers was an unaccompanied woman.[15] In order to travel great distances at the usual speed of between 5 and 7 miles an hour in summer – slower in winter – the coaches had to leave their inns in the early hours of the morning and not arrive at their destination until late at night. Travelling by coach forced passengers to socialise with each other; four strangers who were thrust together in the confines of a coach for up to 18 hours at a time, with breaks to share meals at roadside inns, generally found it easier to talk to each other than to endure awkward silences. When Sarah travelled by coach, she was probably able to pick up information from her new-found travelling companions about the wealth, political views and religious leanings of individuals in a particular district and other gossip that might point her in the direction of a potential new target.

As can be seen from the cost of the trip from Kendal to London, travelling by coach was not cheap. One way of saving money journeying by coach was to travel half-price as an outside passenger. Until much after Sarah's time when seats were fitted on the roofs of coaches, travelling as an outside passenger was not for the faint-hearted. You either had the choice of sitting on the curved roof of the coach with only a handle to hold on to as the coach bounced over the uneven roads, or travelling in the basket at the back of the coach, sharing the space with loose and heavy iron-nailed and sharp-cornered luggage as the coach hurtled downhill. Whichever option was taken, there was no protection from the weather.

A much safer way of travelling cheaply was to travel by waggon. This is a method that Sarah may have used for some of her journeys. As well as carrying goods, the covered waggons usually had planks or benches for passengers. The waggons were large carts covered by a canvas hood, pulled by up to eight strong horses. Waggons had the advantage that the passenger fares worked out at about only a penny a mile and were less attractive to highwaymen than coaches or chaises because of the imagined poverty of the passengers. However, the waggons usually travelled at walking pace and covered no more than 30 miles a day.

London

The London Sarah knew in the 1760s was a filthy, stinking, noisy, dangerous city that covered the 5 miles east to west from Limehouse to Hyde Park Corner and about 2½ miles north to south from Shoreditch to the last buildings in Blackman Street, Southwark. Into that space was crammed a population estimated at around 750,000 (at a time when the next largest town in England, Bristol, had a population of about 50,000).[16]

As her coach drew near to London, Sarah would almost certainly have smelled London before she saw it, surrounded as it was by a chain of smoking brick kilns, pig farms, rubbish heaps and laystalls.

The laystalls were great mounds of human waste mixed with cartloads of animal dung and other filth that had been shovelled off the streets. Night-soil men, otherwise known as rakers, collected the shit in buckets from the bog-houses of buildings with gardens and from the cesspits in the basements of buildings without gardens. They emptied their buckets into carts and drove to the outskirts of town to dump their load.

The (very) minor poet, Charles Jenner, feigning frustration in his search for pastoral bliss in the countryside surrounding London, wrote:

Alas for me! What prospects can I find
To raise poetic ardour in my mind?
Where'er around I cast my wand'ring eyes,
Long burning rows of fetid bricks arise,
And nauseous dunghills swell in mould'ring heaps,
While the fat sow beneath their covert sleeps.[17]

The smells of the brick kilns, the hogs and the laystalls that circled the town were supplemented by the smells of London itself. The stink of sea-coal smoke combined with the other city smells and the stench of the Thames, which was an open sewer, meant that when the wind was in the right direction, people could smell London from several miles away.

The French travel writer Pierre-Jean Grosley was also in London when Sarah was there in 1765. He said there was a constant fog covering London that was caused by smoke from:

The sea-coals made use of in kitchens, apartments, and even the halls of grand houses; and by coals burnt in glass-houses, in houses where earthenware is manufactured, in blacksmiths and gunsmiths shops, in dyers yards, &c. all which trades and manufactures are established in the very heart of London [...] This smoke, being loaded with terrestrial particles, and rolling in a thick, heavy atmosphere, forms a cloud, which envelops London like a mantle; a cloud which the sun pervades but rarely [...] The vapours, fogs, and rains, with which the atmosphere of London is loaded, drag with them in their fall the heaviest particles of the smoke; this forms black rains, and produces all the ill effects that may justly be expected from it upon the cloaths of those who are exposed to it.[18]

The Kendal coaches set down at the Bell in Wood Street.[19] The Bell was one of the inns that served the coaches and carriers from the north of England. The first plate of Hogarth's *Harlot's Progress* shows Moll Hackabout alighting from the York Waggon outside the Bell and being greeted by the brothelkeeper, Mother Needham.

If we were to try to imagine the things that Sarah saw, heard and experienced in London after she left her coach at the Bell by walking in her shoes, we would have had to tread carefully. The streets were shared between pedestrians and vehicles, and where there were pavements, pedestrians had to avoid being jostled by porters carrying goods unloaded from the river, and move aside to avoid being knocked down by burly chairmen rushing past carrying sedan chairs. The pavements were obstructed by shopkeepers' stalls, unloaded goods and cellar doors projecting into the street, forcing people into the road. The streets and the pavements were often covered in filth:

> Fishmongers and Butchers do not hesitate to throw out Quantities of offensive Offal; Oyster Women throw out their shells, which in a few hours are ground to mud; Grocers, Cheesemongers, and many others, sweep the Saw-dust and Rubbish of their Shops into the Streets [...] Scavengers Carts filled to the Brim, and with the Jolts of bad Pavements are usually half emptied again before they reach the Lay-stalls.[20]

That last comment echoed an observation the philanthropist and reformer Jonas Hanway made back in 1754 that the night-soil men, by the motions of their carts:

> Not only drop near a quarter part of their dirt, and render a street, already cleaned, in many spots very filthy, but it subjects every coach, and every passenger, of what quality soever, to be overwhelmed with whole cakes of dirt, with every jolt of the cart; of which many have had a most filthy experience.[21]

Sarah would also have had to make her way past the dung-hills that stood in many corners of the streets. There were dunghills in Fleet Market, Fleet Bridge and around Temple Bar. The stand of coaches at Temple Bar filled the street with 'horse-dung and litter, which I am sorry to see now and then encreased with ashes and filth thrown out by the inhabitants'.[22] In 1762 the dismembered remains of a woman and eight infants were found in a dunghill at the foot of Westminster Bridge.[23] A letter to the *Gazetteer* warned that 'in hot weather the effluvia of [...] the lay-stalls for night-soil which are established in almost every corner of the town [...] may insensibly be an assistant cause of diseases amongst us.'[24]

Night soil was not the only problem. In 1765 a correspondent objected to the people who 'make water under the Gate-way at St James's, as it is not only indecent, but offensive to many of the Courtiers, it being the very Place where Carriages stop to set them down'.[25] Another person wrote about the 'horrid Stench of Urine at the Horse-guards, and in every Avenue leading to it [and] the Puddles and Ponds of stagnated stinking Water'.[26] Grosley commented that:

In the most beautiful part of the Strand and near St Clement's Church, I have during my whole stay in London, seen the middle of the street constantly foul with a dirty puddle to the height of three or four inches; a puddle where splashings cover those who walk on foot, fill coaches when their windows happen not to be up, and bedawb all the lower parts of such houses as are exposed to it.[27]

The dead added to the smells of the city. In August 1765 a person living in St Martin's Lane wrote to the *Public Advertiser* that in the churchyard behind his house:

Are daily brought several dead Bodies, which are there left in the Ground [...] as close as they can possibly be laid to each other, with no other Covering than a few Boards placed over the Mouth of the Grave, neither Dust or Earth being thrown over them [...] A Nusance this of the most shameful Nature, considering what an intolerable Stench must necessarily arise, this hot Weather, from such a number of Corpses, yet green and festering in their Shrouds.[28]

These burial pits, known as poor holes, were a feature of many London churchyards and were said to be 'one of the great sources of putrid disorders [...] so offensive, as frequently to oblige the Ministers and others, upon funeral duty, to stand at a considerable distance, to avoid the horrid stench arising from them'.[29] A person wrote to *Lloyd's Evening Post* pointing out that in a lane near Cavendish Square there were 'many carcases of horses which lie unburied in a state of putrefaction, insomuch that it is a real nuisance to every one passing that way'.[30]

The droppings from the herds of cattle that were driven through the streets on their way to Smithfield added to the stench of the streets. The cattle also increased the dangers of walking in London: scarcely a week went by without reports of horned beasts running wild in the streets tossing and goring pedestrians. No part of the city was safe from them. In 1765 the incidents included an 'over-drove ox' which 'did great damage in Hosier-lane, West Smithfield, and gored a shoemaker's apprentice so dangerously in the belly, that he was carried off for dead'; a woman killed by an 'over-drove bullock' in Chick Lane; an over-drove ox which 'ran furiously up Snow-Hill, and terribly gored a Youth [and] afterwards ran down the Little Old Baily, and into the Session's-House Yard, at which the People attending the Session, were greatly alarmed; from thence he ran into a Coffee-house, and did considerable Damage'; a lad was tossed and killed by an ox in Fleet Street; a bullock tossed several persons in Charing Cross; on a separate occasion a bullock ran down the Strand

and injured several people before goring a man's eye out at Charing Cross; a pregnant woman from Aldersgate Street was killed by an ox; an ox gored a woman in Berkeley Square; a drover was gored to death by an ox in Monmouth Street; a bullock tossed a woman in Gray's Inn Lane; a man was gored by an ox in St James's Street; an ox killed a woman in Holborn; and a bullock tossed several people on Oxford Road (now Oxford Street).[31] Mad dogs running loose on the streets were another hazard.

The roads and the lanes were crammed with hackney coaches, private coaches, stagecoaches, drays and other waggons. To deal with the volume of traffic moving in and out of the city, there were at least seventy-five coaching and carrying inns within London.[32] As an indication of the amount of traffic arriving and departing for the country, if we take just those timetabled coaches and carrier's waggons that left London every week for Coventry, we find that the Flying Machine left the Castle and Falcon, Aldersgate Street, on Mondays, Wednesdays and Fridays at ten o'clock at night, and the ordinary coach left the Swan with Two Necks, Lad Lane, on Mondays, Wednesdays and Thursdays at three o'clock in the morning. Coventry waggons left the George and White Hart, Aldersgate Street, on Mondays, Tuesdays, Thursdays and Saturdays at noon; the Saracen's Head, Snow Hill, at ten o'clock on Saturday mornings and another at six o'clock in the evening; the Ram, Smithfield, on Wednesdays at nine o'clock at night; the Bell, Smithfield, on Mondays, Tuesdays, Thursdays and Saturdays at ten o'clock in the morning; the George, Smithfield, on Mondays and Saturdays at noon; the Castle and Falcon, Aldersgate Street, on Mondays, Tuesdays, Thursdays and Saturdays at ten o'clock in the morning; and the White Horse, Friday Street, on Mondays, Tuesdays,

Thursdays and Saturdays at noon.[33] These do not include the coaches and waggons that passed through Coventry on their way from London to further destinations such as Chester, Holyhead, Shrewsbury, Liverpool, Whitehaven and Carlisle.

It is difficult to imagine just how noisy London was. The multitudes of street sellers hawking their fruit, milk, hot pies, newspapers and other goods needed strong and penetrating voices to make themselves heard above the cries of London from their competitors, the rumble of carts and coaches rattling over the cobbled streets, the ballad singers and street musicians, the clangour of bells, the piercing shriek of the knife grinder's wheel and the hammering of the metal-bashing trades. It is little wonder that Sarah frequently escaped to the country to pursue her adventures.

'I Suppose, Madam, Miss Can Sing Too'

While she was in London, Sarah visited George Jackson, the Secretary to the Navy Board. Shortly before Mr and Mrs Jackson were due to have their dinner, a hackney coach drove up to their door; the coachman knocked and told the servant that a lady in the coach wanted to speak to Mr Jackson. The servant replied that his master was out. Sarah then called out asking whether Mrs Jackson was in. The servant tried to get rid of her by saying that Mrs Jackson was also not at home. Sarah then ordered the coachman to tell the servant that she was ill and to beg the favour that she might come in for a minute or two.

The servant let her in and, pretending to be in a weak state, Sarah asked to be allowed to sit down. Mrs Jackson came to see her. Mrs Jackson noticed that her visitor had a speck in her eye. Sarah told Mrs Jackson that she was the Honourable Miss Mollineux, a daughter of Lord Mollineux, and a near relation of Lord Derby. She said she believed that Captain Jackson of the India Company was related to Mr Jackson and that Captain Jackson had been a particular friend of her late mother. She said that she was in a distressed state because her father had treated her cruelly and forced her to leave home. She was sure that if she could see the captain, he would be willing to help her for the sake of his former friendship with her late mother.

When Mr Jackson arrived home with some friends, he said he would send a servant to find the captain. He invited Sarah to dine with his family and friends. Sarah replied that her sorrows were so great that so much company would be too much for her spirits. Mr Jackson asked his daughter to keep Miss Mollineux company by dining alone with her in a separate room. When the meal was over Mr Jackson told Sarah that the servant was unable to find the captain, and so invited Sarah to take tea; he asked his daughter to entertain her by playing the harpsichord. After Miss Jackson had played a couple of pieces of music Sarah turned to Mrs Jackson and said, 'I suppose, madam, Miss can sing too.' This is one of only two examples of reported speech that we have from Sarah. It shows qualities of boldness, nerve, self-assurance, impudence, pushiness and rudeness, all in one simple phrase.

Sarah was beginning to feel secure and comfortable in her new surroundings. She thought herself lucky that the captain was not able to be found. However, Mr and Mrs Jackson, who suspected that Miss Mollineux might not be who she said she was, told Sarah that they had no room for her to stay the night. Later their suspicions were confirmed when they learned about some of the other adventures of the lady with a speck on her eye.[34]

On 3 December 1765 Sarah went into Mrs Davenport's shop in the Haymarket when Mrs Davenport had been away. Sarah was very shabbily dressed, but told Mrs Davenport's niece that she was born in high society. She described how her relations had forced her to marry a foreign count against her will and that the count had then abandoned her to want and misery. She told the niece that all she had left in the world was a note for £100 payable personally by Robert Child, the banker (Robert Child was the proprietor of London's oldest bank and MP for Wells; his country estate was Osterley Park). Sarah showed the girl the note that probably some dishonest scrivener of her acquaintance had forged for her. She said that Robert Child had known her in happier times, but her present appearance was so much beneath her birth and dignity that she was ashamed to approach him dressed as she was.

The compassionate girl, moved by this sorrowful account of a young lady of quality whose birthright had been taken by a wicked foreigner, took Sarah into her house, gave her bed and board for two or three days, 'and then equipped her very prettily out, in order to enable her to receive her hundred Pounds, without exposing her Poverty by her Dress'.

On a day when Sarah knew that Robert Child would not be at the bank, she told her new benefactress to accompany her to Child's Bank in Fleet Street so she could claim her money and pay the girl for the clothes and her hospitality. They hired a coach to take them to the bank and entered together. With an air of great confidence Sarah strolled up to one of the clerks and told him that she wanted to see Mr Child. The clerk replied that he was not at the bank that day. So Sarah told the coachman to drive them to Mr Child's town house in Lincoln's Inn Fields. When they arrived, Sarah asked the girl to wait in the coach while she went in to see Mr Child.

Sarah knocked on the door. A servant answered and Sarah asked to come in as she needed to speak to Molly, one of the maidservants. The servant let her in, but when Molly appeared, Sarah exclaimed, 'Lord, Ma'am, I beg pardon, if your name is Molly, you are not the person I wanted!' Sarah then said that she needed to go to Clare Market, and as they had a back door in Portugal Street, she would be very grateful if they could let her go out that way, as it would save her a long walk.

Mrs Davenport's niece, after waiting for nearly an hour in the coach, eventually plucked up enough courage to knock on Mr Child's door to ask how long the countess was likely to be. The poor girl then discovered the cruel trick that Sarah had played upon her humanity and credulity.[35]

This episode demonstrates a considerable amount of planning on Sarah's part. She worked out when Mrs Davenport would be away from her shop, when Mr Child would be away from his bank, the layout of Mr Child's house and garden, and that he had a servant called Molly.

After that incident Sarah left the foul air, noise and smells of London. The next sighting we have of her is on Christmas Day 1765 when she arrived dressed 'in a very shabby camblet riding habit' at the Nag's Head in Spon End in Coventry. The Nag's Head was one of the large coaching inns that served the many stagecoaches that stopped at Coventry on their journeys to the north-west. It was owned by Thomas Dullison, who was also the proprietor of the Coventry flying machine and a partner in the Birmingham flying machine.[36] A flying machine was a stagecoach that changed horses at inns every 10 or 20 miles. The fresh teams meant that the coach would travel faster than one with the same jaded team dragging the heavy coach for its full journey of 100 miles or more and having to stop to rest from time to time.

In the winter season the Coventry machine used to leave London from the Castle and Falcon in Aldersgate Street at eleven o'clock at night, and arrive at Coventry the following evening. The fare was £1 1s,[37] the equivalent of £175 at 2018 prices. If Sarah used an ordinary coach to travel the 90 miles from London to Coventry, her journey would have taken two days in the winter season, and would have involved the additional expense of an overnight stay at an inn on the way.

Cheshire

Sarah might have been suspected of being a vagrant when she arrived at the Nag's Head, as she was referred to Mrs Bott, the vagrant carrier's wife, who lived nearby. Sarah told Mrs Bott that she had come from London in a coach and was on her way to see Lord Derby, who was her uncle, and Lord Strange, who was her cousin.[38]

Mrs Bott let Sarah stay at her house for a few days, and put some money in her pocket to send her on her way.[39] However, it seems that Sarah had sufficient funds of her own to carry her the 90 miles from Coventry by coach to the Cock Inn near Great Budworth in Cheshire, on the road between Northwich and Warrington. Using the standard rate of 3d per mile for an inside seat on a long-distance coach, this would have cost her £1 2s 6d.[40]

Sarah stayed a while at the Cock to pick up information about the families who lived in the district before sallying out. She first called on Thomas Deane, a wheelwright. She showed him several letters, which she said were from noblemen, and told him that she had escaped from her father, who was a lord near London. She said her father would have forced her to marry someone she detested, had she not run away. She said her mother was dead and she had an independent fortune that she would receive on her twenty-first birthday in May. Until then she planned to hide away. She added that when she received her fortune she would marry a young nobleman for whom she had the greatest affection. She said that if Mr and Mrs Deane could conceal her in their house and let her board with them until she came of age, she would give them so much money that Mr Deane would never have to do another day's work in his life. The Deanes were suspicious and didn't want to get involved with any quarrel between the young woman and her family, so Sarah went off to try her luck elsewhere.

Sarah walked northwards, away from Great Budworth in the direction of Warrington, until she reached the next house, where a miller and his wife lived. As it was getting late, and the miller and his wife were fearful for the safety of a young woman wandering alone in the dark, they let her stay the night. When she left the following morning she told the miller that she would reward their kindness by settling an annuity on them when she came of age.

Sarah carried on walking northwards until she came to the small village of Seven Oaks. She called on Richard Frith, a yeoman who owned houses and land in Seven Oaks and in the villages of Crowton and Antrobus.[41] She introduced herself as Viscountess Lady Willbrihammon and related her misfortunes of being a Protestant when her father was a Catholic. She told him she had £40,000 in the bank, three large halls, and several manors and estates, all of which would be hers when she came of age in May. She added that shortly after she gained her independence, she would marry a landed gentleman named Irving. If Mr Frith and his family could maintain her until May, and keep the whole affair a secret, she would 'make them all gentlefolks'.

Mr Frith sent Sarah to his son, also named Richard, at Crowton Hall, about 4 miles from Seven Oaks. Crowton Hall was described as a timber farmhouse of the early part of the seventeenth century.[42] Young Richard and Elizabeth, his wife, conscious of the future wealth they anticipated Lady Willbrihammon would bestow on them, spared no expense in providing their guest with the very best of wines and food. Sarah offered Richard the post of steward of her estates with a salary of £200 a year – a very comfortable sum in those days. Her every wish was their command. It seems that she lazed around all day while Richard and his family ran around attending to her every need. They even washed and dressed her, and served her meals on their knees. They gave her money and bought clothes for her, including a nankeen riding habit, a white hat with a blue feather and cockade with gold tassels. She diverted 'herself and the family with music, singing, &c'.[43] The report does not specify what instrument Sarah played. The account of the evenings Sarah spent in London with Thomas Boxall and his friends said she 'sung and played the guitar to perfection'.

In the 1760s there was something of a guitar craze in Britain, particularly among women. In 1770 Hoyle's *Dictionary* gave the definition, 'Guittar or Guittara, a stringed instrument [...] much in use among the ladies of Great-Britain'.[44] The popularity of the guitar among women was partly due to Ann Ford, who was immortalised by Thomas Gainsborough's 1760 portrait of her seated with her guitar on her lap. Ann was said to have had a beautiful singing voice and to have played several stringed instruments. Although her father allowed her to give concerts at home for family friends, accompanied by leading professional and amateur musicians, he forbade her from performing in public. They quarrelled so violently about this that she left home and moved in with a friend, announcing that she would support herself with her music, an unacceptable step for a woman of her class. Her father had her arrested and taken back home. Undeterred, she escaped again and announced a series of five subscription concerts at the Little Theatre in the Haymarket, the first of which she gave on 18 March 1760. This series raised £1,500 in subscriptions. Her father arranged for Bow Street Runners to surround the theatre in an attempt to disrupt the first concert, but they were dispersed by Charles Bennet, 3rd Earl of Tankerville, one of Ann's aristocratic supporters, who threatened to send for a detachment of the guards.[45]

In 1771 Charles Burney observed that 'there is hardly a private family in a civilised nation without its flute, its harpsichord or guitar'.[46] The newspapers carried advertisements from people offering to teach the guitar 'in a most easy Manner. Able to play 12 Tunes in the first Month, and in three Months to be so far a Master of the Instrument to be able to play any common Piece of Music on Sight, on the low Terms of Half a Guinea a Month'.[47] They included advertisements from the versatile N. Hart. As well as teaching his clients how to play the guitar, he said he also taught the violin, German flute, how to dance a minuet and country dances, and fencing. He also prepared and sold his 'Strengthening Pomatum' to make bald people's hair grow again, liniment to remove unwanted hair, 'hair liquid' to turn hair black or brown and various concoctions to remedy defects in the skin.[48]

For those who could not afford to be taught by a master, there were a number of teach-yourself manuals, including

Robert Bremner's *Instructions for the Guitar* (1758), Ann Ford's *Lessons and Instructions for the Guitar* (*c.* 1761) and *The Compleat Tutor for the Guitar* (1763). Like the guitar craze of the 1950s, most players were self-taught.

Advertisements for sheet music specified that they were set for the guitar; for example, an edition of the music for Thomas Arne's opera *Artaxerxes* was set for the German flute, violin and guitar.[49] The *Monthly Melody; or, Gentlemen and Ladies Polite Amusement* was 'a Collection of Vocal and Instrumental Music [...] adapted for the Violin, German Flute and Guitar'.[50] Rees's *Cyclopaedia*, looking back at the 1760s, commented that 'during the guitar paroxysm, not a song or ballad was printed, without it being transposed, and set for that instrument, at the bottom of the page'.[51]

Following the fame and example of Ann Ford, upper-class women were switching from harpsichords to the guitar. The guitar became so popular as a ladies' instrument that Kirckman, the harpsichord maker, saw it as a threat to his livelihood. So he bought a number of cheap guitars and gave them away to girls in milliners' shops, to prostitutes and ballad singers in the streets in order to lower the guitar's status and to try to destroy its reputation as an instrument played by 'respectable' women.[52]

In 1764 the *Gazetteer* reported that a female street singer near the Tabernacle at Moorfields, 'with the assistance of her guitar [...] so enchanted her audience, that she cleared £1 3*s* 8*d* after paying 2*s* 3*d* halfpenny for her supper, at an alehouse in that neighbourhood'.[53] In the same year a (supposedly) humorous letter printed in the *Public Advertiser* included 'No enthusiasm for the Guitar' in the list of the qualifications of a wife.[54] According to the music historian Sir John Hawkins, looking back from 1776, the guitar was 'the common recreation and amusement of women and their visitors in houses of lewd resort'.[55]

Guitars, then, were very popular in the 1760s and were played by women of all classes. They seem to have been relatively cheap to buy and easy to learn compared with other instruments. We know nothing about Sarah's upbringing, but even if she came from a lowly, or even semi-criminal, background, we should not be surprised that she had managed to learn how to play the guitar.

One day in February Sarah told Richard that she needed to visit her northern estates, and asked him to carry her on horseback as far as Kendal, a distance of around 90 miles. She gave him some excuse about why she needed to be in Westmorland on her own. She spent at least some of that time at Robert Hudson's at Brough. After three weeks Sarah wrote to Richard from Robert Hudson's address asking for him to collect her from Kendal. Richard replied to her at that address saying he would meet her at 'the house where we lodged at Kendal' and would bring a horse for her.[56]

Not long after Richard brought Sarah back from Kendal, Elizabeth Frith gave birth to a daughter and the parents asked Sarah to be the child's godmother. The child was baptised at St Mary's, Weaverham, on 1 May 1766 in the name of Sarah Charlotta Irvin Frith.[57]

A few days after the christening Sarah and Richard set off for London for Sarah to take possession of her estates and the large sums of money that were being held for her, and for Richard to enter into his stewardship. They arrived in London on 10 May and stayed 'at a principal inn'. Two days later Sarah went out and never returned. Richard searched for her, but in vain. After paying the innkeeper's 'large bill of expenses', he was left penniless and had to walk back to Crowton, a journey of some 180 miles, 'there to relate his folly and disappointment to his credulous family and friends.'[58]

Coventry

On 16 June 1766 the Earl of Denbigh, whose seat was at Newnham Paddox, 12 miles west of Coventry, wrote to Alderman John Hewitt. He said he had been visited by a young woman who arrived in a post-chaise and who had previously visited Lord Craven at Coombe Abbey, Lady Leigh at Stoneleigh Abbey and other landed families in the district. He said that the young woman had called herself 'Miss Wilberham and a woman of fashion and fortune'. She had told him a 'very improbable story'.

Sarah seemed to have selected the grandest aristocrats who lived in the great houses of Warwickshire for her visits. It must have taken quite some nerve to arrive unannounced at their mansions with her 'very improbable story'. Coombe Abbey was a very imposing building set in a park of some 500 acres. Stoneleigh Abbey was a similarly imposing structure. When Jane Austen visited it with her mother and sister in 1806, it had changed very little over the forty years since Sarah had been there; in a letter from the abbey to her daughter-in-law Mary, Mrs Austen described the house:

There are forty-five windows in front, which is quite straight, with a flat roof, fifteen in a row. You go up a considerable flight of steps to the door, for some of the offices are underground, and enter a large hall. On the right hand is the dining-room and within that the breakfast room [...] on the left hand of the hall is the best drawing-room and within a smaller one [...] Behind the smaller drawing-room is the state-bedchamber – an alarming apartment, with its high, dark crimson velvet bed, just fit for an heroine.

One can visualise Sarah climbing the steps of Stoneleigh Abbey, rehearsing in her mind the story she was hoping to tell Lady Leigh – a story possibly along the lines that she was applying to her because her late mother was distantly related to a distant relative of Lady Leigh, that she had become estranged from her father or for some other reason was forced to leave home, and was now in need of some temporary financial support.

Denbigh said the young woman was either mad or an imposter. If she were disordered in her senses, her friends needed to be told where she was so that they could look after her. If she were an imposter, she deserved to be punished. He asked Hewitt to investigate, trusting in his 'known diligence and activity as a magistrate.'[59]

John Hewitt was three times mayor of Coventry, an exceedingly zealous magistrate and thief taker, and a supreme self-publicist. As well as writing a short booklet about Sarah called *Memoirs of the Celebrated Lady Countess Wilbrahammon, alias Mollineux, alias Irving, Countess of Normandy, and Baroness Wilmington, the greatest Impostress of the present Age,* he also wrote *The Proceedings of J Hewitt, Alderman, and one of His Majesty's Justices of the Peace for the City and County of Coventry in the year 1756; A Guide to Constables and all Peace Officers;* and *A Journal of the Proceedings of J Hewitt, Senior Alderman, of the City of Coventry, and one of His Majesty's Justices of the Peace for the said City and County, in his Duty as a Magistrate during a Period of Thirty Years and upwards.*

In his *Journal of the Proceedings* Hewitt boasted of his actions in suppressing a notorious gang of coiners, pursuing and apprehending 'that numerous and dangerous gang, called the Coventry Gang', and his proceedings against various murderers, highwaymen and housebreakers. He reprinted copies of letters he received from various dignitaries thanking him for his actions. However, his writings have the distinct tone that his efforts were not as appreciated by those in power as he considered they should have been.

Denbigh told Hewitt that the young woman was staying at the Rose and Crown, on the High Street in Coventry. When Sarah stayed there it was probably the most important inn in the city, supplying post-chaises and drivers at 7*d* per mile from Coventry to the Angel at Coleshill and to the Saracen's Head at Daventry, which were the next stages north and south on the turnpike road between London and Chester.[60] The price for those journeys was kept down to 7*d* per mile because it was based on the probability that the driver would find a passenger for the return trip to Coventry. Generally, the hire of a chaise and pair cost 9*d* per mile in the 1760s.[61] To hire post-chaises by the day, as Sarah appeared to have done in order to visit the stately homes of Warwickshire, would have been an extremely expensive undertaking. When Parson Woodforde travelled from Oxford to Ansford in Somerset in 1774, setting off at half past five in the morning and arriving at eight o'clock in the evening, the trip cost him £4 8*s* including tips, meals and turnpike charges.[62] Post-chaises were light four-wheeled coaches with a single seat for two. They were generally drawn by two horses, with the post boy riding the nearside horse. At the end of each journey, the post boy would expect a tip.

Following the Earl of Denbigh's letter, Hewitt went to the Rose and Crown, where he waited until Sarah returned in her chaise. During the course of his interview with her, she told him that her name was Wilbrihammon, and that her father lived at Corby Castle, near Carlisle. She said her father was a Roman Catholic and her mother, who was a Protestant, had died recently. Her mother had brought her up as a Protestant, but now that her mother was dead her father had tried to compel her to change her religion and become a Catholic. To avoid this, she had run away from home; in the six weeks since, she had visited Mr Strickland at Sizergh House near Kendal; Lord Molynaux, presumably at Croxteth Hall near Liverpool; and Lord Derby; and that she was going to visit the Duke of Leeds as she was very intimate with that family. She also said that she had recently married a person she called the Honourable Mr Irving at Great Budworth, but she didn't know where he was at present.

Hewitt asked her to name some of the principal families that lived in Cumberland in the vicinity of Corby Castle, but she was unable to do so. He told her that he knew for a fact that the family who lived at Corby Castle were not called Wilbrihammon. He told her that he believed she was an 'arrant impostress' and that he would commit her as such.

He took from her a letter case on which 'Richard Frith Esq; of Crowton-Hall, Cheshire' was written in gilt letters, which she had obviously stolen. He asked her who Richard Frith was. She answered that he was her steward. He examined her papers and found the two marriage certificates, the evidence that she had travelled all over the country, that she had given herself the title of Lady Viscountess Wilbraham, the Honourable Miss Mollineaux and the Honourable Mrs Irving, and that:

Although she had pretended that she had not been in London for two years, by her papers it appeared, that she had very lately been at several inns in town within a few weeks, and was just coming out of the West, wherein she hath, it's more than probable, imposed upon the generous and well-disposed, and under these several borrowed names and false pretences obtained considerable sums of money.

Hewitt kept the letters. It is a shame that he did not leave an archive where the full extent of Sarah's documents could be examined. He said he found several letters where he claimed to have recognised the handwriting as being the same as on certain forged documents he had seen. He also found a series of letters that Richard Frith had written to her that included some poems he had composed in her honour, of which the following extract is typical:

The heavenly grace your Ladyship imparts,
I hope is deeply rooted in our hearts.
God by your favours deigns to interpose,
And lift our souls above our impious foes,
Henceforth therefore may th' Almighty Pow'rs,
Blessings on you bestow in never-ending showers;
Oh! May you happy be, and always bles'd
Of ev'ry grace, of ev'ry wish possess'd!
May plenty dissipate your worldly cares,
And smiling peace bless your revolving years.

Hewitt asked Sarah whether she had any friends who could testify to her character. She gave him the addresses of George Jackson of the Navy Board and George-Lewis Scott.

Hewitt told her that he was going to London that night, and while he was there he would check on those references. In the meantime he would leave her in the care of the landlord of the Rose and Crown and a constable at the inn.

The landlord thought that Hewitt had made a terrible mistake. He was convinced that Sarah was a lady of quality and was horrified at the disrespect Hewitt had shown towards her while she was a guest at his inn.

When Hewitt returned from London, he found a letter waiting for him from the Earl of Denbigh's steward telling him that the landlord of the inn had let her go to Banbury in his post-chaise. He said that Sarah had promised to pay the post-chaise driver the £3 11s 6d she owed the landlord when she reached Banbury, but had disappeared without paying. The steward added, 'She vended many imprecations against you for detaining her pocket-book, and attempting to examine her ladyship.'[63]

A report in the newspapers of her visit to Coventry, obviously sourced from Hewitt, ended:

This notorious vagrant and impostress made her escape from Coventry, and went for Banbury in Oxfordshire. The following description of her is given by way of a caution, and to prevent her farther success, viz. a short, slender-made woman, of a pale or sallow complexion, a little deformed, a speck or kell over one eye, had on a lightish-coloured riding habit, white hat, blue feather and cockade, with gold tassels, and said she was about 20 years of age.[64]

The clothes were those Richard Frith had bought for her.

In Banbury, according to Hewitt, she defrauded a 'Mr C' of 10 guineas before moving on.[65]

Lancashire and St Albans

According to newspaper accounts Sarah turned up in Lancaster on Thursday 16 October 1766 in a return chaise and on the Friday she 'practised her usual arts in the neighbourhood'. In the evening she hired a horse to Bolton in the Sands, and went from there to Kirkby Lonsdale. The papers said that she concealed the speck in her right eye for some time by excessive winking. They added:

> Her story is adapted to move the compassion of those she visits. She has bad nerves, and seems in great disorder of mind, which she pretends to be owing to the ill usage of her father [...] She attempts to borrow money of waiters, servants, and chaise boys, and offers to leave something in pawn with them to the value. Her name is supposed to be Sarah Wilson.[66]

This is the first reference to what appears to have been Sarah's real name.

There is another gap in Sarah's history until July 1767 when she arrived 'in the dusk of the evening' at Holloway House in St Albans, one of the seats of Lord Spencer. She was attended by a man dressed in livery, whom she called her second coachman. She asked to see Lord Spencer, but as he was away, the steward was called to deal with her. She told the steward that she was Lady Wilmington, Countess of Normandy, that she had met with the misfortune of having her carriage break down on the road to St Albans, and that she had left the broken carriage on the road with one of her attendants and had brought the other with her. She said that she was most disappointed at his lordship being away from home as he was an intimate acquaintance of her mama and papa.

The steward believed Sarah's story. He had a bed prepared for her and laid on an elegant supper. For a while she was treated by the household as an honoured guest, but the absence of a broken carriage on the road and the disappearance of her retinue attracted suspicion. Her presence in the town came to the attention of the mayor of St Albans, and he questioned her closely about the title she assumed. As she was unable to give indisputable evidence that she really was Lady Wilmington, Countess of Normandy, the mayor committed her to the house of correction as a vagrant and impostress.[67]

Devizes

It appears that Sarah did not stay imprisoned in St Albans for long; shortly after July 1767 she travelled west and called on Lord Botetourt of Stoke Gifford, just outside Bristol, the Countess of Shelburne at Bowood House near Calne, and other West Country gentry.[68]

It may seem odd to us that a complete stranger could just turn up at a country house and gain admittance. But in the eighteenth century visiting the seats of the nobility and gentry was an accepted part of domestic tourism. Road books such as *The Traveller's Pocket-Book*, which went through five editions between 1760 and 1770, and Paterson's *Roads* (various editions from 1771) contained 'an Account of Seats of the Nobility and Gentry that lie near the Road', inviting the traveller to depart from the road at the relevant points to visit those places of interest.

Elizabeth Bennett and the Gardiners' fictional visit to Pemberley in *Pride and Prejudice* shows that there was a presumption of access to grand houses. Owners were not obliged to open their houses, but many did so from a sense of *noblesse oblige*. Allowing visitors to view the house, its decoration, furniture and the owner's collection of art and antiquities was a way of showing off the owner's taste and education, reinforcing the landed elite's claim to cultural and political leadership. Those who did not permit entry could be heavily criticised, as was the case when the diarist John Byng was denied entry to Lyme Park.[69]

Generally, visiting took place in the months when the family were likely to be absent and the housekeeper acted as a guide. In order to gain entry, potential visitors needed to have the appearance of gentility, or at least look as if they were able to give the housekeeper a generous tip. Sarah would have looked the part, arriving in style in a post-chaise. Horace Walpole once remarked that he should have married his housekeeper as she had grown rich by showing visitors around Strawberry Hill.

Landed families were likely to be staying at their town houses during the London season, which coincided with the sitting of Parliament. In 1766 the parliamentary session ended on 6 June; in 1767 on 2 June. However, Sarah's tour of the seats of the nobility of the Midlands in 1766 and the West Country in 1767 took place after those dates. This was when the families were more likely to be at home in the country and less likely to open their houses to strangers. Sarah was no doubt working on the assumption that they might have been ready, perhaps, to open their purses to a fellow member of the nobility who claimed a distant relationship with the family and had arrived with a hard-luck story to tell.

On 5 September 1767 someone sent a letter from Devizes to the London newspapers that:

> This day one Sarah Wilson, alias Nixon, was committed to our Bridewell, as a notorious cheat and impostress: she has defrauded several Gentlemen, Ladies, Tradesmen and others, of considerable sums, under pretence of being a Woman of Family and Birth, and used to stile herself the Countess of Normandy. She is about 20 years of age, of fair complexion, a little pockfretten, short of stature, and slim in person, and is supposed to be the same Woman who lately played so many pranks at Lichfield, Coventry and places adjacent.[70]

Unfortunately there appear to be no records of the pranks she was supposed to have played at Lichfield.

Charles Garth, the recorder at Devizes, sent Sarah to Devizes Bridewell to await trial as a result of information that she had been 'endeavouring to impose false and crafty representations of her distress on sundry persons in Devizes'. Sarah remained in Devizes Bridewell for about two months, with a brief interval when she appeared before the quarter sessions on 9 October 1767.

Devizes Bridewell also served as the town jail. It had two night rooms for women and two for men; both sexes mixed freely in the day room and the courtyard. Prisoners were allowed three-halfpennyworth of bread a day and a pint of small beer.[71] Devizes Bridewell achieved some notoriety some years later when a prisoner was found dead in his cell whose body was in 'a most emaciated condition'. The unanimous verdict of the coroner's jury was that he had died of hunger and cold. 'The cries of the deceased was heard by other prisoners, as many of them testified on oath.'[72]

At the quarter sessions Sarah gave her name as Sarah Boxall, explaining that she was married to farmer Boxall of Frensham in Surrey. She said her maiden name was Wilson and her own relations were living in London. The newspaper reports said:

> It seems this woman has, for some time past, been travelling through almost all parts of the Kingdom, assuming various titles and characters, at different times and places: she has presented herself to be of high birth and distinction, as well foreign and English, and accordingly stiling herself a Princess of Mecklenburgh, Countess of Normandy, Lady Countess Wilbrahammon, &c. &c. and under some or other of such names making promises of providing, by means of her weight and interest, for the families of, and also borrowing money and giving notes for the payment to, the ignorant of the lower class of people; unto those of higher rank in life she has represented herself to be in the greatest distress, abandoned and deserted by her parents and friends of considerable family, either upon account of an unfortunate love affair, or of religion, pretending to be a Protestant against the will of her relations, who were Roman Catholicks, and always varying the account of herself as she chanced to pick up intelligence of characters and connections of those she intended to deceive and impose upon [...] She is a short woman, slender made, of a pale complexion, something deformed, has a speck or knell over one eye, and dresses in a lightish coloured riding-habit.[73]

Sarah's claim to be a princess of the House of Mecklenburg had a particular resonance in 1760s England. For those who believed her, it meant that they were in the presence of greatness – a woman related to royalty, a woman therefore with great powers of patronage. One of the princesses of the House of Mecklenburg, Charlotte of Mecklenburg-Sterlitz, had married King George III and was now Queen of England.

The court convicted Sarah under the Vagrancy Act 1744 and deemed her to be a vagabond. The 1744 Act listed those who could be prosecuted under the law. The list was a long one, including:

Patent gatherers, gatherers of alms under pretence of loss by fire, or other casualty;

Fencers and bear wards [those who travel with a bear or dancing bear];

All persons concerned with performing interludes, tragedies, comedies, operas, plays, farces or other entertainments for the stage, not being authorised by law;

Minstrels and jugglers;

Persons pretending to be gypsies, or wandering in the habit of gypsies;

Those pretending to have skill in physiognomy, palmistry, or fortune telling;

Those using subtle crafts to deceive and impose, or playing or betting on unlawful games;

All persons who run away and leave their wives and children;

Petty chapmen and pedlars, not duly licensed;

All persons wandering abroad and lodging in alehouses, barns, outhouses or in the open air, not giving a good account of themselves;

All persons wandering abroad and begging, pretending to be soldiers, mariners, seafaring men, pretending to go to work in harvest; and

All persons wandering abroad and begging.

The court ordered that 'after the time of the punishment ordered upon her conviction is expired', Sarah should be conveyed by a pass to Frensham as that was the place of her husband's settlement. This meant that she would be passed from constable to constable through all the parishes on the way to Frensham. Unfortunately the Devizes quarter sessions papers for the period have been lost, so we don't have any details of Sarah's trial or for how long she was sentenced to remain in Devizes Bridewell before she was due to be released to begin her journey. As the court had convicted her as a vagabond, they could have sentenced her for up to six months.[74]

For three weeks in October 1767 an advertisement appeared in the *Salisbury Journal* promising that a book entitled *A Plain Narrative of Facts, relating to the Person who lately passed under the assumed name of the Princess WILBRAHAMA, lately detected at the Devizes* would be published on 2 November, price 1s.[75] Indeed the *Salisbury Journal* for 2 November 1767 headed the advertisement with 'This Day is Published'. However, there is no trace of this publication, and it is not known whether it was ever issued.[76]

Sarah did not remain in Devizes for the full length of her sentence. The reports in the newspapers of her conviction, including the description of her having 'a speck or knell over one eye', came to the attention of the authorities in London, and while she was still in jail an order came to take her to London. The trick that Sarah had performed to obtain upmarket clothes from Mrs Davenport's shop way back in December 1765 had finally caught up with her.

PRISON

Sarah was taken from Devizes Bridewell and escorted to London. On 18 November 1767 she appeared before the 'Blind Beak', Sir John Fielding, at the Public Office in Bow Street.

Bow Street Magistrates' Court

The public office was actually part of Sir John's residence. It had been his half-brother Henry Fielding's house when Henry was the Westminster chief magistrate, and the home of Henry's predecessor, Sir Thomas de Veil, before that, but Sir John had turned the house into a magistrates' office unlike anything that had gone before.

As well as being the office where prosecutors and witnesses came to make their statements and undertook to appear to prosecute or bear witness at the next quarter sessions, and where Sir John conducted his pre-trial examinations of the suspected offenders, it was the place where people could report information about crimes that had been committed and the likely perpetrators. It was where Sir John commanded his Bow Street Runners, sending them out to investigate crimes and apprehend suspects. It was also the base from which he used the London press, particularly the *Public Advertiser*, to broadcast reports of crimes, descriptions of suspects and offers of rewards.

Sir John was keen on opening up the pre-trial process to the wider public so they could see that the system was working. The thinking behind this was that it would give people the confidence to believe that if they reported crimes in a timely manner, there could be a quick response from the Bow Street Runners and effective action by the magistrates. It could also bring in the victims of unsolved crimes who might attend pre-trial hearings in the hope of identifying those who attacked them or who had stolen their property. In order to encourage visitors and make it easier for victims to find a magistrate before whom they could lay charges, get help in finding their attackers and recover their stolen goods, Sir John extended the hours that the office was open. He did this by persuading the government to provide stipends to two other magistrates: William Kelynge and Thomas Kynaston. The three magistrates shared the work in rotation, enabling the office to be open every day.

So, when Sarah arrived at Bow Street, she would have been confronted with the hustle and bustle and the comings and goings of victims arriving to report crimes, messengers leaving with notices for the newspapers, Bow Street Runners rushing in and out to report on their investigations and receive instructions, prosecutors and witnesses laying charges, suspected offenders attending their pre-trial hearings, journalists and the idly curious.

In the midst of this confusion, a clerk would have been taking notes of the day's proceedings which a scrivener would then write up on individual sheets of vellum. In Sarah's case the record was as follows:

Westminster To wit: Jane the Wife of Samuel Davenport Gent & Jane the Wife of Thomas Chapman of the same, widow, acknowledge on pain of imprisonment Upon condition that they do personally appear at the next Quarter Sessions of the Peace to be held for the said City and Liberty at the Guild Hall, in King-Street, Westminster, then and there the said Jane Davenport to prosecute the Law with Effect, and the said Jane Chapman to give Evidence on his Majesty's Behalf against Sarah Wilson otherwise Wilbraham for knowingly and designedly by false pretences obtaining from the said Davenport one pair of Stays one Shift one Petticoat and other Apparel with intent to defraud the said Samuel Davenport.

And if the Bill be found a True Bill and returned so by the Grand Jury, that then they appear in Court, and prosecute and give Evidence upon that Indictment. And do not depart the Court.

> Taken and acknowledged the
> 18th day of November 1767
> Before me[1]

On the same day Fielding committed 'Sarah Wilson otherwise Charlotte Wilbraham' to Tothill Fields Bridewell 'on Oaths of Jane Davenport and others for knowing & Designedly by False Pretences obtaining from the sd Jane a Quantity of Wearing Apparrell with intent to Cheat and Defraud the sd Jane thereof Contrary to the Statute &c'.[2]

Tothill Fields Bridewell

Tothill Fields Bridewell, otherwise known as the Westminster house of correction, was originally designed as a bridewell for vagrants where 'sturdy beggars and valiant rogues' were put to work beating hemp. During the reign of Queen Anne it was converted into a jail for prisoners.[3] Tothill Fields Bridewell should not be confused with the Bridewell Palace (usually referred to simply as 'Bridewell'), which was the house of correction for the city of London, or with Clerkenwell Bridewell, which was the Middlesex house of correction.

William Smith MD visited Tothill Fields Bridewell in the 1770s and reported that:

> There are sometimes 150 prisoners contained in this gaol at one time [...] There are no baths or bathing tubs [...] The prisoners in this gaol are a miserable set of objects; some of the very lowest order of abandoned women, covered with filth and vermin, eat up with the bad distemper, and broke down by every species of intemperance [...] The inconveniences attending this gaol in common with others I have visited, are a want of a certain allowance of food, more regular medical attendance, a sick ward, some cloaths or covering for those that come in almost literally naked [...] There is in this gaol such a constant fluctuation, some going out, while others are brought in, that it is impossible to keep it free from itch, filth and vermin [...] [The keeper] complains that it is out of his power to keep [the prisoners] from rioting and drunkenness, particularly on Sunday, when numbers of their friends and associates come to them.[4]

Smith, writing about prisons in general, said:

> Few, accustomed to any degree of cleanliness, could
> bear the stench of such places, or stand the shock of
> such misery. Vagrants and disorderly women of the very
> lowest and most wretched class of human beings, almost
> naked, with only a few filthy rags almost alive and in
> motion with vermin, their bodies rotting with the bad
> distemper, and covered with itch, scorbutic and venereal
> ulcers [...] are drove in shoals to gaols, particularly to
> the two Clerkenwells and Tothil-fields, there thirty, and
> sometimes forty of these unhappy wretches are crouded
> or crammed together in one ward [...] In the morning,
> before the turn-keys attempt to open the doors of the
> different wards, which are more like the black hole in
> Calcutta than places of confinement in a Christian coun-
> try, they are obliged to drink a glass of spirits to keep
> them from fainting, for the putrid steam or miasma is
> enough to knock them down. They are very frequently
> seized with such violent retchings, that nothing will lie
> upon their stomachs.[5]

Jacob Ilive, one of the minor characters of Grub Street, was
sentenced to three years' hard labour at the Clerkenwell
house of correction for writing, printing and publishing 'a
most blasphemous book [...] denying in a ludicrous manner
the divinity of Jesus Christ [as well as] all revealed religion'. He
described Sundays in that house of correction:

> As for Drunkenness, both the Men and the Women
> Prisoners are all guilty of it, getting drunk but as often
> as they can, which usually happens on a *Sunday*, for

that Day, being a kind of Holiday with the lower Class of People, they resort hither, and often treat the Prisoners to Excess. And this generally appears in their Fighting and Quarrelling, Swearing and Blasting of a *Sunday* Night, more than all the Nights and Days in the Week put together.[6]

Tothill Fields Bridewell had a licence for beer and wine. The prisoners were allowed a penny loaf a day each. As the weight of a penny loaf varied according to the price of ingredients, the degree of the prisoners' hunger varied with the price of bread. The prisoners were also allowed a penny a day. The keeper, George Smith, stated that this county allowance of twopence a day was insufficient for the maintenance of the convicts, and that they had to rely on the assistance of their friends.[7]

'Garnish' was 1*s* 4*d*. Garnish was an entrance fee that the prisoners demanded newcomers pay into a common fund, otherwise they would have to give up an article of clothing, 'pay or strip', and be denied access to what meagre comforts the other prisoners enjoyed. Using the Marshalsea as an example, in that prison garnish allowed access to the common room, the use of boiling water from the fire, the cooking of food and the reading of newspapers.

The night rooms had barrack beds but no straw or bedding. Unless the prisoners had their own straw or rags to lie in, they had to sleep on the bare boards.[8] When Jonas Hanway visited Tothill Fields Bridewell, he noted that it contained several felons: 'the sessions seldom receiving less than 6 or 7 from hence, who are capitally convicted.'[9] A prisoner who escaped from Tothill Fields Bridewell in 1756 said she did so because she was so hungry she was 'obliged to eat the cabbage stalks off the dunghill.'[10]

Hogarth based Plate IV of his series *The Harlot's Progress* on Tothill Fields Bridewell. It shows Moll Hackabout beating hemp. It is thought that Hogarth had Katherine Hackabout in mind when he used Tothill Fields Bridewell as a model for the print. Sir John Gonson, the Westminster magistrate, sentenced her to hard labour beating hemp at Tothill Fields Bridewell in August 1730.[11] As Moll is wearing fine clothing, totally inappropriate for prison life, Hogarth might also have been referencing Mary Muffet, 'a Woman of Great Note in the Hundreds of Drury'. The justices 'appointed for suppressing the Night-houses and other disorderly Houses' committed her to Tothill Fields Bridewell when she expected to have been either bailed or discharged. So she was, 'now beating Hemp in a Gown very richly laced with Silver'.[12]

Sir John Fielding sent Sarah to Tothill Fields Bridewell along with Lewis Repinder, Catherine Carson and Thomas Chesterman, whom he also committed on 18 November. Fielding committed Repinder on suspicion of having stolen a bond for the payment of money; he was transferred to Newgate on 5 December, but was subsequently released without charge. Catherine Carson was accused of 'knowing and designedly by false Pretences obtaining [from the church-wardens or overseers of the poor] Several Sums of Money with Intent to Cheat & Defraud the Parishioners of the Parish of St Paul's Covent Garden Contrary to the Statute'.[13]

Fielding committed Thomas Chesterman on suspicion of 'having knowingly & feloniously wrote and sent to Mrs Mary Cope a certain Letter without a Name subscribed there threatening to murder her and burn her house against the statute'. John Warrington, Esq. swore that he believed that it was Mrs Cope's servant Thomas Chesterman who wrote the letter signed 'One and twenty bold Fellows' that was sent to Mrs Cope at Hackney, 'not only on account of the hand-writing but for several other reasons'. Thomas Chesterman remained with Sarah in Tothill Fields Bridewell until 3 December 1767 when he was removed to Newgate before being tried at the Middlesex sessions at Hicks Hall in St John Street, Clerkenwell. The Hicks Hall justices sent him to the New Prison, Clerkenwell, for a year. He was released on 13 December 1768.[14]

Also on 18 November, Thomas Kynaston sent Thomas Williams to Tothill Fields for being 'a loose idle Disorderly Person'. Kynaston released Williams seven days later on 25 November.[15]

Tothill Fields Bridewell contained a mix of prisoners: there were those like Sarah who were sent there to await their trials at the next sessions, and others like Thomas Williams, who were sent there for short periods simply as a punishment. The numbers of prisoners varied from day to day as new prisoners arrived and others were released. On the day Sarah arrived at Tothill Fields there were at least thirty female and twenty male prisoners there, some of whom remained with Sarah waiting to take their trials at the next Westminster quarter sessions.

Tothill Associates

Sarah was in Tothill Fields Bridewell for the best part of two months, so she would have developed friendships with her fellow prisoners. Apart from those who were sentenced to hard labour, the prisoners had no employment. In the ample leisure time available to them they would have exchanged stories of their exploits and learned something about each other's lives. Most of her fellow prisoners were victims of being born into a sub-culture of chronic poverty and petty criminality. They were excluded from mainstream culture, in which the rewards of its economic aspirations were all too visible, but which were unattainable to them as a result of uncertain work and low wages.

The women who were Sarah's roommates were mostly thieves and prostitutes. They would have been little different from those Jacob Ilive knew during his term at Clerkenwell Bridewell:

These Molls, who have neither Friends nor Money to support them, fare very hard, and their Condition is very miserable. This Want exposes them to the Lust of every Felon, or other Man here confined, who never fail of improving the Civility they confer on these Girls, of giving them a Mouthful of Victuals, and a Swill of Strong Beer, to their own wicked and debauched Ends. One Felon of the last Session, who spent a good deal of Money on two such needy Girls, it was currently reported, that he was seen in Bed between both of them [...] As to their Conversation, it generally, nay, I may say, always turns on the Obscene; they hourly, even while they are beating Hemp, sing the most lewd Songs, Men or Devils have invented. They can scarce speak a Word, without Swearing, Blasting or Profaning the Sacred Name of GOD [...] They take great Delight in sitting in a Ring, and telling Stories of their own Adventures; how many Men they had bilked, what Sums they had robbed 'em of, and how many Watches they had masoned. Tell who had their Maidenheads; how they were first debauched; how long they had been in Keeping; how many Children they had had, and what was become of them [...] how often, and where they had been in Confinement; whether for Debt or Hard Labour [...] As for their Diversions, when they are not beating of Hemp, they chiefly turn upon, Hunting the Slipper, Thread my Needle Nan, and Prison and Bars. The Men play at Chuck-Farthing, Tossing-up, Leap-Frog, &c. They both take a particular Delight in the Fairy Dance, called Rolly Powly, which is a very merry Exercise, but abominably obscene.[16]

Here are some of the women who were already in Tothill Fields Bridewell when Sarah arrived. Catherine Potts was accused of stealing two diaper tablecloths, value 9*d*. Ann Kelly had been sent to Tothill Fields by Sir John Fielding for 'feloniously taking & Carrying away a Pewter Quart Pott, value 10*d*'. Sarah Clark, otherwise known as Sarah Stevens, was a pickpocket charged with stealing a silk handkerchief, valued at 10*d*. Jane Connor was committed for stealing several linen clothes and one pair of shoes, the whole lot valued at 10*d*.

The justices valued most items that were said to have been stolen at less than a shilling, irrespective of their actual worth. Stealing goods valued at more than a shilling was classed as grand larceny, which could attract the death penalty.

Elizabeth Stevens or Stephenson arrived on 4 November accused of stealing a cloth coat from Daniel Murray, valued at 3*s*. She remained at Tothill Fields with Sarah until 3 December, when she was removed to Newgate to take her trial for grand larceny at the Old Bailey. The report of her trial demonstrates the messiness of such women's lives:

Daniel Murray deposed he had known the prisoner two or three years; that she came to him in the morning, and asked him for a dram; they had one, she paid for it; then they had three or four more; after which she spent a shilling; then he paid for another quartern of gin; that she sent him of on [*sic*] errand, and he left her in his stall till he returned, he missed a coat he had to mend; that he never knew any harm of her before; after he took her up, she first said she had pawned it, and after that brought a Jew, who bought it out: at one time she said she got a shilling of the pawnbroker, and another time she got two, and another time she said she got but a shilling for it of the Jew; that he never got it again, and could he have got it again he would have forgiven her.

Unsurprisingly, she was acquitted.[17]

Margaret Matthews and Anne Cordiner were accused of the same sort of offence as Catherine Carson committed. Sir John Fielding sent Matthews, otherwise known as Stephens, to Tothill Fields for 'knowing and designedly by false pretences obtaining [from the churchwardens or overseers of the poor] Several Sums of Money & 3 Pair of Shoes with Intent to Cheat & Defraud the Parishioners of St Paul Covent Garden'. William Kelynge committed Anne Cordiner for dishonestly obtaining several sums of money from the overseers of the poor for the parish of St George Hanover Square.[18]

When Sarah arrived, Anne Cordiner appeared to be in good health. However, about three weeks later, according to Jane Stevens, a fellow prisoner, Anne was seized with a pain in her side and was 'otherwise out of order'. Despite the attendance of Mr Purdue, an apothecary, Anne grew worse and had almost lost the use of her limbs. She died in the prison between three and four o'clock in the morning of 23 December. The verdict of the coroner's jury was that Anne had died of a fever.[19]

Mary Baker, Charlotte Smith and Elizabeth Shepheard were sentenced to hard labour until the sessions by Sir John Fielding on 28 October for being 'loose Idle Disorderly Persons of Evil Fame & Common Prostitutes'. Despite his original sentence, Sir John discharged Mary Baker on 12 December and the other two on 18 December. Similarly, Thomas Kynaston on 3 November had sentenced Lucy Hudson and Ann Spencer to hard labour to the next sessions for being 'loose Idle Disorderly Persons of Evil Fame and Common Night Walkers', but discharged Lucy on 3 December and Ann on 18 December. Mary Calf, Ann Riddle, Elizabeth Fox, Jane Smith, Jane Lambeth and Mary Hoskins were also sentenced to hard labour for similar offences and discharged at various dates in December after they had served between one and two months.

So when Sarah arrived, she would have seen at least eleven ladies of the night engaged in beating hemp with mallets. The work of beating hemp was done in prisons because it was so arduous, boring and back breaking that nobody outside was prepared to do it. In the houses of correction in some counties, for example, Bedfordshire, Cambridgeshire and Warwickshire, beating hemp was men's work, while the women spun wool or flax.[20] Once broken, hemp was used to make rope, including hangman's rope. A 'hempen collar' was a slang term for a hangman's noose and a 'hempen widow' was a woman whose husband had been hanged. A hanged man was said to have died of 'hempen fever'.

Mary Calf, one of the 'Common Night Walkers', had appeared at the Old Bailey earlier in the year. She had been indicted for stealing 8 guineas from William Roberts, the landlord of the Noah's Ark public house in Clerkenwell. Mary was employed as a servant, probably a barmaid, at the pub.

She stayed there for three days, then she disappeared, and so did the money. William Roberts found her drinking in the Stationer's Arms in St John Street and called a constable. Mary admitted to the constable that she had taken some money, but no more than 3½ guineas. At her trial, she claimed that William Roberts told her that if she admitted taking the money he would let her go. She said she had confessed to a crime she hadn't committed on the strength of William Robert's assurance that she wouldn't be confined. She said her mother gave her the 3½ guineas. The jury, probably out of compassion rather than belief in her story, gave her the benefit of the doubt and acquitted her.[21]

Two days before Sarah arrived, Sir John Fielding sent Charlotte Lyons to Tothill Fields for being a 'loose Idle Disorderly Person of Evil Fame and Common Prostitute'. Charlotte was discharged on 26 November 1767 so Sarah would have only known her for little more than a week. Charlotte was only aged 20 on 22 August 1768 when she was admitted to the workhouse at St Martin's in the Fields. She died there four days later.[22]

When Sarah was in Tothill Fields, a male prisoner, Joseph Blatchford, died. The sole witness at the inquest was a female prisoner, Elizabeth Dyer. She had been sent there for assaulting and beating one Thomas Stoddart. Elizabeth told the coroner that she had been a prisoner at Tothill Fields Bridewell for the past nine weeks and Joseph Blatchford was 'brought prisoner to the said prison' about six weeks ago. She said he appeared to be in ill health and consumptive, but he was able to eat his daily allowance. He grew worse and died at about four o'clock in the morning on Saturday, 2 January.[23]

This example shows that, although there was separate accommodation in Tothill Fields Bridewell for men and women, the sexes mixed freely.[24] Sarah would therefore have developed friendships with the male prisoners as well as other women. Many of the male prisoners were charged with picking pockets. George Trotman was committed by Sir John Fielding on 16 October for picking pockets and 'feloniously taking and carrying away a Handkerchief the Property of a Certain Person as yet unknown, value 10*d*.'[25] He had previous: in November 1766 he had appeared at a court held at Bridewell Hospital charged 'on the Oath of John Barton for Picking his Pocket of a Handkerchief of small value last Night & for being an Idle and Disorderly Person and giving no good Account of himself.'[26]

Other pickpockets waiting to take their trials when Sarah arrived included John Williams, also known as John Blake, charged with picking the pocket of a Dr Frere and stealing his pocketbook; George Edwards, charged with stealing a linen handkerchief, value 10*d*; John Porter, charged with an identical offence; Richard Price, charged with stealing six linen handkerchiefs, value 10*d*; and Thomas Grey, charged with stealing a silk handkerchief, value 10*d*.

George Kingston was another pickpocket. He was committed by Sir John Fielding for stealing a silk handkerchief, value 10*d*.[27] In 1764 he was sentenced at the Old Bailey to be transported for seven years for entering a shop, grabbing the wooden till, value 3*d* and containing 3*s* 4*d*, and running off with it. It is not clear whether he actually was transported. He might have been let off on account of his age. In July 1767 he was accused in his absence of stealing a silver watch on 1 June from a house in Bunhill Row. A witness described him as a 'boy [who] always bore the character of a pickpocket.'[28]

Some of these lads might well have been graduates of the thieves' kitchen, or one similar, that was described in this 1765 newspaper report:

On the examination of the boy admitted evidence against others it appears that the Publican in custody had an association, or club, where they drank punch, and, at proper intervals, he instructed them in picking pockets, and other iniquitous practices, beginning first with picking a handkerchief out of his own pocket, and next his watch, so that at last the evidence was so great an Adept, that he got the Publican's watch four times in one evening, when he swore he was as perfect as one of 20 years practice. The pilfering out of shops was the next art; his Pupils instructions were, that as many Chandlers, or other shops, as had hatches, one boy was to knock for admittance for some trifle, whilst another was lying on his belly, close to the hatch, who, when the boy came out, the hatch on jar, and the owner withdrawn into their little parlour, crawled in, on all fours, and took the tills, or anything else he could meet with, and retired in the same manner, unobserved.[29]

On 3 November Thomas Kynaston sent John Blanch to Tothill Fields for picking a pocket of a linen handkerchief, value 10*d*. Back in July Blanch had appeared at the Old Bailey accused of stealing six shifts, two pairs of worsted stockings, one pair of thread stockings, two linen aprons, four handkerchiefs, one sheet, one linen gown, one flannel petticoat, five pewter plates, four flat irons, a copper chocolate-pot, a copper saucepan, three brass candlesticks, and three leather pocketbooks. Those items had been left temporarily in an empty house while the owner was moving to a new address. Blanch claimed that he found them in an alley, but was found guilty of grand larceny and branded on the thumb.[30]

On 29 October Sir John Fielding committed Joseph Stevens, otherwise known as Richard Stevens, to Tothill

Fields for stealing ten pairs of silk stockings, twelve pairs of women's leather gloves, a black silk sack and petticoat, two riding habits, a black silk gown and petticoat, two bed gowns, three white petticoats, shifts, and other items that were in a big leather trunk owned by the Earl of Thanet.

Stevens remained at Tothill Fields until 3 December, when he was transferred to Newgate to take his trial at the Old Bailey. At his trial on 9 December, Joseph Smith, one of the Earl of Thanet's servants, testified that on 28 October the earl and his wife set out in a post-chaise with four horses and two postilions to come to London about six in the evening. The large leather trunk was safely secured behind the carriage, but when the carriage arrived at its destination, the trunk was gone. Smith found one of the straps between the perch and the axletree of the carriage which appeared to have been cut by two or three attempts with some instrument. He made an account of the trunk's principal items and went immediately to Sir John Fielding. Fielding arranged for handbills describing the missing goods to be delivered about town.

The following day Stevens offered to sell a pair of silk stockings for 3*s* to Jane Lowrey, a second-hand clothes dealer in Rosemary Lane, where Rag Fair was held every afternoon. Mrs Lowery said she would give him 2*s*. He agreed that price and said he had eleven more pairs. She then suspected he had stolen them. She told him she did not have enough money but she could borrow some at a house a little way off. She took him to the Crooked Billet and asked him to wait there while she got the money, but instead she alerted a peace officer. Mrs Lowery returned to the Crooked Billet and sat down next to Stevens. The officer and a colleague entered the pub shortly after. The officer told the court, 'I went and sat down by the prisoner; and said to the woman, Madam, am I right; she said

I was. In a little time I told him I was an officer, and he was my prisoner.'

Although Stevens claimed that he took no part in the actual robbery, which he blamed on his brother, and led the officers to where the rest of the clothes were, he was found guilty and sentenced to be transported.[31] He sailed for Virginia in December 1767 on the *Neptune*, captained by James Arbuckle.

Another character Sarah would have met also accompanied Joseph Stevens to Newgate on 3 December to await his trial at the Old Bailey. James Towers had been sent to Tothill Fields on 4 November accused of stealing a silver watch worth 39*s*. When he appeared at the Old Bailey, the prosecutor, William Waddington, said that he (Waddington) arrived back at his lodgings some time after midnight, but he was too late to be let in. He walked around, but he was cold and tired. Eventually he noticed that the Red Lion in Piccadilly was open. He went in and bought a pint of beer. At ten past three in the morning he looked at his watch. That was the last he could remember before he fell asleep with his head on the table. When he woke up two hours later his watch was gone. He told the landlord he had lost his watch and gave him his address so the landlord could let him know if anyone found it. The following Wednesday someone from the Red Lion took him to a pub in the Haymarket to meet a coachman named Couch who had bought the watch from Towers without realising it was stolen. They then went to the White Bear Inn where they found Towers and took him to Sir John Fielding. The court found Towers guilty of taking the watch from the sleeping man's pocket and sentenced him to be transported for seven years. He sailed with Joseph Stevens on the *Neptune*.[32]

On 14 November Robert Petterson was sentenced to fourteen days' hard labour at Tothill Fields for unlawfully collecting the sea-coal dust and ashes from the inhabitants of the parish of St George, Westminster, the property of the official collector.[33]

These, and the other inmates, were the prisoners to whom Sarah paid her garnish money and who gave her an introduction to the jail. After Sarah arrived, and as the quarter sessions drew closer, the prison began to fill up as the new arrivals outnumbered those who were discharged before the date of the sessions. When the new arrivals entered the prison the existing prisoners would surge around them demanding their garnish money and seeking details of the offences they were charged with.

Two days after Sarah arrived she was joined by William Dunk, John Heatley, William Warner and Richard Cave, who were committed for robbing Richard Hassell and his son of their gold watches and money on the King's Highway near Barnet in Hertfordshire on 2 November. Dunk, Heatley and Warner were moved to Newgate on the 25th. Cave was separated from his accomplices and remained at Tothill Fields as he had decided to give evidence against his fellow highwaymen in a bid to save his neck.[34]

In February 1768 Dunk, Heatley and Warner were escorted from Newgate to the county jail at Hertford to await their trial at Hertford assizes for highway robbery. At the assizes Dunk and Warner were found guilty and Heatley was acquitted. The judge sentenced Dunk and Warner to death, but reprieved Warner on condition of being transported for fourteen years, leaving Dunk for execution. However, the royal clemency was later extended to Dunk on condition that he be transported for the rest of his natural life.[35]

On 28 May 1769, William Jones of Queen Court, Great Queen Street in St Giles in the Fields was woken in the middle of the night by a noise at his parlour window. All of a sudden the shutter burst open, a square of glass smashed, and there was the sound of someone trying to unscrew the sash. Jones ran to the street door and shouted, 'Stop thief!' The burglar ran off, but was pursued and captured by a watchman named William Goodall. The burglar turned out to be William Dunk. At the Old Bailey on 28 June 1769 Dunk was acquitted of the burglary on a technicality. There was a word missing in the indictment. But he was found guilty of returning from transportation and sentenced to death.[36]

On the morning of 26 July 1769 Dunk and three others – Thomas Mellor, Robert Merry and Richard Belcher – left Newgate in two carts to begin their journey to the gallows at Tyburn. Even before they left the prison they would have heard the mourning bells of nearby St Sepulchre's church reminding them of their fate and ringing out the news to Londoners that an execution was about to take place.

Hanging days occurred only eight times a year and were treated as holidays. Outside the gates and all along the route raucous crowds gathered on the roads and people were hanging out of windows of houses, all trying to catch a glimpse of Dunk and his three companions. No one was allowed to get very near to the cart: there had been attempts at rescuing prisoners before, so the city marshal, who was present, ensured that the cart was surrounded by armed guards on horseback. It probably took them three hours to travel the 2½ miles because of the crowds obstructing the streets that needed to be cleared away.

The route from Newgate to Tyburn (near where Marble Arch now is) passed along Holborn, St Giles and the Tyburn Road (Oxford Street). While they were passing through St Giles, 'the horse of one Mr Giles, a Sheriff's Officer, started and threw his rider, who pitching on his head, dislocated the vertebrae of his neck, and died upon the Spot'.

It was the custom for the condemned felons to have a few drinks on their last journey, stopping off at the Bowl Inn at St Giles and the Masons Arms in Seymour Place, and possibly other pubs, to fortify them against the ordeal ahead.

When they arrived at Tyburn there was a huge crowd waiting for them. There was the noise and bustle of hawkers shouting their wares of food and souvenirs, women selling copies of the prisoners' last dying speeches that had been printed days before those last words had been spoken, and massed ranks of pickpockets, undeterred by the example dangling before them. The newspaper account of Dunk's execution said that it was 'attended by a prodigious concourse of people, the greatest part of whom were females'.[37]

After the execution, a mob attacked the undertaker who was taking away the bodies of Merry and Belcher for burial, and 'used him so cruelly that his life is despaired of', in the mistaken belief that he was going to sell the bodies to the anatomists. Although Dunk and Thomas Mellor, who had been condemned for a rape, had not known each other before they met in Newgate, they had built up such a friendship, being thrown together within the confines of the prison and finding themselves in the same situation, that they asked to be interred in the same grave.[38] This was an example of how prisoners confined together could develop strong bonds with each other in a relatively short period of time.

As for Richard Cave, on 17 March 1768 he was found guilty at the Old Bailey of stealing a leather pocketbook, valued at 2s, by pushing against the owner and grabbing the book as he left the Royal Exchange. The book contained bills totalling £3,500. When he was caught he was found to have been carrying eleven handkerchiefs and two or three pocketbooks. He was found guilty of grand larceny and sentenced to be transported for seven years. The report of his trial commented: 'The prisoner is the person who gave evidence against Dunk and two others, who were capitally convicted at Hertford last assize, for a robbery near Barnet. It appears that the prisoner was the person who acted the most in that robbery.'[39]

Three days after Sarah arrived, eighteen women and girls described as 'Common Night Walkers' joined her in the women's side of the jail. On 30 November twelve more arrived. They were sentenced to hard labour until the sessions. Nearly every day women described as 'Common Night Walkers' or 'Common Prostitutes' were added to the number of prisoners (I have yet to find a committal of an uncommon prostitute). One 'Common Night Walker' who arrived at Tothill Fields on 24 December was shown in the list of committals as rejoicing in the name of Twiddy Hartsthorne.

On 30 November Charles Stevens added to the Hogarthian picture of Tothill Fields Bridewell. He was sentenced to hard labour for a month for being an 'Idle Disorderly Apprentice refusing to obey his Master's Lawful Commands Contrary to the Statute'. It is not known whether he shared the same fate as Hogarth's Idle Apprentice.

On 11 December Elias Perry was committed for obtaining a suit of clothes from a tailor by false pretences. He told the tailor that his name was John Eaves and that he was a printer who worked for Mr Faden in Peterborough Court, Fleet Street. He said that James Hudson, who also worked for Mr Faden, and was a regular customer of the tailor, had recommended him. He ordered a suit which he said he needed in order to accompany Mr Hudson to an event on the next Friday evening, and would pay him the next Saturday. He thus managed to walk off with a cloth coat worth £3, a cloth waist-coat and a cloth pair of breeches, both valued at £1.[40]

On 14 December Sir John Fielding sent James Blakey to Tothill Fields on suspicion of stealing a cloth coat and waist-coat. Blakey was transferred to Newgate on 7 January. At the Old Bailey session on 14 January 1768 the owner of the clothes said that Blakey admitted that he had pawned them; Blakey had been 'out of bread, and had nothing valuable in his chest'. He said that he thought 'it was poverty, rather than a bad wicked heart that drove him to it'. Blakey was found guilty of stealing goods to the value of 10*d* even though the indictment said that the coat was valued at 12*s* and the waistcoat was valued at 6*s*. He was sentenced to be whipped and then released.[41]

Sir John Fielding committed John Upton on 21 December for stealing a knife from one Oliver Dowle. Upton was also accused of stealing from a summerhouse in Camberwell a silver watch and a brass-mounted blunderbuss. It was thought that he had either pawned them or left them in a pub. On 30 December Upton was further accused of assaulting and robbing Henry Martin on the King's Highway in Surrey.[42]

Sarah Mason arrived at Tothill Fields on 29 December. She was accused of receiving money from the overseers of the poor of the parish of St Margaret's Westminster by falsely claiming that her husband lived in that parish and was lately dead and had left her with four children and big with a fifth. She was also accused of receiving money from the overseers of the poor of the parish of St John the Evangelist by claiming that the fictional dead husband lived in that parish.[43]

Others who joined Sarah to await their trials at the quarter sessions included William Miller, who was com-mitted for stealing three linen handkerchiefs; Mary Wall, for stealing 50lb of potatoes in Covent Garden Market;

George Thompson, for 'unlawfully Breaking into the Dwelling House of Lady Catherine Pelham in White Hall with intent to Commit Burglary there'; William Mahany, for stealing a lead pipe weighing 10lb and a brass cock from someone's house; and Thomas Howard, for stealing 9 yards of satin.[44]

On 2 January 1768 William Kelynge sent Joseph Smith to Tothill Fields Bridewell. The newspapers described Smith as follows:

> He is about forty years of age, about six feet two inches high, and stout made in proportion, at present wears his short black hair, but is supposed to have lately wore a wig, his now dress a second mourning coat, and scarlet gold-laced waistcoat, says he was born in Derbyshire, but appears to have spent some time in Holland, speaks Dutch fluently, and hath gone by the names of Wild and Frederick-Theodore Birckenfeld, has been a soldier in and deserted from one of the English regiments of Foot, and is supposed to have sometime supported himself in England, especially in town, by begging of gentlemen at their houses in the character of a distressed gentleman from misfortunes, and particularly by imposing on many of the dissenting ministers.[45]

This colourful character was committed 'on the oath of Job Gardner on suspicion of being guilty of Buggery on the Body of a Mare in the County of Gloucester against the Peace'.[46] There appear to be no records of what happened to him after his committal, but presumably he was conveyed to Gloucester.

Westminster Quarter Sessions

The general quarter sessions for the City and Liberty of Westminster were held at the new Guildhall in King Street, Westminster, from Thursday, 7 January to Saturday, 9 January 1768. Cases were first considered by a grand jury who decided whether the evidence was sufficient to warrant a trial. If the grand jury decided the evidence was sufficient, the case was approved as a true bill and proceeded to trial in front of a petty jury. Where the grand jury considered the evidence was insufficient, it was labelled 'not found' and the case was dropped.

Sarah Clark and Ann Kelly, who had both been stuck in Tothill Fields Bridewell since October, had their charges declared not found and were released. A few days after her release, Ann Kelly and an accomplice, Anne Martin, met a man named William Bignall in Shoreditch. Bignall told the jury at the Old Bailey that the two women enticed him into Kelly's lodgings. He said he sat on the bed, with the two women on either side of him, and:

> We had not been in the room but about four minutes before Martin took my pocket-book, and Kelly my purse with my money [...] they ran down stairs, I went to run after them; there stood another woman behind the door, and she pushed me about so I could not get out quick enough.

Despite his testimony, Ann Kelly and her companion were acquitted.[47]

Mary Wall (the alleged potato stealer), George Trotman and William Miller were also declared not found. Following his release, William Miller turned highwayman. On the night of Saturday, 9 June 1768 he, Patrick Hanlon and John Leicester, all three armed with pistols, held up a coach on the new road to Hampstead. Sarah Rogers was the only passenger. She said the three men ordered the coachman to stop. One of the men presented a pistol and told her that if she did not deliver her money they would shoot her. He took her purse from out of her hand; it contained money in gold and silver, a Spanish dollar and a crown piece.

As a result of this and other reports of robberies on the new road, Sir John Fielding ordered a decoy coach containing four Bow Street Runners to go down the new road the following night. Sure enough, about two fields before the Tottenham Court turnpike, the three highwaymen attempted to rob the coach. When they stopped the coach, the Bow Street Runners leapt out. They managed to capture Leicester, but the other two got away. Leicester decided to save his neck by turning evidence and told the runners where Miller and Hanlon lived. Miller and Hanlon appeared at the Old Bailey on 19 October 1768 and were sentenced to death. They were hanged at Tyburn on 23 November 1768.[48]

The fate of some of the other characters whom Sarah had got to know was as follows. The grand jury found a true bill for Catherine Potts but the petty jury found her not guilty of stealing the two tablecloths. Jane Connor, John Porter, Thomas Grey, Thomas Patterson, George Thompson, John Blanch and George Edwards were all found guilty and sentenced to be whipped.[49]

Although Blanch had been branded for picking pockets, and now was sentenced to be whipped for a similar offence, he carried on as before. On 28 October 1768 he was caught picking a pocket of a linen handkerchief in Fleet Street.

He was found guilty at the Old Bailey and sentenced to seven years' transportation.[50] He left England on the convict ship *Thornton* in January 1769 bound for Maryland.

Sarah Mason and Margaret Matthews were also sentenced to be whipped. In Sarah Mason's case, she was sentenced to be whipped from the Gatehouse to the Broadway, Tothill Street. Margaret Matthews was sentenced to be whipped round the rails of Covent Garden on the first Friday in February. The petty jury found that Margaret Matthews:

> Being a person of Evil Name and Fame and of Dishonest Conversation and not minding to gain her Livelihood by Truth and Honest Labour but going about and daily continuing and intending to Cheat and Defraud the honest Subjects of our said Lord the King of their Goods and Monies on the Tenth Day of July came to one of the Overseers of the Poor of the Parish of Saint Paul Covent Garden and then and there prayed Relief for herself and three Children as being legally settled in the said Parish of Saint Paul Covent Garden and then and there unlawfully fraudulently and wilfully did falsely pretend that she was the Widow of William Matthews dec'd & that she was married to him at the Fleet fourteen Years ago and upwards and that her said Husband lived as a yearly hired Servant with Mr Venables at the Bedford Arms under the Piazza within the Parish of Saint Paul Covent Garden Victualler for the space of four Years at the Yearly Wage of Ten Pounds [...] and that she had three Children then living by her said Husband [...] and did obtain [...] five shillings of lawful money [and] three pairs of leather shoes the value of five shillings and two pence [...] whereas in Truth and in Fact the said Margaret was not

the Widow of the said William Matthews and never had three Children [and] was not legally settled in the said Parish of St Paul's Covent Garden.

The document went on to describe a similar offence of claiming a settlement in the parish of St George Hanover Square and obtaining money from the parishioners by pretending to be the widow of one John Stevens.

Elias Perry was fined and sentenced to be imprisoned for a further month. John Williams, alias Blake, Richard Price, George Kingston, John Upton, William Mahany and Thomas Howard were sentenced to be transported for seven years. James Crosby and Thomas Probert, who were committed directly to the quarter sessions, were also sentenced to seven years' transportation. James Crosby was described as 'an Irish Lad, about 22 Years of Age, 5 Feet 8 Inches high, very fair Complexion, and a little Cross-Eyed.'[51] He was found guilty of stealing a hat, value 10*d*.

In Sarah's case, the grand jury found a true bill, and the petty jury that was selected to decide her case found her guilty. Some of the details of the offence shown in the court documents differed from the newspaper account. According to the court documents the jury found that Sarah:

On the third day of December in the sixth year of the reign of our Lord Sovereign King George the third [1765] [...] unlawfully knowingly and designedly did falsely pretend [...] that her (the said Sarah Wilson's) name was Sarah Charlotte Wilbraham and that she was a young Lady of fortune and had then run away from her Boarding School because her friends [meaning relatives or guardians] wanted her to marry against her Will and that she was agoing to Mr Child's a Banker near Temple Bar to receive money for a hundred pounds note and that if she (the said Jane) would lend her Cloaths to go on that she would return them in the Evening and make her a very handsome present for the use of them by means of said false pretences she the said Sarah did then and there unlawfully, knowingly and designedly obtain [the clothes listed below] of the Goods and Chattels of the said Samuel [...] To the great deception of the said Jane and damage of the said Samuel in Evil Example of all others in the like Case.

The clothes that, 'by means of said false pretences', Sarah did 'unlawfully, knowingly and designedly obtain' were:

One Linen Cap of the value of one shilling;
One Bead Necklace of the value of one shilling;
One Sattin Hat of the value of three shillings;
One silk cloak of the value of Twenty shillings;
One linen Handkerchief of the value of one shilling;
One pair of stays of the value of Twenty shillings;
One linnen Shift of the value of Two Shillings;
One linen petticoat of the value of five shillings;
One pair of linen sleeves of the value of one shilling;
One pair of stone shoe Buckles set in Silver of the value of five shillings;
One pair of Stone Sleeve Buttons of the value of two shillings;
One pair of stuff shoes of the value of four shillings;
One pair of Cotton stockings of the value of three shillings;
One pair of linen Ruffles of the value of three shillings;

One linen Apron of the value of three shillings;
One pair of linen pockets of the value of one shilling;
One pair of silk mittens of the value of three shillings.[52]

Sarah had therefore got away with goods valued at £3 18*s*, the equivalent of about £650 at 2018 prices.

It seems unlikely that anyone would trust a total stranger with such valuable clothes on the strength of a promise to bring them back in the evening, so the newspaper account of Sarah and Mrs Davenport's niece travelling together to see Mr Child seems more credible. Unlike the trials at the Old Bailey, there was no shorthand writer to provide a verbatim account of the trial to be sold in the streets as a fourpenny pamphlet, so we don't know whether the story of Sarah borrowing the clothes and promising to return them that evening was a way of keeping the court record concise, or whether the story of the visit to the bank and to Lincoln's Inn Fields was a piece of journalistic fiction. Whichever version of the circumstances surrounding the crime was correct, the fact remains that Sarah managed to use her actress's skills to enable her to walk off with £3 18*s*-worth of clothes.

There had been other cases in the 1760s of women found guilty of defrauding shopkeepers in London. In 1763 Lucy Bruguiere obtained various items of silk and other cloth on seven separate occasions from a mercer on Ludgate Hill by pretending she was acting on behalf of one of the mercer's established customers, a Mrs Minet. The crime only came to light when the mercer was alerted by a suspicious pawnbroker. The same year Ann Thompson was found guilty of defrauding a Mr Rogers of a crepe sack and petticoat by false pretences. The method she used was not recorded. In 1767 Elizabeth Southern obtained 36 yards of silk ribbon and

12 yards of flowered gauze from a silk weaver's shop in Wood Street, Cheapside. The method she used was similar to that used by Lucy Bruguiere: she pretended to be an employee of a shopkeeper in St James's Street who was a regular customer.[53]

The practice of pretending to be acting on behalf of a customer who had an account with the shopkeeper was a common technique. By contrast, whether Sarah pretended to be the abandoned wife of a count with a note for £100 payable by Mr Child, or a girl with the £100 note escaping from boarding school to avoid a loveless marriage, she showed imagination and ingenuity.

The court sentenced Sarah to be transported for seven years. The brief newspaper account listing the names of those convicted at the session and their sentences added:

> The above Sarah Wilson, otherwise Wilbraham, one of the Transports, is the same Woman who for some Time since appeared at St Albans, at Coventry, and that Neighbourhood, as well as in other Parts of the Country, in the Character of the Countess of Wilbraham, and imposed on several of the Nobility and Gentry.[54]

Newgate

It is not known whether Sarah and the eight men who were also sentenced at the quarter sessions to transportation were taken to Newgate straight away to wait for the next convict ship, or whether they were sent back to Tothill Fields Bridewell and moved to Newgate later. According to John Howard, the prison reformer, prisoners from the Poultry Compter, Wood

Street Compter and Clerkenwell Bridewell who were sentenced to transportation were taken straight from the courts by Mr Akerman. This was Richard Akerman, who was the keeper at Newgate. In John Howard's entry for Tothill Fields Bridewell, he simply said, 'Transports, taken by Mr Akerman', but he didn't say at what point they were taken.[55]

As we have seen, eighteenth-century London was a horribly smelly place, but despite the competing smells, as Sarah and her companions drew within a few streets of Newgate, they would have noticed an even fouler stench coming from the prison that infiltrated the entire neighbourhood. At the Old Bailey sessions in April 1750 the people in the courtroom were 'severely afflicted with a noisome smell [from] the putrid effluvia which the prisoners brought with them in their clothes' from Newgate. Within a week, or ten days at most, many people who were in the court were seized with a malignant fever and sixty-four of them died, including the Lord Mayor of London, two of the judges, several lawyers and five jurymen.[56]

In 1757 the residents of the streets surrounding Newgate petitioned the corporation, 'setting forth their apprehension from their vicinity to Newgate, and from the stenches proceeding therefrom, of being subject to an infectious disease called the gaol distemper'.[57] According to the coroner for Middlesex, 132 prisoners died of the contagion in Newgate between 1755 and 1765, 28 of them in 1763.[58] Gaol distemper, also known as jail fever, was a type of typhus fever spread by ticks and fleas on rodents.

John Howard wrote that the air in prisons was made poisonous by the effluvia from the sick and what else in prisons was offensive. His clothes on visits were so offensive that he was obliged to travel on horseback rather than in a coach, and the pages of his memorandum book were often so tainted that he could not use it until after spending an hour or two disinfecting it before the fire. Describing the state of Newgate as it stood when Sarah was there, he said:

> The Builders of Old Newgate seem to have regarded in their Plan, nothing but the single article of keeping prisoners in safe custody. The rooms and cells were so close, as to be almost the constant seats of disease, and sources of infection; to the destruction of multitudes, not only in the Prison, but abroad.[59]

Samuel Denne, writing in 1771, said that there was no prison in the kingdom:

> Where there are so great a number of abandoned criminals as inhabit Newgate [...] These filthy and miserable wretches disperse their putrid and pestilential vapours far and wide; and, as it is remarked of a species of nasty animals, can annoy at a distance those whom they deem their enemies, without hurting themselves.[60]

When Sarah arrived at Newgate, she had to decide whether to enter that part of the prison known as the Master Felons' Side, or whether to enter the Common Felons' Side. A person needed to have a great deal of money in order to be admitted to the Master Felons' Side; in 1724 the upfront costs were 14s 10d for fees and garnish money, 1s 6d for coals, and 1s to the prisoners who belonged to the newcomer's ward. Other costs included 3s 6d a week for the use of a feather bed.[61]

Batty Langley described the Common Felons' Side as 'a most Terrible Wicked and Dreadful Place'. That side comprised five wards, two of which were for women, and three for men. The first women's ward was a 'very dark and stinking place'. It had an oak plank floor, which was 'all the Bed allotted for its miserable inhabitants'. The second women's ward was a very large room with only one window, which was very small. On each side of the ward were barracks, but without any bedding. He said that the persons imprisoned on the Common Felons' Side were:

> Generally those that lie for Transportation; and they knowing their Time to be short here, rather than bestow one Minute towards cleaning the same, suffer themselves to live far worse than Swine; and, to speak the Truth, the *Augean* Stable could bear no Comparison to it, for they are almost poisoned with their own Filth, and their Conversation is nothing but one continued Course of Swearing, Cursing and Debauchery, insomuch that it surpasses all Description and Belief.
>
> It is with no small Concern, that I am obliged to observe, That the Women in every Ward of this Prison, are exceedingly worse than the worst of the Men, not only in respect to Nastiness and Indecency of living, but more especially as to their Conversation, which, to their great Shame, is as profane and wicked, as Hell itself can possibly be.[62]

It is not known for certain how long Sarah remained in Newgate. It is likely, however, that she was transported on the next available ship, which wasn't until April when the *Thornton* commanded by Christopher Read sailed for Maryland 'with near 200 Felons on board'.[63] We do not know for certain that Sarah sailed on the *Thornton*, but there seems no reason why she would have kept in jail any longer than was necessary. It is just possible that she paid for her own passage to avoid being transported with the other convicts and sold into slavery once she reached America. However, there is no evidence that she made arrangements with the authorities to ensure that she transported herself, so I think it reasonable to assume that she was treated like any other convict and sailed on the *Thornton*.

TRANSPORTATION TO AMERICA

Most people know that Britain transported convicts to Australia. The joke is that (white) Australia is populated by the descendants of convicts. However, the same could be said for America, albeit to a lesser extent. Before the American War of Independence, Britain transported tens of thousands of convicts to America. It is reckoned that transported felons made up a quarter of all British immigrants who arrived in the American colonies in the eighteenth century.[1]

'Lewd and Dangerous Persons'

Richard Hakluyt was probably the first person to come up with the idea of sending English convicts to America. In his *Discourse Concerning Western Planting* written in 1584 he noted that:

Many thousandes of idle persons are within this realme, which, havinge no way to be sett on worke, be either mutinous and seeke alteration in the state, or at leaste very burdensome to the common wealthe, and often fall to pilfering and thevinge and other lewdnes, whereby all the prisons of the lande are daily pestred and stuffed full of them, where either they pitifully pyne awaye, or els at lengthe are miserably hanged.

He recommended that 'these pety theves mighte be comdempned for certen yeres in the western partes'.

However, it was not until the Order of 23 January 1615 that the Privy Council authorised the reprieve of prisoners from capital punishment so that they might 'yeald a proffitable service to the commonwealth in partes abroade where it shal be found fitt to emploie them'. In 1656 the Council of State ordered the transportation to America of 'lewd and dangerous persons who have no way of livelihood'.

By the early years of the eighteenth century it was clear that the existing arrangements for transportation were inadequate. Not enough people were being transported. Jailers were reluctant to hand their prisoners over to the shippers because they would lose their fees and the charges they were able to extract from their inmates. Ships' captains were unwilling to carry convicts because of the dangers they posed to both vessel and crew. Merchants, who were dependent on sales for their profits, were reluctant to ship anyone without saleable skills. There was no proper system in place to make sure that those who were sentenced to be transported actually were transported; many never left the country. Courts therefore saw little point in including transportation in their range of sentences.

In the meantime, the system of law and order was in crisis. Employment opportunities for the poorer elements of society had not kept pace with the growth in population, and wages had not kept pace with the cost of living. Between a quarter and a half of the population subsisted in poverty, leaving many of them little alternative but turning to 'pilferinge and thevinge and other lewdnes'. Unemployed soldiers returning after the end of the War of the Spanish Succession in 1714 helped to swell an already growing jail population.

The overcrowded London jails were so unhealthy that many inmates died from disease or starvation. The movement of people from the countryside to London and the major cities meant that they were no longer kept in check by their communities. Once a person moved from their village or small town to London, they no longer had to suffer the humiliation and embarrassment of having to undergo the old public punishments of whippings, brandings and the pillory in front of their relations and neighbours. As those punishments were now performed in front of strangers, they had little effect and were less likely to shame lawbreakers into reforming their behaviour.

The failure to renew the Licensing Act in 1695 meant that pre-publication censorship had been abolished. Anyone could now set up a printing press anywhere in the country. The resultant flood of printed material in the early years of the eighteenth century included reports of highwaymen, footpads and housebreakers in the newspapers, transcripts of trials in the Old Bailey Sessions Papers, the dying speeches of executed criminals and criminal biographies in chapbooks and pamphlets. This proliferation of stories about crime and criminals strengthened the perception that crime was running out of control. There was widespread concern that the existing penal policy had failed to act as a deterrent to wrong-doers. A new solution had to be found for the increasing numbers of felons overrunning London.

At the same time there was a shortage of workers in the American colonies. This was especially the case in Virginia and Maryland, where the production and export of tobacco had become the main source of income after John Rolfe shipped the first marketable harvest of *Nicotiana tabacum* to England in 1614. As the cultivation of tobacco spread, the demand for workers increased. This demand at first was satisfied by indentured servants who came mostly from England, worked for a fixed number of years for those who paid their passage, and then became 'free' planters them-selves. In the middle decades of the seventeenth century, crop failures in England and Wales prompted many to leave to start afresh in the New World. However, political sta-bility after the Glorious Revolution of 1688 and improved economic conditions in Britain resulted in a reduction in the numbers of those who were willing to go to America as indentured servants. By the eighteenth century, the rapidly expanding tobacco and grain economies and ironworks of Maryland and Virginia needed increasingly large amounts of cheap labour.

Tobacco was a very labour-intensive crop, requiring many workers who all needed feeding. Plantation owners therefore also grew corn, wheat, beans and other food crops. Maryland was also becoming a major centre of iron production – by the 1770s it had eighteen furnaces and twenty forges – and as the planters, farmers, ironmasters and other settlers could no longer rely on an influx of indentured servants, they faced the problem of trying to find workers at a price cheap enough to enable them to grow their businesses.

Sir William Thornton was a prominent lawyer who had long recognised that the existing punishments had failed to deter people from committing crimes such as robbery, burglary and larceny. Juries were often reluctant to find people guilty of capital offences, and they would underestimate the value of stolen goods to save the person from hanging. Because the jails were not intended for long-term incarceration, criminals escaped with a whipping or a branding and were then released back onto the streets to commit more crimes.

Sir William was convinced that a proper system of convict transportation was necessary. When he became Solicitor General in 1717 he was able to put his belief into practice by drafting a bill that would add transportation to the list of sentencing options judges could use. He persuaded parliament that transportation would kill two birds with one stone by getting rid of unwanted criminals and helping to satisfy the American colonies' need for cheap labour. In other words, the British government would be ridding the mother country of a serious nuisance, while at the same time arguing that its actions were benevolent.

The Transportation Act

The preamble to the Act For the Further Preventing of Robbery, Burglary and Other Felonies, and For the More Effectual Transportation of Felons, and Unlawful Exporters of Wool; and For the Declaring the Law upon Some Points Relating to Pirates (4 Geo. I, c.11), otherwise known as the Transportation Act 1718, made it clear that the Act was intended to meet those twin purposes:

It is found by experience, that the punishments inflicted by the Laws now in force against the offences of robbery, larceny and other felonious taking or stealing of money and goods have not proved effectual to deter wicked and evil-disposed persons from being guilty of the said crimes [...] and [...] in many of his Majesty's colonies and plantations in America, there is a great want of servants, who by their labour and industry might be the means of improving and making the said colonies and plantations more useful to this Nation.

The act provided that those who were guilty of capital offences could be reprieved on condition of transportation for fourteen years or life. Those guilty of lesser offences could be sentenced to be transported for seven years. The act also specified that those who returned to England before the term of their sentence had expired were liable to be sentenced to death.

People who were sentenced to transportation were passed to convict merchants who had contracted with the courts to 'convey or cause to be conveyed on board some ships [...] bound for America all and every malefactors [...] lying under sentence of transportation without excepting or refusing by reason of age, lameness or other infirmities [...] at his own [expense]'.[2] John Stewart, who was the main contractor for transporting convicts sentenced to transportation by the courts of London, Middlesex and the Home Counties at the time that Sarah was transported, was paid £5 for each convict. Before each voyage, Stewart and the captain of the ship entered into a bond that they would:

Transport or cause to be Transported effectually all and every of the Convicts [...] to some of his Majesty's Colonies and Plantations in America [...] and shall procure from the Governor or Chief Customhouse Officer of the Place whereunto they shall be sent an Authentic Certificate of their landing there (Death and Casualties of the Sea excepted).

Once the convicts had been conveyed to the merchants, the government ceased to have any responsibility for their care; they had become the private property of the merchants, who were free to dispose of them for their own profit. The merchants, who were generally shippers who dealt in tobacco, recouped the cost of transportation by auctioning off the convicts to plantation owners and others on arrival in America.

Between 1718 and 1775, more than 90 per cent of the transported convicts were shipped to Maryland and Virginia,[3] where the demand for labour was such that a better price could be had for them. The second advantage to the merchants was that they could fill their ships for the return voyage from those two colonies with tobacco, wheat, corn and pig iron.

Alexander Cluny, writing in 1769, said that in the previous three years Maryland and Virginia had exported an average of 96,000 hogsheads of tobacco a year worth £768,000; £35,000-worth of iron; £40,000-worth of wheat and £197,000 of other goods. The tobacco trade gave 'constant Employment to 330 Sail of Ships, and 3,960 Sailors.'[4]

Women and Crime

After the passing of the act, transportation became the main punishment at the courts' disposal. From May 1718 to 1776 (when the American War of Independence brought an end to the practice of transportation to America), over 70 per cent of those who were found guilty at the Old Bailey were sentenced to be transported, compared with less than 1 per cent in the period from 1700 to March 1718.[5]

Between 1718 and 1776 some 52,200 convicts had been consigned to British merchants and transported to the American colonies, of whom around 20 per cent were women. A census for Maryland showed that in 1755 there were 1,574 male convict servants (1,507 men and 67 boys aged under 16) and 407 female convict servants (386 women and 21 girls aged under 16).[6] The females represented 20.6 per cent of the total.

That around 1,000 people a year were banished from the shores of Great Britain was the result of the rapid demographic changes during that period that helped create the conditions for rising crime. This particularly affected women. During the eighteenth century, the technological developments associated with the Industrial Revolution meant that the traditional means of female employment – spinning and weaving – moved from the cottage to the mill, and from the country to the town. Enclosure and the enhancement of landed estates often resulted in the cottage disappearing along with the cottage industry. Due to the declining employment opportunities in agriculture and cottage industries, there were few jobs available in the countryside for women and many moved to London and other large cities in search of work.

Sir John Fielding, writing in the *London Chronicle*, said:

The infinite variety of professions, trades, and manufactures, joined to the army, navy, and services, leave few men idle, unless from choice; whilst women have few trades, and fewer manufactures to employ them: Hence it is, that the general resource of young women is to go into service; and it is for that reason that there is always in London an amazing number of women servants out of place [...] and as the chief of these come from the country, and are far distant from their friends, they are obliged, when out of place, to go into lodgings, and there to subsist on their little savings [...] till their all is spent.[7]

Many young women who moved to London faced a number of problems. If they failed to obtain work quickly, they might easily find themselves destitute. If they did find work, their pay was considerably lower than that for men. James Boswell once asked Samuel Johnson:

What is the reason that women servants, though obliged to be at the expense of purchasing their own clothes, have much lower wages than men servants, to whom a great proportion of that article is furnished, and when in fact our female house servants work much harder than the male?

Boswell said that Johnson could not answer and that he never found anyone else who could.[8]

Women's work tended to be more seasonal, especially for those who worked in market gardens or who peddled goods in the streets. Even those who managed to find a live-in job as a servant might find themselves out on the streets when the family returned to the country at the end of the London season. During periods of unemployment or underemployment the women were forced to consider other means of supporting themselves, which might include prostitution or crime. A number of women were transported because they had been found guilty of stealing from their lodgings. Some had simply sold the goods they had taken. Others, in the absence of any mechanism for obtaining short-term loans, had pawned the goods in order to eat, and fully intended to redeem and return the goods when they had the means to do so. Many of the offences for which women were transported were crimes of theft, brought about by economic necessity rather than greed.

For many women, being sentenced to transportation filled them with horror. The thought of being exiled from all that was familiar was bad enough, but it was heartbreaking for mothers sentenced to be separated from their babies or from young children whom they might never see again. Unless there was a close family member who could take care of the children, the older ones were left to fend for themselves and the younger ones became pauper inmates of the London workhouses. In many London parishes in the 1760s the death rate among workhouse children aged under 12 months was between 80 and 100 per cent, and the figures for those aged over 12 months weren't much better.[9]

While the sentence of transportation was likely to have been a shock to Sarah, she probably took it better than most. She was a loner with no fixed roots and apparently with no close family. Even so, she must have been anxious about what lay in store for her in a strange country: a land of cruel masters, savage Indians and wild beasts. She would also have been anxious about the dangers of the crossing, fearful of shipwreck and drowning.

Most newspapers at the time carried a number of short paragraphs under the heading 'Ship News', listing the arrivals and departures from London and the other ports, and the ships lost at sea. By this means shipowners, merchants and insurers could keep track of their investments, and families could learn of the safe arrival – or otherwise – of their loved ones.

The massive human tragedy caused by the losses of ships was reduced to one sentence per ship:

> The *Young William*, Clancy, from Malaga, for Dublin, is lost on the Coast of Lancashire, and all the Crew except the Master and one Boy, perished.
> The *Isabella*, Jordan, from Leith, to Plymouth, is lost.[10]

Occasionally, readers were given a first-hand account from a survivor of a shipwreck, as in the case of the narrative that appeared in both the *Gentleman's Magazine* for July 1737 and the *Political State of Great Britain* for the same month, where the survivors had to resort to cannibalism.

Not all convict ships arrived safely in America. The *Mary*, with fifty-two convicts on board, was lost at sea.[11] The *Plain Dealer* bound for Maryland with 136 convicts from Newgate was taken by the *Zephyre*, a French man-of-war; Captain Dobbins, most of his crew and some of the convicts were put on board the *Zephyre*, and about thirty-five of the male convicts and all the female convicts were kept on board the *Plain Dealer*, which was taken as a prize and sailed for France. The *Plain Dealer* was lost near Brest and all on board were drowned except seven Frenchmen.[12] Shipwreck was an ever-present fear.

'Draining the Nation of its Offensive Rubbish'

While transportation was a more humane substitute for hanging, only a small minority of those who were transported were guilty of a capital crime. For the vast majority transportation was a much harsher punishment than they would have received before the Transportation Act. Men and women who would have been whipped or branded on the thumb and then set free were now being transported across the seas to be sold as slaves for seven years.

According to George Ollyffe, the vicar of Wendover, transportation served the purpose of 'draining the Nation of its offensive Rubbish, without taking away their Lives'.[13] While some saw transportation as a severe punishment by exiling convicts to seven or fourteen years of forced servitude, others regarded transportation as offering rehabilitation to the convicts by giving them the opportunity to make a new life in a new country away from the temptations of their old haunts. *Moll Flanders*, published in 1722, was a piece of propaganda supporting transportation's supposed redemptive powers. Defoe compared the destructiveness of imprisonment with what he saw as the benefits of transportation. He was careful to show Maryland and Virginia in a favourable light.

While the plantation owners and ironmasters of Maryland and Virginia welcomed the influx of cheap labour, other Americans, particularly those in the northern colonies, were less enthusiastic. After a spate of crimes in Maryland and Virginia in 1751, Benjamin Franklin wrote to the *Pennsylvania Gazette*. Referring to the 'mother country' preventing colonial assemblies from making laws for preventing or discouraging the importation of convicts from Britain on the grounds that such laws would 'prevent the Improvement and well peopling of the Colonies', he suggested that America should export rattlesnakes in return for the convicts:

Such a tender *parental* Concern in our *Mother Country* for the *Welfare* of her Children, calls aloud for the

highest *Returns* of Gratitude and Duty [...] In some
of the uninhabited Parts of these Provinces, there are
Numbers of these venomous Reptiles we call Rattle-
Snakes; Felons-convict from the Beginning of the World:
These, whenever we meet with them, we put to Death
[...] however mischievous those Creatures are with us,
they may possibly change their Natures, if they were to
change the Climate; I would humbly propose, that this
general Sentence of *Death* be changed for *Transportation*
[...] some Thousands might be collected annually, and
transported to Britain. There I would propose to have
them carefully distributed in St. James's Park, in the
Spring-Gardens and other Places of Pleasure about
London; in the Gardens of all the Nobility and Gentry
throughout the Nation; but particularly in the Gardens of
the *Prime Ministers,* the *Lords of Trade* and *Members of
Parliament;* for to them we are *most particularly* obliged
[...] Our *Mother* knows what is best for us. What is a little
Housebreaking, Shoplifting, or *Highway Robbing;* what
is a *Son* now and then *corrupted* and *hang'd,* a Daughter
debauch'd and *pox'd,* a Wife *stabb'd,* a Husband's *Throat
cut,* or a Child's *Brains beat out* with an Axe, compar'd
with this 'Improvement and well peopling of the
Colonies!' [...] I would only add, That this Exporting of
Felons to the Colonies, may be consider'd as a *Trade* [...]
And *Rattle-Snakes* seem the most *suitable Returns* for the
Human Serpents sent us by our *Mother* Country. In this,
however, as in every other Branch of Trade, she will have
the Advantage of us. She will reap *equal* Benefits without
equal Risque of the Inconveniencies and Dangers. For
the *Rattle-Snake* gives Warning before he attempts his
Mischief; which the Convict does not.[14]

Franklin returned to the theme in a letter to the *London Chronicle* in 1759 where he dismissed the claims about the redemptive nature of transportation:

> The same indolence of temper and habits of idleness that make people poor and tempt them to steal in England, continue with them when they are sent to America, and must there have the same effects, where all who live well owe their subsistence to labour and business, and where it is a thousand times more difficult than here to acquire wealth without industry. Hence the instances of trans-ported thieves advancing their fortunes in the colonies are extreamly rare, if there *really is* a single instance of it, which I very much doubt; but of their being advanc'd there to the gallows the instances are plenty. Might they not as well have been hang'd at home? We call Britain the *mother* country; but what good mother besides, would introduce thieves and criminals into the company of her children, to corrupt and disgrace them? And how cruel is it, to force, by the high hand of power, a particular coun-try of your subjects, who have not deserv'd such usage, to receive your outcasts, repealing all the laws they make to prevent their admission, and then reproach them with the detested mixture you have made. The emptying their jails into our settlements (says a writer of that country) is an insult and contempt, the cruellest perhaps that ever one people offered another; and would not be equal'd even by emptying their jakes on our tables.[15]

Those opposed to transportation claimed that not only did the convicts bring their criminal ways to the colonies, they also brought their diseases with them. The *Maryland Gazette* for 9 July 1767 reported that a Mrs Blake and 'near Thirty' of her slaves had died as a result of being infected by jail fever communicated by, 'one of the *Felons*, sometime since imported on a *Convict* Ship'. However, a defender of transportation attributed the deaths to the overcrowded conditions of the slaves' living accommodation. He said that such reports were spread by 'a few Gentlemen [who] seem very angry that Convicts are imported here at all, and would, if they could, by spreading this Kind of Terror, prevent the People's buying them'. He argued that 'a young Country cannot be settled, cultivated, and improved' without the use of convicts, and that, 'Gentlemen, who have had the sale of them for near Twenty Years, and have attended every Ship, and have been constantly among them during the Sales, have found no ill Effects in their Healths from it'.[16]

A correspondent in a subsequent edition of the paper accused the last writer as being:

Sway'd by the most sordid selfishness [...] that he would [...] endeavour to disarm the People of all Caution against such imminent Danger, lest their just Apprehensions should interfere with his little Schemes of Profit [...] and being [...] an Advocate for the Importation of Felons, the Scouring of Jails, and the abandoned Outcasts of the British Nation, as a Mode in any Sort eligible for the peopling of a young Country.

Another writer waded in and said the supporters of transportation were 'extolling the general Utility of importing Rogues, Felons and Diseases, from the long infected Walls, and deeply corrupted Mansions of NEWGATE'.[17]

4

THE ATLANTIC
CROSSING

In the early hours of Monday, 4 April 1768 Sarah and the other convicts who were due to be transported were chained together two by two, and marched through the streets from Newgate down to the quay at Blackfriars in a crocodile, like children on an outing from primary school. Any who were too ill to walk would have been drawn down the hill to Blackfriars in a cart.

The pickpocket, George Barrington, described the march from Newgate to Blackfriars, which was treated by some as a piece of street theatre:

About a quarter before five, a general muster took place, and, having bid farewell to my fellow-prisoners we were escorted from the prison to Blackfriars bridge by the city guard, where two lighters were waiting to receive us. This procession, though early, and but a few spectators, made a deep impression on my mind; and the ignominy of being thus mingled with felons of all descriptions, many scarce a degree above the brute creation, intoxicated with liquor, and shocking the ears of those they passed with blasphemy, oaths, and songs, the most offensive to modesty.[1]

On 3 October 1768 the *Gazetteer* printed the following report of the march to Blackfriars of the convicts who were transported on the *Justitia* bound for Virginia:

> Saturday morning, between four and five o'clock, the transports, to the number of eighty, were conveyed from Newgate, and put on board a close lighter at Black-friars, in order to be forwarded to the British plantations. They went off very merry, huzzaing; and declared that they were going to a place where they might soon retain their lost liberty.

Leaving England

When Sarah and her fellow convicts arrived at Blackfriars, they were put on board a lighter, which was a large, open flat-bottomed vessel used for carrying goods between the quays and the ships further downriver. The lighter carried them down the Thames to the *Thornton* at Blackwall. Blackwall was the nearest cargo-lightening port upstream that was deep enough for fully laden merchant ships of the type used for transporting convicts.[2] While they were going down the river to Blackwall, some of the convicts cut the main chain on board the lighter, but were prevented from making their escape.[3]

Once on board the *Thornton*, Sarah and her fellow convicts were chained together in groups of six and clapped under hatches, either stowed in the damp and dirty hold, or crammed into the suffocating area between the hold and the main deck which was only about four and a half feet from floor to ceiling. Some ships had partitions to separate the male and female convicts.

The year before Sarah sailed, an enterprising convict had tried to maintain his pickpocketing skills on the *Trial* transport ship: 'Yesterday the Felons in Newgate, under Sentence of Transportation, were put on board the Trial, in order for their Voyage to America, pursuant to their Sentence. While the Securing Chain was putting on them, the Hand of one of them was caught in the Captain's Pocket.'[4]

The Earl of Fife, who in 1770 went to find a convict named Kennedy shortly before his ship was due to sail downriver, described the condition in which he found Kennedy when he arrived at the ship:

> I went on board, and, to be sure, all the states of horror I ever had an idea of are much short of what I saw this poor man in; chained to a board, in a hole not above sixteen feet long; more than fifty with him; a collar and padlock about his neck, and chained to five of the most dreadful creatures I ever looked on.[5]

It has not been discovered what sort of ship the *Thornton* was. Anecdotal evidence suggests that the ships used for transporting convicts were old and in poor condition; a few of them had served as slave ships.

After Sarah and the other Newgate convicts had been put on board the *Thornton* it remained at Blackwall for a further two days until Wednesday, 6 April, possibly waiting for convicts to arrive from the county jails.[6] Once it had finished loading, the *Thornton* sailed down the Thames from Blackwall with its cargo of convicts, who came from the courts of London and Middlesex, from the Home Circuit of Essex, Hertfordshire, Kent, Surrey and Sussex, as well as from Buckinghamshire.[7]

On the *Thornton* Sarah was reunited with George Trotman. After he was released, Trotman continued picking pockets until he was caught again. At Hicks Hall on 20 February 1768 he was convicted of petit larceny and sentenced to be transported for seven years.[8] Sarah might also have recognised William Warner, the highwayman, who with William Dunk was briefly in Tothill Fields Bridewell. Warner came on board with the Hertfordshire contingent of convicts.

On 14 April the *Thornton* was anchored at the Downs between Deal in Kent and the Goodwin Sands to wait for favourable winds to take it out to sea while the wind was blowing fresh and westerly.[9] It sailed for America the following day.[10]

Sarah's Fellow Passengers

Once the ship reached open water the women had their fetters removed, but they were still packed tightly together. During their period of enforced acquaintance Sarah and the other women would have got to know each other well and shared each other's stories.

Elizabeth Carter was found guilty at the Old Bailey of stealing two china bowls, a silk hat, a linen gown, a silk cardinal and two linen waistcoats from Sarah Gardener's rooms in a lodging house. A neighbour who lodged in the same building saw Elizabeth on the stairs with the items and Sarah

Gardener's door open. The neighbour detained Elizabeth and got her daughter to summon Sarah Gardener from Fleet Market where she kept a vegetable stall. Sarah Gardener confirmed that the items were hers.

Jane Willson had lodged with a silk dyer and his wife at Three Fox Court, Long Lane for one and a half years, during which time she had been stealing various items belonging to her landlady and pawning them. She was convicted of stealing a silk gown, a bed gown, a pair of ruffles, a pair of stockings, a laced handkerchief, two pieces of black silk, two bed curtains, a damask napkin and other items from her lodgings. The jury valued the whole lot at 10*d* to save it from being a capital offence. Her defence was that 'I have worked day and night for the prosecutor's wife, and she would hardly give me a bit of bread to keep life and soul together'.

Jane Heley was also transported for stealing from her lodgings. She was seen carrying a large bundle out of the house while her landlord and his wife were out. She stole a linen gown, a cotton gown, a stuff gown, a stuff petticoat, a linen petticoat, a pair of stays and a satin hat. She sold two gowns and the two petticoats to an old-clothes man in the Minories, and pawned another gown for 6*s* and the pair of stays for 18*d* somewhere in Moorfields. At her trial, her unsuccessful defence was as follows:

> These people, my prosecutors, keep a disorderly house in East-Smithfield; she drawed me away from my mother, a green grocer; she lives now in New Rag-fair; what money I got from men, this woman made me give it to her; when I threatened to go from her she said she would lay me rotting in a gaol [...] she and her husband get their living by unfortunate girls, and when they are

for going away from them they threaten to put them in gaol.

Mary Pain, who lived opposite, told the court that she saw Jane Heley take a bundle 'as much as she could carry' from the house. She said the prosecutor was a baker who rented a house from her husband. When asked, 'Does he carry on baking?' she replied, 'No, he does not.' The court then asked how the prosecutor got his living and whether he kept a respectable house. She replied, 'I never hear no noise, they always pay me honestly, and I have no business further.'

Anne Griffith was the servant to a hosier who lived on Lombard Street. Every Sunday morning her friend, Jane Dixon, used to visit her at Lombard Street; and every Sunday morning at the end of the visit Jane used to leave with a bundle of goods from the shop. This went on for some months, until a suspicious pawnbroker told the hosier that he had some goods that he believed were his. The thefts then came to light. The formal charge concerned the theft of twenty pairs of silk stockings, fifteen pairs of silk gloves, six pairs of silk mitts, two pairs of worsted hose, four pairs of thread hose and eight pairs of cotton hose, although it was thought that much more than this had been taken. Jane blamed Anne, saying that Anne gave the goods to her when she visited; Anne blamed Jane, saying that Jane used to go behind the counter and take what goods she had a mind to. Both Jane and Anne were found equally guilty and were sentenced to be transported for seven years. All the witnesses said that Jane Dixon's husband was a very honest man and knew nothing about the thefts. I can imagine Mr Dixon's friends and acquaintances asking after his wife's health, and him having to explain that she had been transported to America.

Of the nine women on the *Thornton* who were sentenced to transportation at the Old Bailey, four were married (Elizabeth Carter, Jane Willson, Jane Dixon and Elizabeth Gordon). They left their husbands behind in England.

Elizabeth Brice and Anne Clifford were convicted of stealing 5 guineas, a half guinea, 2 quarter guineas and a pair of leather breeches. On the night of 26 January 1768 a drunken farmer from Edmonton was locked out of his lodgings in Ormond Yard. He was wandering around somewhere near the Coach and Horses in Holborn when he met Elizabeth Brice, Anne Clifford and Mary Clifford. They told him they could take him to some good lodgings, but first they asked him to take them to the Coach and Horses and buy a glass of gin for them to share. This enabled the women to notice that he paid for the drink with money from the purse in his breeches pocket. They then took him to a house in a place called Jacob's Court at the back of Blackboy Alley, off Chick Lane, once home of the notorious Blackboy Alley Gang. While Mary Clifford stood by the doorway, the other two women took off his boots and flung them to the other side of the room. They then pulled off his leather breeches. Mary blew out the candle and the three women ran out of the house with his breeches and his purse. A watchman told the court, 'I heard a man call, for God's sake, watchman make haste, I am stripped and I shall be murdered.' Another peace officer explained that they had to borrow a pair of breeches before they could take the farmer before the justice to report the crime. Elizabeth Brice and Anne Clifford were sentenced to seven years' transportation and Mary Clifford was acquitted.

Anne Berry's crime was similar. She was charged with grand larceny and her partner, David Johnson, was charged with receiving. On 18 January 1768 Henry Ratman from

Hamburg was about to board a ship when a woman asked him 'for a dram' and tempted him to enter a house. He gave her money 'to get a dram'. He told the court:

> There were women came about me, one sat on my knee, and got half a guinea and five shillings out of my pocket; the woman at the bar [Anne Berry] asked me what it was o'clock; I took my watch out, and had it in my hand; she said it is a very fine chain, and got hold of it; she snatched the watch from me, and ran downstairs; I followed her; then Johnson appeared, and called me dirty fellow, and bid me go about my business, or he would murder me, and kicked and cuffed me about, and drove me out of the house.

Later, Johnson sold the watch chain to a watchmaker. Anne Berry was sentenced to be transported for seven years for stealing and David Johnson for fourteen years for receiving.[11] David Johnson was described as 'about 5 Feet 8 Inches high, and 28 Years of Age [...] he is very remarkable, his left Hand being off at the wrist'.[12]

The courts generally imposed fourteen-year sentences for receiving, as they considered that receivers facilitated and encouraged theft. Another of Sarah's fellow passengers, Elizabeth Gordon, was also transported for fourteen years for receiving. Three boys stole two pieces of cotton, amounting to 50 yards, from the back of a cart in Whitechapel; they sold the pieces to her and she cut out the identification marks. One boy turned evidence, another disappeared and the third, Thomas Collop, aged 13, was transported for seven years.

Thomas Collop was not the only child who was transported with Sarah on board the *Thornton*. James Callaghan and Henry Williams were both 12; Callaghan was transported for picking a pocket of a silk handkerchief, and Williams for grabbing a handful of money from an open till in a chandler's shop and running off with it.[13]

While Sarah would have spent more time with the female convicts both in Newgate and on board the *Thornton*, she would also have become acquainted with some of the male convicts on the long voyage.

One of the stranger characters Sarah would have met on the ship was John Harvey. On the night of 5 January 1768 Harvey managed to steal a pig, a cock, six hens, a woollen horse-cloth and a silver-plated spur from a house in Leytonstone. As the watchman at Bromley-by-Bow was calling the hour of five in the morning he saw John Harvey try to slink by. He caught up with Harvey and searched the basket Harvey was carrying and discovered the menagerie. Harvey was unable to give an adequate explanation of how he came by the animals or the silver spur the watchman found in his pocket. A witness at his trial said that Harvey was known to have been in custody several times, 'but he always shams mad and so gets cleared'. When asked if he had any defence, Harvey replied, 'The peace of God be with you, I make no defence.'

Thomas Mitchell and William Taylor were transported for stealing eleven live turkeys and four live chickens. They entered the empty house at Mile End, where the animals were kept, by breaking in through the cellar. They tied the animals' legs together and carried them off to Leadenhall Market where they sold them to a poulterer. Mitchell and Taylor were also found guilty of a separate offence of stealing one dead hare, sixteen dead ducks and nine dead rabbits.

Thomas King was another of the 'King's Passengers' who was transported for animal theft. On the evening of

26 December 1767 he grabbed two geese that were hanging from the window of a poulterer's shop in Whitecross Street and ran off with them slung over his shoulder. The poulterer's son-in-law chased after him and caught him; with the help of some other people they took him to a public house and tied his hands while the son-in-law went in search of a constable. When the constable arrived, King 'got loose and knocked down several people that assisted the constable; he vowed revenge when he got his liberty'.

William Peterson stole various items from his lodgings. When his landlord accused him of taking the items, he admitted what he had done and gave the landlord the details of the pawnbrokers where the goods were. William Peterson told the court, 'I was out of work, and greatly distressed for want; I made use of these things to get my own out of pawn.'

George Blessett was one of the more stupid criminals who sailed with Sarah. On 10 February he had gone into James Chapman's shop three times and just looked around. He had apparently decided that Chapman was doing a good trade and there was money to be had there. At about quarter to eleven that night, Blessett and another idiot knocked on James Chapman's door. As soon as Chapman opened the door, Blessett and his companion rushed in. Blessett clapped a pistol to Chapman's breast and said, 'Deliver, or you are a dead man,' but Chapman wrenched the pistol from his hand and called for help. Chapman's three lodgers came running down the stairs and together they managed to secure the two intruders and carried them to Covent Garden Roundhouse. Blessett was found guilty and his accomplice was acquitted, presumably of the grounds that he was an innocent who had been led astray. The moral of this tale is, do not to try to rob a house that is full of able-bodied lodgers.[14]

Henry Levi was almost as daft. He was transported for grabbing a man's hat from his head and running off with it, but not fast enough.

Benny Daniel, who had been drinking, walked into Elias Mordecai's shop and took two wooden tubs containing 38lb of butter from behind the counter. Mrs Mordecai told the court, 'I heard my daughter cry, somebody was gone out with two tubs of butter; a neighbour said to me do not make yourself uneasy, Daniel has got them, we will go and see after him'. The neighbour said:

> I was coming home three nights before Christmas, I met the prisoner next door to Mordecai's; he fell down, I helped him up with his tubs; he went about four doors farther, and fell down again; he had two tubs, one full of butter, the other about half full. When the woman complained of being robbed, I told her of Daniel.

Benny Daniel lived down an alley in Whitechapel. When they arrived at his house, he jumped out of a window, and his wife showed them where the butter was.

Thomas Robinson was transported for an equally foolish crime: he walked into a chandler's shop in Wapping and stole 33lb of bacon. The chandler said he was in the back kitchen when he heard his 8-year-old daughter cry out, 'O daddy, daddy, the bacon is gone.' He ran out of the shop and saw by the light of a lamp a man further down the street with something bulky. When Robinson saw the chandler, he ran off. The chandler caught up with him and the bacon about 200 yards from the shop.

Richard Dodd was caught in the act by two watchmen ripping lead off the roof of a building. The watchmen were passing by when they heard the sound of something falling; they went over to investigate and saw a ladder against the building. The watchmen hid. After about ten minutes, a piece of lead fell to the ground, followed by a hatchet. When Richard Dodd climbed down the ladder, the watchmen were ready to pounce. Dodd had ripped 160lb of lead from the building.

John Dixon was caught stealing a bag of pimento red chili peppers from a Thames-side quay near Billingsgate. He lashed out at his captors with his feet so they had to tie his hands and feet together and carry him to London Bridge before they could put him in a cart to take him to the Compter (either Wood Street Compter or Poultry Compter).

John Brown was another quayside robber. At about half past eleven on the night of 14 December 1767, he climbed on board what he thought was an empty ship that was tied up at Dice Quay and entered the captain's cabin. He took a fish-skin case, three razors, a pair of scissors, an iron key, an iron tobacco box and other items. However, he did not realise that the captain of the ship was asleep in the cabin; the captain told the Old Bailey that rattling of the tobacco box woke him up and, 'I catched him by the hind part of the neck, as he was examining my coat and waistcoat pockets.'

Joseph Smith was convicted of attempted highway robbery. William Bewley told the court:

I was coming towards Hackney, and when I was betwixt Lea-bridge turnpike and Clapton turnpike, the prisoner met me; he demanded my money, saying I was a dead man if I did not deliver, and produced a pistol tinder-box, and held it to me as if it had been a pistol; I told him I was a poor man and had nothing for him, and away I ran from him, and he after me; I got the heels of him;

I met with the watchman, and described the prisoner's cap he had on, and his person; they took him; he was searched, and the pistol tinder-box found upon him.[15]

David Miller, also known as John Miller, was transported on the *Thornton* for stealing a silver-mounted sword from the side of a man as he left Drury Lane Playhouse. Someone told Thomas Fellows, the High Constable for the City of Westminster, that they had overheard Miller at the Crooked Billet at the bottom of Wych Street trying to offer the sword for sale. Fellows went to the Crooked Billet and found the sword hidden under Miller's coat. Fellows took Miller to Sir John Fielding's office, where he found that the sword was the same as that advertised as having been stolen outside Drury Lane Playhouse. When Fellows searched Miller's lodgings he found two pocketbooks that had been reported missing.

Miller had appeared at the Old Bailey before. In 1764 he was indicted for stealing two gold rings from a goldsmith's shop, having walked into the shop and said he wanted to buy one. He asked the shopkeeper's wife to open the glass case full of rings so he could have a closer look, and while doing so, ran his hands over them. She told the court:

He kept his hands over them for some time; then he said, Your servant, madam, I'll come tomorrow; and was turning to go. I said, Harkee, Sir, and took him by his two hands, and took a ring out of each hand; they seemed as if they stuck there with something; my daughter got hold of him also; he got away and left his cane.

Miller told the court that he was looking at the rings when the shopkeeper's wife accused him of trying to steal them, and in the confusion he left his cane in the shop. As the case against him could not be proved, he was acquitted.

In 1766 he was at the Old Bailey again. This time he was accused of stealing three pairs of pistols from a gunmaker's shop in Norfolk Street, off the Strand. When the gunmaker went to open the shop he noticed a hole in the window and that three pairs of pistols had been taken from the hooks near the hole. Some days later Miller sold a pair of pistols to a silversmith at Hatton Garden and said he had some other things of value to sell. After he left, the silversmith suspected that the pistols might have been stolen, and resolved to stop Miller when he came again. When Miller returned the next day with another pair of pistols the silversmith tried to stop him. Miller ran out of the shop. The silversmith shouted, 'Stop, thief', and Miller was caught. In court, Miller claimed he found the pistols lying in the street and he produced a witness who said he was there when Miller found the pistols. Again, he was acquitted.

Two years after the *Thornton* sailed for America, on the night of 14 May 1770, Nicholas Bond, a Bow Street Runner, saw two men looking down an area in Denmark Court. He asked them what they were looking for. One of the men muttered a reply which he did not understand so he asked the question again. As the man turned towards him he recognised the man as David Miller. Bond told the court:

> I said, Is it you, David Miller? You can be about no good here; what business have you here? He said his name was not David Miller, it was John Read. Then I said, John Read, you shall go along with me. As I was bringing him along the court, he said, What is your name? I said my name is Bond. I put my hand down, and felt something in his pocket then I took out this pocket pistol.

Miller's defence was that his name was John Read, he had never been transported, and Bond had planted the pistol on him. However John Heley, a Bow Street Runner, and Thomas Fellows, who had been appointed in 1769 as one of his Majesty's Justices of the Peace for the City of Westminster, both testified that the man in the dock was David Miller. Justice Fellows said he knew him by the great cut on his jaw and, when he came to speak, he knew him by his voice.

When Miller was found guilty of returning from transportation and sentenced to death, he thanked the jury and told them that he would rather die than live a transport, as no man knew the misery of such a state, but those who felt it. It was so intolerable that, having failed in several attempts 'to escape from his slavery and bondage', he attempted to hang himself, which he said he was fully determined to do, had he not succeeded in his last escape. He was hanged at Tyburn on 4 July 1770.[16]

David Miller was not the only convict who was with Sarah on the *Thornton* who escaped from his master after being sold in America. It is not known whether any of the following were recaptured, or whether they made a new life for themselves in America, or whether they made it back to England and remained undetected.

William Simmons was transported on board the *Thornton* for stealing six bushels of green peas worth 12s, six pecks of French beans worth 8s and three hempen sacks.[17] In America, he, David Johnson and James Crosby were bought by William Duvall. On 12 July 1768 Duvall advertised that the three of them had run away and 'it is supposed they will pass for Sailors, and make for *Chester*, in *Pennsylvania*. They were seen near *Baltimore-Town*, on Tuesday last'.[18]

William Roberts was transported for breaking into a house in Ropemaker's Alley, Moorfields, at one o'clock in the morning on 19 January 1768 and stealing twelve linen shirts, 3 yards of silver lace, three silver teaspoons and some other items. James Bailey and two others were transported for stealing canvas, cable rope and cordage from a ship lying near Union Stairs, Wapping.[19] In America Roberts and Bailey were both bought by the same master, who lived near Georgetown in Frederick County, Maryland. They were advertised as having escaped from him in July 1769.[20]

The convicts from Essex included a group who were sentenced to death at Chelmsford Assizes: William Cracknell, James Heard and William Tomlin, for housebreaking; William Green, for sheep stealing; William Pennock, for stealing a cow; Henry Pomfret, for horse stealing; and Thomas Corder, for stealing five bullocks.[21] They were subsequently reprieved on condition of being transported for fourteen years.

John Cole, George Tremble, Thomas Wayte and Thomas Griffiths from Surrey were also sentenced to death but had their sentences commuted to fourteen years' transportation. Cole, Tremble and Wayte were convicted of highway robberies and Griffiths for horse stealing.[22]

The convicts from Kent included John Humphries (or Humphrey) and David Toole. In July 1769 Richard Weedon of Sandy Point, Anne Arundel County advertised that Humphries and two others had escaped and, 'went off in a small Boat, and is supposed to have gone down the [Chesapeake] Bay'. Weedon described John Humphries as, 'about 20 Years of Age, fair Complexion, brown Hair, red Beard, and is lame in his left Arm'. David Toole also escaped from his master. In July 1771 he and a convict boy aged about 14 or 15 ran away together from their plantation some 10 miles from Baltimore, taking a supply of spare clothing with them.[23]

Seasickness, Fever and Dysentery

Lice were constant companions on board ship and rats were not unknown. Sleeping was difficult on boards that were only 18in wide. Some of the convicts may have come on board suffering from jail fever, smallpox or some other contagious disease. It would not have taken long for the contagion to spread round the hot, cramped and suffocating space where the convicts were held.

There were examples of considerable loss of life aboard convict ships. The convicts on board the *Rappahannock Merchant* were heavily infected with jail fever; of the eighty-four on board, thirty-eight had died before the ship arrived in Virginia. The fever spread to the crew, and the captain also died. Of the seventy-six convicts on board the *Forward*, bound for Maryland, fifty-eight had died.[24] By the time Sarah was transported the proportion of convicts who died during the voyage had fallen, but even so the death rate was still around 10 per cent.

Duncan Campbell, the transportation contractor for ships leaving London during the final years to transportation to America, told a House of Commons committee:

That he transported on an Average of seven Years, 473 Convicts Annually; that he carried from One to Two hundred Persons on a Ship; that the ordinary Passage was about Two Months, during which Time, and in the Gaol, where they were confined frequently Two Months before their Embarkation, rather more than a Seventh Part of the Felons died, many of the Gaol Fever, but more of the Small Pox.[25]

It is possible that for part of her journey Sarah was sitting next to a corpse before it was taken up on deck to be flung overboard. In March 1764 seven Newgate convicts were buried in Greenwich burying ground, their infected bodies found on the shore having been thrown out of a transport ship.[26]

Most of the women had never been to sea before. Many would have been seasick. Their vomit would flow backwards and forwards around their feet as the ship was tossed by the waves. In the rough Atlantic seas the sickness was worse. The sharp smell of vomit mingled with the stink from the tubs of excrement and with the stale odour of bodies that had worn the same clothes for too long. An advertisement offering a reward for the capture of two convicts, 'just imported from London, in the *Justitia*', said: 'To those used to the smell of servants just from a ship, they will be easily discovered, unless they have procured new clothes.'[27]

Gottlieb Mittelberger was an organist and schoolmaster who left Germany in 1750 to sail to America. This is his description of the voyage from Cowes, Isle of Wight, to Philadelphia:

> During the voyage there is on board these ships terrible misery, stench, fumes, horror, vomiting, many kinds of sea-sickness, fever, dysentery, headache, heat, constipation, boils, scurvy, cancer, mouth-rot, and the like, all of which come from old and sharply salted food and meat, also from very bad and foul water, so that many die miserably.
>
> Add to this want of provisions, hunger, thirst, frost, heat, dampness, anxiety, want, afflictions and lamentations, together with other trouble [...] the lice abound so frightfully, especially on sick people, that they can be scraped off the body. The misery reaches the climax

when a gale rages for two or three nights and days, so
that everyone believes that the ship will go to the bottom
with all human beings on board. In such a visitation the
people cry and pray most piteously.

When in such a gale the sea rages and surges, so that
the waves rise often like high mountains one above the
other, and often tumble over the ship, so that one fears
to go down with the ship; when the ship is constantly
tossed from side to side by the storm and waves, so
that no one can either walk, or sit, or lie, and the closely
packed people in the berths are thereby tumbled over
each other, both the sick and the well – it will be readily understood that many of these people, none of whom
had been prepared for hardships, suffer so terribly from
them that they do not survive it.[28]

Unlike the male convicts, who were generally kept in chains for
most of the voyage for fear of mutiny, the women were allowed
on deck singly or in small groups to allow them to get away
from the smell and stale air and in order to get some fresh air
and exercise. On some ships the sailors, many of whom had
venereal disease, regarded the women convicts as fair game for
harassment and rape.[29] On those ships sexual activity took place
whether the women were willing or not. In the case of Susanna
Ball and Anne Ellis in 1774 it seems that both were willing and
were fond of their new partners. In America they were advertised as having run away, having recently been transported, and
were thought to have been making their way back to Norfolk,
Virginia, in order to get back on board the same ship:

As one of them was kept by the second mate, who
parted with her with much reluctance, and the other

120

was connected with a silversmith who came passenger, who lives in Norfolk, and would have married her if her temper had not been too disagreeable.

The advertisement described Anne Ellis as 'a full faced, lusty woman, of a ruddy complexion, has black hair, and is much addicted to swearing.'[30]

In December 1757 the Welsh poet Goronwy Owen sailed to America with his wife and children as passengers on board the *Trial*, a convict ship, in order to take up a teaching post at the College of William and Mary. While the *Trial* was waiting at Portsmouth Harbour for a convoy of ships to gather (Britain was at war with France and there was safety in numbers) he sent a letter to a friend describing conditions on board:

> The seamen are a frightfully vile bunch of men. God be my keeper, every one of them has taken to himself a strumpet from amongst the she-thieves and do no work except whoring wanton in every corner of the ship. Five or six of them have already contracted the pox from the women [...] Do you remember how this tadpole of a captain promised that my wife could have one of the she-thieves to serve her whilst at sea? One of them is here in the cabin, but it is to serve this husband's penis, and not to wait upon my wife, that she was brought here.[31]

Nonetheless, as the captains received a commission from the sale of convicts once they reached America, it was in their interest to try to make sure that as many as possible survived the journey and arrived free from disease. It was also in their interest, and that of the convict merchant, to try to make the convicts appear as presentable and sale-worthy as possible. The captains would make sure the convicts washed themselves before arriving in port. In 1773, the convict merchant Duncan Campbell ordered gowns, petticoats, shifts, handkerchiefs and yarn hose to be sent to Captain Finlay Grey of the *Justitia* which was due to sail with forty-six female convicts.[32] This might not have been necessary for all the female convicts; some would have arranged to have their own trunks of spare clothes and other possessions taken on board ship.

While it was in the captains' interest to make sure the convicts survived the voyage so they could receive their share of the sale proceeds, the convicts on board ship in many cases were treated worse than slaves. The captains had more reasons for trying to make sure the slaves survived; the death of a slave was a more material loss than the death of a convict, as slaves commanded a much higher price. Slaves were more attractive to potential buyers than convicts: they were more trustworthy as they didn't have a criminal record; they were generally fitter, stronger and healthier; and they were sold for life, whereas most convicts were sold for seven-year terms. Slaves were sold for between £30 and £60. Most male convicts were sold for between £10 and £14, while most women went for between £5 and £9.[33] Convicts were often bought by poorer planters who could not afford to buy slaves.

One of the reasons why women were sold so cheaply was because potential buyers suspected that many of them had contracted venereal disease, either on the assumption that most of the women were prostitutes, or that they had been the subject of sexual assault by the sailors during the voyage. As the colonists mainly used the women as domestic servants, they feared infection. And there were those masters who were frightened of contracting the disease because they considered convict servant women to be their sexual property. A study in one Maryland county showed that 20 per cent of the women who had arrived as servants wound up in court for having illegitimate children, some of whom were likely to have been seduced or raped by their masters.[34]

In good weather the voyage from Blackwall to America could take as little as seven weeks. When a voyage took longer than eight or nine weeks, the diet was restricted to sharply salted food and foul water, and many of the convicts developed scurvy as a result. Gottlieb Mittelberger described the water on the last stages of his voyage as 'very black, thick and full of worms, so that one cannot drink it without loathing, even with the greatest thirst', and that, 'toward the end we were compelled to eat the ship's biscuit which had been spoiled long ago; though in a whole biscuit there was scarcely a piece the size of a dollar that had not been full of red worms and spiders' nests.'[35]

In September 1767 the snow *Rodney* left England with ninety-two convicts on board, bound for Maryland. Beset by fierce Atlantic storms, the ship beat about on the coast of America trying to land for several weeks until it was forced to bear away for the island of Antigua in the West Indies, where it landed on 21 January 1768. By the time it landed eleven of the convicts had starved to death and the rest were:

Reduced to the necessity of eating their shoes and breeches to sustain life, not having provisions of any kind to subsist on. Their condition is truly miserable; full of sores and ulcers, very low, and having lain for three weeks absolutely in water, the vessel being almost torn to pieces, by the many severe storms she encountered.[36]

The voyage of the *Thornton* took twelve weeks; it eventually arrived at the Ferry Branch of the Patapsco River in Baltimore Harbour on or slightly before 28 June 1768.[37] It seems that the reason for the *Thornton*'s delay was that it was caught in one or more fierce Atlantic storms. There was a violent thunderstorm on 17 June 1768 that passed through Pennsylvania on its way out to the Atlantic; hailstones, many of which were 9in in circumference, flattened crops, smashed windows and killed cattle.[38]

If the *Thornton* did encounter a storm, Sarah and her companions would have been terrified by the violent buffeting of the ship flinging them to and fro; the sounds of crashing waves, groaning timbers and the shouts of the sailors. They would also have been terrified by the water rushing over the decks, splashing through the planks and cracks and joints, drenching them in the darkness below. They would have felt that the ship was about to sink with them trapped and helpless in the hold. Anything that was not tied down would be flung backwards and forwards as the ship violently dipped and rose.

After the dangers and discomforts of the voyage, the sight of land must have come as a tremendous relief. But it was also a time of trepidation, worrying about who would be their master, what kind of work they would be made to do, and what hardships they might have to endure in this strange new land.

The broom maker's cottage. (Postcard, *c.* 1910)

Frensham church. (Supplement to the *Gentleman's Magazine*, 1797)

The Bell Inn, Wood Street. (William Hogarth, *A Harlot's Progress*, 1732, Plate 1. Wellcome Collection)

COVENTRY MACHINE on Steel Springs, (In Two Days, for the Winter Season) SETS out from the CASTLE and FALCON Inn in Alderſgate Street, London, and from THOMAS DULLISON's, in Coventry, every Monday and Thurſday Mornings at Six o'Clock. Each Paſſenger to pay One Guinea ; Children on Lap, and Outſides, to pay Half Fare.

Performed by { THOMAS DULLISON, : And GILES TOTTINGHAM.

N. B. For the Conveniency of Ladies and Gentlemen travelling farther, the Machine gets to Coventry by Three o'Clock in the Afternoon the Second Day.

Advertisement for the coach to the Nag's Head, Coventry. (*Public Ledger*, 27 October 1761)

LIVERPOOL and Warrington New Flying Machine, to carry six Paſſengers in Two Days. By Way of Newcaſtle, Sambich, Middlewich and Northwich, ſets out from the Swan with Two-Necks Inn in Lad-Lane, London, and from the Go den Talbot Inn at Liverpool, every Sunday, Tueſday, and Thurſday Nights; from each Place preciſely at Ten o'Clock. Lies at Litchfield down, and Coventry up.

Each Inſide from London to Liverpool - 2 10 0	Middlewich - 2 2 0
Warrington — 2 6 0	Newcaſtle - 1 18 0
Northwich - 2 4 0	Litchfield - 1 8 0
	Coventry - 1 1 0

And ſo in Proportion to any Part of the Road.

Each Paſſenger to be allowed twenty Pound Weight of Luggage; all above to Liverpool, Three-pence per Pound, and ſo in Proportion to any Part of the Road. Outſides and Children in Laps half Price. One half to be paid t king the Place, the other entering the Coach. Parcels to be paid for at taking in. Performed, if God permit, by JOHN HANFORTH, WILLIAM DIMOCK and Co. London.

Advertisement for the Liverpool and Warrington Flying Machine. (*Gazetteer*, 9 April 1765)

This is to give NOTICE, To all Gentlemen and Ladies, THAT they may be ſupplied with Neat Poſt-Chaiſes, on the Turnpike Road from London to Cheſter, with Two Paſſengers, at Seven-pence per Mile; Four Horſes, at Thirteen-pence, at the following Inns:

Green Man at Whetſtone; Saracen's Head at St. Alban's; Bedford Arms, at Dunſtable; Buck and Bell, at Fenny Stratford; Angel, at Towceſter; Saracen's Aead, at Daventry; Roſe and Crown, at Coventry; Hngel, at Core-Hill; Coach and Horſes, at Litchfield; Saracen's Head, at Stafford; Royal Oak, at Fackell; Swan, at Woor; Crown, at Nantwich; Red Lion, at Tarpley; Talbot, at Cheſter; and the Red Lion, at Ditto.

N. B. Thoſe who pleaſe to favour us with their Commands, may depend on good Accommodations of every Kind, at the above Inns; and Gentry may be fetch'd from London at the above Price, by a Penny-poſt Letter, directed to R. Bolton, at Whetſtone.

*** A Letter put in before Seven o'Clock in the Evening, is received the next Day by Two.

Advertisement for the Coventry post-chaise. (*London Evening-Post*, 9 January 1766)

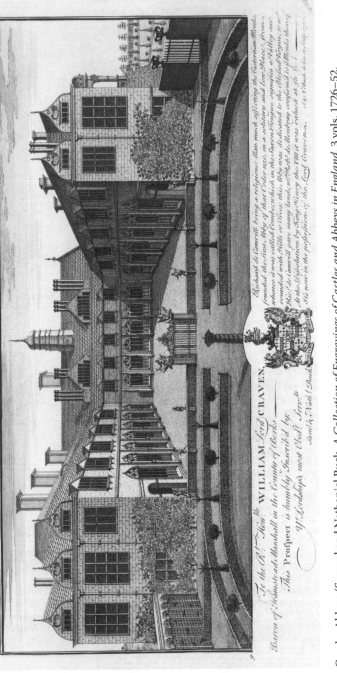

Combe Abbey. (Samuel and Nathaniel Buck, *A Collection of Engravings of Castles and Abbeys in England*, 3 vols, 1726–52. Reproduced with the permission of the Library of Birmingham, ref: AF 728.810942)

View of the **PUBLIC OFFICE** Bow Street, with Sir John Fielding presiding, & a prisoner under examination

Sir John Fielding at Bow Street. (*The Malefactor's Register*, vol. 3, 1779. Wellcome Collection)

Beating hemp at Tothill Fields Bridewell. (William Hogarth, *A Harlot's Progress*, 1732, Plate 4. Wellcome Collection)

The march from Newgate to Blackfriars. (*The Newgate Calendar*, vol. 5, 1773. Chronicle/Alamy Stock Photo)

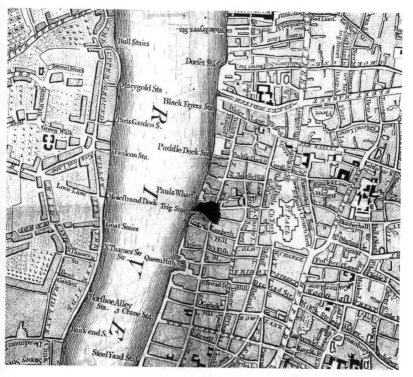

The route from Newgate to Blackfriars. (From John Pine's reduction of Rocque's *Plan of the Cites of London and Westminster etc.*, 1749)

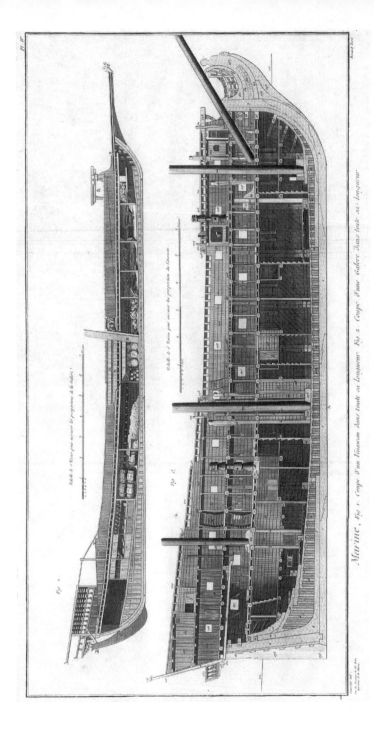

Marine, Fig. 1. Coupe d'un Vaisseau dans toute sa longueur. Fig. 2. Coupe d'une Galère dans toute sa longueur.

Section of the type of ship that was also used to transport convicts. (Denis Diderot, *Encyclopédie*, 1751–72)

June 28, 1768.

THE Seven Years SERVANTS, imported in the Ship *Thornton*, Capt. *Chriftopher Read*, will be expofed to Sale, on board the faid Ship, lying in the Ferry-Branch of *Patapfco* River, on Tuefday the 5th Day of *July* enfuing.——Great Allowances will be made for ready Cafh, and good Bills of Exchange. Crop-Notes will be taken, at a Price then to be agreed on, if tendered, as Pay, on any Account.

*** The Appearance of thefe Servants, muft, without Doubt, recommend them to thofe who chufe to purchafe, they being in Health, and all Young.

ALEX^r. STEWART,
and
WILLIAM RUSSELL.

Advertisement for the sale of convicts from the *Thornton*. (*Maryland Gazette*, 30 June 1768)

‡ A D V E R T I S E M E N T.
Bufh-Creek, Frederick County, Maryland, October 11. 1771.

RUN away from the Subfcriber; a convict fervant maid, named SARAH WILSON, but has changed her name to Lady Sufanna Carolina Matilda, which made the public believe that fhe was his Majefty's fifter, fhe has a blemifh in her right eye, black roll'd hair, ftoops in the fhoulders, makes a common practice of writing and marking her cloaths with a crown and a B. Whoever fecures the faid fervant woman, or takes her home, fhall receive five piftoles, befides all cofts and charges,

WILLIAM DEVALL.

I entitle Michael Dalton to fearch the city of Philadelphia, and from thence to Charlef-town, for the faid woman. (A true Copy)
WILLIAM DEVALL.

Wanted advertisement for Sarah. (*Rivington's New York Gazetteer*, 13 May 1773; reprinted in *Connecticut Journal*, 21 May 1773)

July 9, 1771.

RUN away, yefterday, from the Subfcriber, living near Gunpowder Falls, 9 miles from Baltimore-town, a convict fervant woman, named SARAH HILL, about 22 years of age, of a middling fize, grey eyes and fhort yellow hair, fhe has a boil on one of her arms. Had on when fhe went away, a black bonnet, a red handkerchief bird's-eyed, a blue calimanco gown almoft new, a black quilted petticoat with large diamonds; fhe had neither fhoes nor ftockings; fhe is frefh coloured, and has one or two large marks near her mouth from the fmall-pox.

Whoever takes up faid woman, and fecures her, fo that her Mafter may get her again, fhall have FOUR POUNDS reward, and reafonable charges if brought home, paid by
JOHN CHRISTOPHER.

Example of an advertisement for a runaway convict. (*Pennsylvania Chronicle*, 21 August 1771)

Tryon Palace. (Library of Congress)

The Boston Tea Party. (Woodcut, c. 1850)

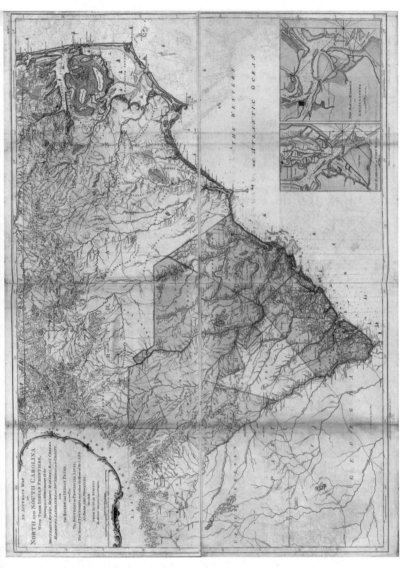

Map of the Carolinas. (Henry Mouzon, *An Accurate Map of North and South Carolina*, 1775. Library of Congress)

THE PUBLIC are hereby informed, That STAVERS's original Stage-Coach, and Poſt Chaiſe, ſets off as uſual, from the Earl of Halifax Tavern in *Portſmouth* every Tueſday Morning for *Boſton*, and returns on Saturday.

Mr. *Stavers*'s was the firſt Perſon that ever ſet up and regularly maintain'd a Stage Carriage in New-England, the Utility of which at all Seaſons has been abundantly experienced for Ten Years paſt ; he flatters himſelf that his honeſt and ſincere Endeavours to oblige the Public, has been for the moſt part ſatisfactory, as they have ſo often honour'd him with their Marks of Approbation ; He therefore humbly hopes that his Carriages will ſtill continue to be preſer'd to any other, that may be ſet up in Oppoſition to them ; eſpecially as his Carriages are univerſally allow'd to be as convenient, genteel, and eaſy, and his Horſes as good *(if not better)* than any that have as yet travelled the Road. Single Perſons are carried in the moſt genteel and expeditious Manner from *Boſton* to *Portſmouth*, at the ſmall Price of Twelve Shillings Lawful Money, and from *Boſton* to *Newbury-Port* for Nine Shillings, and any ſhorter Diſtance in the ſame Proportion ;—the greateſt Care will be taken of all Bundles and Packages.

N. B. Good Entertainment at the Earl of Halifax Tavern, and Horſe-keeping equal to any on the Continent.

Said *Stavers*'s puts up at Mrs. *Bean*'s, at the New-bury-Port Tavern in King-Street, *Boſton*, where all Perſons may apply for Paſſages or any other Buſineſs.

Advertisement for Stavers's Boston and Portsmouth stagecoach. (*Boston News-Letter*, 29 August 1771)

Rev. Manasseh Cutler's Parsonage. (Edwin Erle Sparkes, *The United States of America, Part 1: 1783–1830*, 1904)

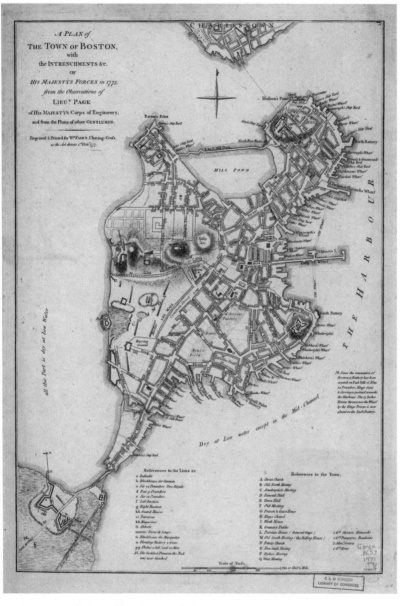

Map of Boston. (William Faden, *A Plan of the Town of Boston*, 1777. Library of Congress)

State Street, Boston. (James Brown Marston, *State* Street, 1801. Library of Congress)

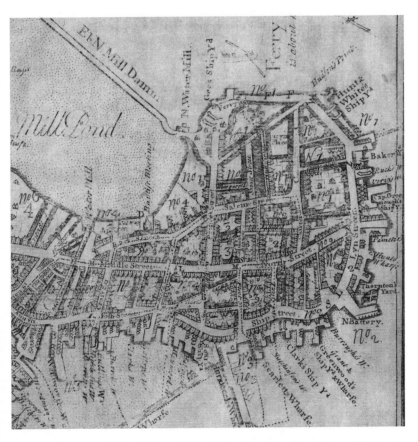

North End, Boston. (From William Price, *A New Plan of ye Great Town of Boston ...
to the Year 1769.* Library of Congress)

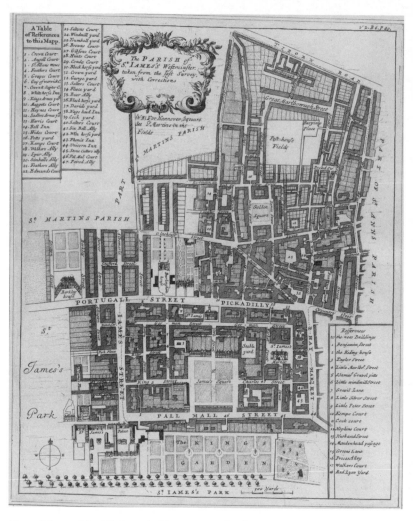

Map of the parish of St James's, Westminster. (Richard Blome, from Strype's edition of Stow's *Survey of the cities of London and Westminster* (1755) © The British Library Board, source, Maps. Crace. 12.3)

From a Certain Princess

To the Worthy Mrs Mary Stedman,

My Dear Friend,

We humbly hope that these few Lines will come safe & find you, and your Consort Capt. Stedman, & the whole of your Family in the Sweet Shades of good health, & happiness, heartily wishing at the same time, that both you & ours May be in the Royal Arms of Almighty Love & Mercy.

We beg Leave to inform you that We prepose to Leave BOSTON, in a very Shorte time, for the Southward, if the Blessed God, be willing, by Reason of having had the happiness of seeing The Hon.ble William Langborne, Esq.r of Virginia, a Gentleman who knowed, on our first arrival on the Continent, & Lady, Langborne, his Mamma, was our Sincere Friend, tho now no more on the Shore of time, & our Dear Friends in that quarter have requested M.r Langborne, to find us out, for the word, is to return to them again, & they will endeavour to make us, as comfortable & happy as We can with in all Langland, Lady-Ann. L. Mosey, has sent me word, if I'll return she will send her Coach &c to meet me in the Jerseys, & that her Ladyship's arms, will be ready to Seal in me, with the warm Love, &c

I now beg Leave to inform you that I was Extreemly that not the pleasure of seeing you when you was so kind to Call on us, Miss Furber, was very sorry that you did not Light & have Tea and that found her in her disable, by he as on our Friend M.r Grant, being so Extreemly Ill! & still so Main so that he I not Expected to Live — Miss Furber, presents her Love to you & shall be proud to wait on you, any time you come to Boston,

Be pleased to give my sincere Love to the whole of your Family, & except, & Same your self, Tell M.r B. Frap, as often as Meditated are what I Say'd to when you — ing to Boston, if he has not & inablow &c will L—

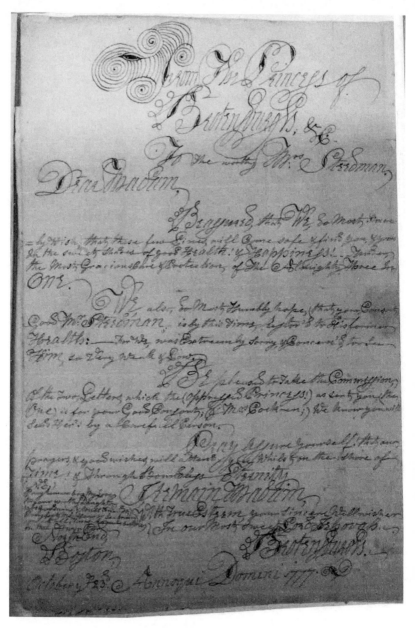

Letter dated 23 October 1777. (American Antiquarian Society, *Three Letters from a Person Calling Herself the Princess Brotensburg*)

5

AMERICA: THE SOUTH

Sarah's first sight of land did not mean that her voyage would soon be over. Once the *Thornton* arrived at the mouth of the Chesapeake, it had a further 175 miles to sail up the river to Baltimore. When the Englishman William Eddis first sailed up the Chesapeake in 1769 to take up his job as the surveyor of customs at Annapolis, the sight of the river made a great impression on him. He said the Thames had been the biggest river he had ever seen, but, 'it is now, comparatively, reduced to a diminutive stream.'[1] He was amazed that the Chesapeake, 'in its narrowest part, is at least ten miles broad, and runs a course of near three hundred, navigable for the largest ships.'[2]

'Seven Years Servants'

When the *Thornton* finally arrived at Baltimore an official came on board to examine the convicts. He compared their names with those on the list held by Captain Read, noted any deaths and issued an arrival certificate for the captain to take back to England to prove that the surviving convicts had been delivered to America. When he was back in England Captain Read passed the certificate to the convict merchant to be presented to the Treasury for payment for each convict safely delivered.

In the meantime, as soon as the *Thornton* arrived at Baltimore, the American partner of the convict merchant placed an advertisement in the *Maryland Gazette* announcing that a sale of convicts was about to take place. The advertisement referred to Sarah and her companions as 'Seven Years Servants'. This was a euphemism for transported convicts, reflecting the fact that a convict was the property of the purchaser for the full seven years. In other words, the term of the sentence did not begin until the convict was sold, irrespective of the amount of time that might have elapsed between being sentenced in England and sold in America.

Because the convicts became the property of the purchaser, they appeared in inventories along with the owner's goods, chattels and farm animals. Comparing the conditions of convicts with those of slaves, William Eddis said that slaves were 'under more comfortable circumstances than the miserable European, over whom the rigid planter exercises an inflexible severity [...] they groan beneath a worse than Egyptian bondage'.[3]

Sarah and her fellow convicts were kept prisoner on the *Thornton* until 5 July 1768, when it was time for them to be exposed for sale.[4] They were then lined up on deck to be inspected by potential purchasers. The buyers would have asked Captain Read about Sarah's health, her conviction, what he knew of her origins and what skills she possessed, in order to see whether she was a worthwhile investment.

Skilled or semi-skilled workers (joiners, coopers, black-smiths, carpenters, tailors, dressmakers, cooks, etc.) were likely to be sold first. Those without a saleable skill were examined to see whether they were fit and strong enough to be productive labourers in the ironworks or on the plantations. Those who had spent all their lives in London would have had little or no experience of agricultural work, and would have been concerned about how they would cope.

James Revel, in *The Poor Unhappy Felon's Sorrowful Account*, described the sale process in verse:

Against the Planters did come us to view,
How well they lik'd this fresh transported Crew,
The Women from us separated stood,
As well as we, by them to be thus view'd;
And in short Time some Men up to us came.
Some ask'd our Trade, others ask'd our Name.
Some view'd our Limbs, and others turn'd us round
Examining like Horses, if we were sound [...]
Some felt our Hands, others our Legs and Feet,
And made us walk, to see we were compleat,
Some view'd our Teeth, to see if they were good,
And fit to chew our hard and homely Food.[5]

The captains needed to make sure that the convicts were sold quickly. They could then load their ships with tobacco and other saleable goods for the return voyage. Any convicts who were left over after the sale were sold in bulk at a cheap price to dealers who were known as 'soul-drivers', such as William Walters and Richard Gattrell of Frederick County, Maryland.[6] As the women were more difficult to sell, many of them being not hardy enough to work in the ironworks or the plantations, they were more likely to fall into the hands of the soul-drivers. The soul-drivers herded their purchases out of Baltimore, travelling inland to the back country along rough roads and walking trails, or by boat along the many rivers and creeks that ran through Maryland, selling the convicts singly or in groups as they passed each settlement. This method meant that small planters and farmers who were unable to travel to Baltimore or Annapolis where the convict auctions took place were still able to buy convict workers.

William Green, who was transported on board the *Sally* in 1762, was purchased by soul-drivers. He described his experience as follows:

> The next day we were put all on shore in couples, chained together and drove in lots like oxen or sheep, till we came to a town called *Fike*, where there was a great number of men and women, young and old, came to see us; they search us there as the dealers in horses do those animals in this country, by looking at our teeth, viewing our limbs to see if they are sound and fit for their labour, and if they approve of us after asking our trades and names, and what crimes we have been guilty of to bring us to that shame, the bargain is made.[7]

It is unlikely that Sarah would have been one of the first to be snapped up by an eager buyer. She had no sought-after skills apart from those of an actress, and she probably looked too delicate to be a very productive labourer on a plantation. From a newspaper report in 1773 (see below) it appears that she was bought by one William Devall of Bush Creek, Frederick County. This has been taken to refer to William Duvall, who owned some 3,000 acres in Frederick County.[8] Bush Creek is about 50 miles inland from Baltimore and 5 miles south-east of the town of Frederick. Although it is possible that William Duvall or an agent acting on his behalf bought her directly from on board the *Thornton* in Baltimore, it is more likely that he bought her from a soul-driver who was passing through Bush Creek or Frederick.

Sarah was transported towards the end of the colonial era. By that time, settlers had taken most of the land situated on or near the banks of the Chesapeake. As a result, more and more pioneers were moving west from the Chesapeake seeking new land. Once they had settled, they needed extra hands to clear and cultivate the land. Increasing numbers of convicts were being employed in the backcountry; of the thirty-nine convicts landed from the *Hercules* when it arrived at Baltimore in 1773, thirty-two were bought by soul-drivers and taken into the backcountry.[9]

The Queen's Jewels

On 13 May 1773 *Rivington's New York Gazetteer* printed the following report:

NEW-YORK, MAY 13.

Some time ago, one SARAH WILSON, who attended upon the Hon. Miss Vernon, sister to Lady Grosvenor, and Maid of Honour to the Queen, having found means to be admitted into one of the royal apartments, took occasion to break open a cabinet, and rifled it of many valuable jewels: for which she was apprehended, tried, and condemned to die, but through the gracious interposition of her mistress, the sentence was softened into a transportation, she accordingly in the fall of 1771, was landed in Maryland, where she was exposed for sale, and purchased by Mr W Devall, of Bush-Creek, Frederick County; after a short residence in that place, she very secretly decamped, and escaped into Virginia, travelled through that colony, and through North, to South-Carolina, when at a prudent distance from Mr Devall, she had assumed the title of the Princess Susanna Carolina Matilda, pronouncing herself to be an own sister to our sovereign lady the Queen, she had carried with her clothes that served to favour that deception, had secured a part of the jewels, together with her Majesty's picture, which had proved so fatal to her; she travelled from one gentleman's house to another under these pretensions, and made astonishing impressions in many places, affecting the mode of royalty so inimitably, that many had the honour to kiss her hand; to some she promised governments, to others regiments, with promotions of all kinds, in the Treasury, Army and in the Royal Navy. In short, she acted her part so plausibly as to persuade the generality she was no imposter. In vain did many sensible gentlemen in those parts exert themselves to detect, and make a proper example of her, for she had levied heavy contributions upon some persons of the highest rank in the Southern colonies, but at length appeared the underwritten advertisement, together with Mr Michael Dalton, at Charlestown, raising a loud hue and cry for her serene highness; but the lady had made an excursion a few miles to a neighbouring plantation, for which place the messenger set out, when the gentleman who brought us this information left Charlestown. How distressing to behold a lady of this exalted pedigree and pretensions, thus surprized into the hands of her inexorable enemies.

ADVERTISEMENT

Bush-Creek, Frederick County, Maryland,
October 11, 1771.
RUN away from the Subscriber; a convict servant maid, named SARAH WILSON, but has changed her name to Lady Susanna Carolina Matilda, which made the public believe she was his Majesty's sister, she has a blemish in her right eye, black roll'd hair, stoops in the shoulders, makes a common practice of writing and marking her cloaths with a crown and a B. Whoever secures the said servant woman, or takes her home, shall receive five pistoles, besides all costs and charges, WILLIAM DEVALL. I entitle Michael Dalton to search the city of Philadelphia, and from thence to Charlestown, for the said woman. WILLIAM DEVALL

This report was reprinted in several American newspapers.[10] It also crossed the Atlantic to appear in English newspapers and magazines.[11] The *London Magazine* ended its report by saying that 'there is no doubt but her highness will be soon stripped of her royalty, and suffer the punishment due to her crimes'. None of the English journals recognised that this was the same woman they had written about a few years earlier. In fact, the only contemporary who appeared to have realised this was Alderman Hewitt, writing in 1778:

After her adventures in St Albans, and other places, was transported to America, where she imposed on the credulous, and pretended to be allied to the Royal Family, calling herself the Princess Louisa, producing some valuables as jewels, supposed to be taken from one of the royal palaces.[12]

The report in *Rivington's New York Gazetteer* is a mixture of things that are clearly untrue, things that appear to be true as they are substantiated from other sources, and things that *could* be true as there is no evidence to the contrary.

The story of Sarah stealing the queen's jewels is obviously a piece of fiction. If the queen's jewels had really been stolen, gossip about such an event would have made it into the newspapers, but there is no record of such a robbery taking place. Besides, we know why Sarah was transported. Where this story came from remains a mystery – maybe it came from Sarah herself, perhaps telling it to the people in Bush Creek who knew she was a convict in order to make herself seem interesting. Sarah collected information about royalty and the aristocracy to further her deceits. She was probably aware from the newspapers that Caroline Vernon was one of Queen Charlotte's six maids of honour.[13] The story of the queen's jewels inspired some other wild stories about her that were invented in the nineteenth and twentieth centuries (see Appendix 4).

The reference to landing in Maryland in the autumn of 1771 is also wrong. Although we cannot be absolutely sure that Sarah sailed on the *Thornton* in the spring of 1768 with the others who received the same sentence at the quarter sessions, the authorities would not have kept her in England until 1771 before transporting her. Even if she had agreed to pay for her own passage to avoid being sold into slavery, she would not have been allowed to remain in England until 1771. If she did not pay for her own passage, she would have been put on the first available convict ship, which was the *Thornton*.

The reference to 1771 might have been due to confusing Sarah Wilson with Mary Wilson, who appeared at the Old Bailey in April 1771. Mary and her friend Susannah Hancock had lured William Blunder into Susannah Hancock's house and robbed him of one and a half guineas. Blunder said that Hancock told him that if he tried to prosecute them, she would tell the justice that he 'gave her the half guinea for to bugger her'. Both women were sentenced to transportation for seven years.[14] They left England for America on the *Scarsdale* in July 1771 and would have arrived in America in the autumn of 1771.[15]

Sarah probably knew Mary Wilson, as they were both in Tothill Fields Bridewell at the same time. Mary arrived there on 30 November 1767 with seven other women, all eight having been sent there for being 'Loose Idle Disorderly Persons of Evil fame & Common Night Walkers' who were sentenced to hard labour until the quarter session the following January.[16]

The statement that Sarah travelled through Virginia and North Carolina to South Carolina was certainly true, as this was supported by earlier reports. Those earlier reports also confirm that she was calling herself Princess Susanna Carolina Matilda or similar names and was claiming to be the queen's sister. It is possible that Sarah brought with her a set of fine clothes 'that served to favour that deception [that she was the Queen's sister]' along with some jewels and a picture of the queen along with her other possessions when she was transported.

The story that she promised government appointments to some and commissions in the army and navy to others and thus 'levied heavy contributions upon some persons of the highest rank in the Southern colonies' is not only in character with what she was doing in England, but is confirmed by other newspaper accounts.

There is no evidence to prove or disprove that William Duvall bought Sarah, and there is no doubt occasioned by the fact that Duvall's name was printed as 'Devall'; such misprints were common where the printer had misread the author's handwriting. Similarly there is no evidence to prove or disprove the story that Duvall's agent, Michael Dalton, captured Sarah in Charleston. We know from other sources that Sarah was in Charleston in 1773. In the absence of any evidence to the contrary, it can be assumed that the newspaper story concerning Duvall was true.

However, the advertisement does seem odd. It would be reasonable to expect it to have been placed in the *Maryland Gazette* or possibly the *Virginia Gazette*, but it was not in either of those papers. Other advertisements for runaways did not specify that an agent was engaged to search for the escapee. This indicates that for some reason Duvall was fairly desperate to get Sarah back. On the other hand a pistole was only worth 16*s*.[17] The description of Sarah as a 'servant maid' suggests that Duvall was employing her as a domestic servant.

'Run Away from the Subscriber'

Apart from the reference to the use of an agent, the advertisement followed the pattern of other advertisements seeking the return of transported women who had run away. They usually began with the words, 'Run away from the subscriber,

a convict servant woman, named ...', and were placed along-
side advertisements for lost or stolen horses and strayed
cattle. In a pre-photographic age, the advertisements tried to
provide sufficient detail to enable the readers to recognise the
runaways if they encountered them. The advertisements usually described the clothes the women were last known to have
been wearing, and provided detailed physical descriptions of
the women, including their age, hair colour, height and other
characteristics, generally in an unflattering way.

The advertisement for the return of Hannah Boyer said
she was 'pitted much with the Small Pox', had a scar on one
of her eyebrows, was not very tall and was a 'robust mascu-
line Wench'.[18] Mary Price had a 'sour down Look, and bloated
under her Eyes'.[19] Sarah Davis had a 'long Visage, a palavering
Tongue' and was 'round shoulder'd [and] pot-belly'd'.[20] Nell
Fitzgerald had 'black hair, is marked with the small-pox, and
is far gone with child'. [21] Mary Clew was 'very talkative and
artful'.[22] Mary Brady had a 'broad Nose [and] a remarkable
Mole on the left Cheek'.[23] Catherine McClue, alias Moore, was
of 'low stature' and had 'coarse features'.[24] Nancy Partinton
was 'about 19 Years of Age, round Face, small black Eyes,
light Eye-brows, sandy colour'd Hair, of a short Stature, very
round shoulder'd, talks very brisk, has a down look, keeps
a Handkerchief tied under her Jaws'.[25] Mary Davis 'always
talks as if she had a bad cold'.[26] Mary Owens was 'born at
Shrewsbury, in England, and speaks in that Dialect [...] lost
some of her Fore-Teeth, has a large Dimple in her left Cheek
when she laughs, takes snuff [...] walks with her Toes inward
[...] she is a sly wilful Hussy'.[27] Margaret Cane 'is fond of Drink
[and] likes Sailors' Company much'.[28] Sarah Knox was 'of a
middle size, brown complexion, short nose, talks broad, and
said she was born in Yorkshire [...] She may pretend to be a

dancing mistress; will make a great many courtesies, and is a very deceitful, bold, insinuating woman, and a great liar.'[29] Catherine Pardon was 'subject to all manner of vice [...] She appears to be with Child, and is an artful, deceiving Hussey'.[30]

Some descriptions of the women indicate that their masters had an intimate knowledge of their bodies. Winnifred Thomas was 'mark'd on the Inside of her Right Arm, with Gun-powder, W.T. and the Date of the Year underneath.'[31] Susannah Cowden, 'a round faced pert saucy Wench [...] has got a large Scar on one of her Legs'.[32] Isabella Pierce 'limps with her right Leg, which, if examin'd will appear to be a large Scar on each Side of the Ancle of her said Leg,' an indication that either during her voyage or while in service, she had worn metal shackles that had cut into her skin.[33]

Some masters shamelessly advertised that they had fitted their servants with iron collars. Mary Burdon 'had on when she went away an Iron Collar', and Margaret Tasker, 'about 18 Years old, of short Stature [...] Had on an Iron Collar, and has sustained the Loss of one Eye'.[34] Hannah Boyer escaped with 'no Shoes or Stockings [and] had a Horse Lock and Chain on one of her Legs'.[35] Sarah Davis had 'many Scars on her Back occasioned by severe Whippings from her former Master'.[36]

Most women ran away on their own, although some escaped with a companion. The advertiser said of Elsa Picke, 'who took a Bottle of Rum and other Things', when she ran away, that it was 'supposed that one John Manning, a Ditcher, carried her off'.[37] Anne Bailey, 'a small likely Huzzy', ran away with John Kelly, 'an artful deceiving Fellow'.[38] Sarah Plint ran away with William Newcombe, another convict servant, and took with them two horses and two saddles.[39] Husband and wife team John and Mary Jackson ran away together. Mary was 'a lusty Woman [...] of a brown Complexion, full Face, and does not want for Impudence [...] she is a great Singer, and they both love strong Liquors'. John was 'much given to Swearing and Lying' and 'plays on the Bagpipes'.[40]

Isabella Watson was another woman who escaped with a fellow convict. In February 1762 the Bridewell minute book described Isabella and three other women as:

> Loose Idle and Disorderly Persons and Common Night Walkers apprehended loitering in the Streets of this City in and about the Old Bailey Attempting to Pick up Men for the purpose of Lewdness and other Immoral Practices and not having a Visible Way of living nor giving a good Account of themselves.[41]

The following year Isabella and another woman met a man in the street at two o'clock in the morning and invited him to their lodgings. When they got there, Isabella grabbed him by the throat, held him backwards over an old bedstead and took 2 guineas from his pocket. At the Old Bailey Isabella was found guilty of stealing the money and sentenced to transportation.[42] She was transported in the *Neptune* where she met James Corrt, a convict from Kent. When the *Neptune* arrived in America in February 1764, Isabella and James were bought by John Priggs of Prince-George's County. In June 1764 Priggs advertised that they had run away together. They were obviously recaptured because in July 1768 they were advertised as having run away together again.[43] It is not clear whether on their second attempt they were any more successful in evading capture.

There is no indication that Sarah escaped with a companion or that she had an accomplice. If she escaped wearing the working clothes of a servant, she would have been likely to have been stopped and asked to produce a pass to show that she was on a legitimate errand. Servants travelling through the countryside had to carry papers showing that they had their owner's permission to be wandering away from their property, and anyone who encountered a person who looked like a servant wandering at large was likely to have asked to see their papers in the hope that they had none, so they could capture them and claim a reward.

In Maryland, transported convicts who ran away had to serve an additional ten days for each day they were absent.[44] Under the law in Virginia anyone who escaped were subject to thirty-nine lashes of the whip and had to serve for two extra days for each day's absence, plus an additional length of service to reimburse their owner for the costs of their pursuit and recovery.[45]

To avoid detection Sarah would have had to travel by night and keep herself hidden by day, meaning her journey from Bush Creek would have been hazardous. Most roads were mere tracks cut through dark and lonely woods. The many rivers and creeks in Maryland and Virginia made travelling by foot extremely difficult. Treacherous ground, deep river banks and unexpected fords were among the dangers for someone travelling at night along unfamiliar tracks.

Even by day the sounds in the dark woods would have been startling to a solitary traveller unfamiliar with the area. By night the strange noises were heartstopping. Strange and dangerous beasts inhabited Maryland and Virginia. One account of Maryland and Virginia written in 1770 said:

The animals natural to this country are [...] a sort of panther or tiger; bears, wolves, foxes, racoons, squirrels, wild cats [...] The reptiles are many; it would be tedious

to enumerate all the kinds of serpents bred here; the
rattle snake is the principal.[46]

Another writer added:

A wild animal resembling a bull, with very long hair,
short legs, large bodies, and great hunches on their backs
near the shoulders. Their horns are black and short, and
they have a great beard under their muzzles, and much
hair on their heads that it hides their eyes, which gives
then a hideous look. They have [...] elks [...] and two
sorts of rats.[47]

From Frederick to Virginia

If, as seems likely, Sarah did bring with her a set of fine clothes
when she was transported and probably a supply of money,
she was likely to have headed for the town of Frederick,
which was only two or three hours' walk from Bush Creek.
In 1771 William Eddis described Frederick as the third place
of importance in the province of Maryland after the capital,
Annapolis, and Baltimore. Frederick was a market town and
political centre. Its shops and warehouses supplied the needs
of the inland population of Maryland and the backcountry.
Eddis said:

This place exceeds Annapolis in size, and in the number
of inhabitants [...] The buildings, although mostly of
wood, have a neat and regular appearance. Provisions
are cheap, plentiful and excellent. In a word, here are

to be found all conveniences, and many superfluities; a lucrative trade is supported with the back country, and a considerable quantity of grain is sent from hence, by land carriage, to Baltimore, for exportation to the European markets.[48]

Frederick's population was described as 'upwards of 2,000' in 1775, which was quite a large settlement by American standards at the time.[49] Once she arrived in Frederick, Sarah could mingle with the crowds and possibly hitch a ride on one of the waggons carrying goods for the south.

Unlike in England, where there had been a long-developed system of roads that, for the most part, were suitable for wheeled traffic, the American road system was still in its infancy. Maryland and Virginia were originally almost entirely covered with trees, but gradually isolated pockets were cleared for tobacco growing. The planters' houses were generally surrounded by forests and mainly accessible by water, with only narrow tracks through the woods. A contemporary guide said that 'every planter has a river at the door, which makes the conveyance of commodities extremely easy.'[50] The many navigable rivers that flowed into the Chesapeake meant that most planters could load their hogsheads of tobacco directly on to ocean-bound ships without the need to develop an extensive network of roads.

In many areas outside the towns, the few extant roads were impassable for carriages for much of the year; most travel was either by water or on foot or on horseback. Some of Sarah's travels in America might have been made on horseback. We know she could ride: Richard Frith brought a horse for her to ride from Kendal back to Cheshire, and the newspapers referred to her hiring a horse at Lancaster to ride to

Bolton-in-the-Sands. As was the case in England, the news-papers' accounts of Sarah's movements in America are so fragmentary that there are large gaps in her story. The modes of travel and the routes she took are often unknown.

From Frederick there were a number of routes that led into Virginia, including the Great Wagon Road, which went through the Shenandoah Valley to Roanoke, and the Carolina Road, which crossed the Potomac into Virginia at Noland's Ferry and passed through Leesburg and Charlottesville on its way to North Carolina. However, it is more likely that Sarah travelled, probably by waggon, down the Georgetown road, crossing the Monocacy River by the Middle Ford Ferry and then through Georgetown to Richmond, Virginia. This was a much-travelled road, used not only by traders moving between the two colonies, but also as a tobacco road. Large barrels of tobacco, weighing as much as 1,000lb each, were rolled to the port at Georgetown to be shipped across the Atlantic.

From Richmond Sarah could pick up information about the Virginia gentry who might be a worthwhile target for her deceptions. From a later letter, it appears that Sarah visited, and probably stayed for a while with, Mrs Susanna Langborne at the Langborne mansion in King William County Virginia, some 25 miles east of Richmond. Susanna Langborne inherited 1,600 acres of land from her father, and was the widow of Captain William Langborne, who died in 1766. Captain Langborne had been wealthy in his own right, owning several plantations and at least eleven slaves.[51]

According to Sarah's entry in *Notable American Women 1607–1950: A Biographical Dictionary*, her victims in Virginia also included Rev. James Horrocks of Williamsburg, the president of the College of William and Mary, and the Pages of Rosewell, although it is not clear where that information came from.[52] If Sarah did visit James Horrocks, she did so before mid-1771, as Horrocks left Virginia for England in summer 1771 and never returned. It might be that someone might have thought it helpful to Horrocks to introduce him to the queen's sister as he was going to England. Horrocks died at Oporto in Portugal the following year.[53]

The Pages lived at Rosewell plantation, across the York River from Williamsburg. Rosewell plantation was one of the largest and most elaborate houses in colonial America, built of brick imported from England and with a frontage of 231ft, including wings. There were twenty-three rooms in its central building, including a great hall with a grand stairway.[54]

John Page had been a friend of Thomas Jefferson since the days when they were classmates at the College of William and Mary. Jefferson was a frequent visitor to Rosewell and is said to have written a rough draft of the Declaration of Independence at Rosewell on one of the occasions when he was staying with Page.

Thomas Jefferson was elected to the Virginia House of Representatives in 1768. He joined its radical wing of those who opposed British rule which was led by Patrick Henry. It was Patrick Henry who famously said, 'Give me liberty or give me death.' It would be nice to think that Sarah and Jefferson met each other at Rosewell and it would be fun to imagine what the republican Jefferson and the queen's sister talked about if they did meet.

After leaving Rosewell, it is likely that Sarah took the ferry back to Williamsburg, which was then the capital of Virginia and had better transport links. The King's Highway from Boston to Charleston passed through Williamsburg. From Williamsburg Sarah could have travelled down the stretch of the King's Highway through Yorktown and Hampton where a ferry crossed the James River to Norfolk, Virginia. From Norfolk, travellers on the King's Highway had to undergo the difficult journey of crossing fords through the lowland swamps of the tidewater areas of Virginia to Nansemond Court House at Suffolk, Virginia, before skirting west to avoid the Great Dismal Swamp on the way south to Edenton, North Carolina. It is more likely, however, that, with money in her pocket, Sarah took the stagecoach that carried the mail from Williamsburg to Edenton by way of the Hog Island Ferry near Jamestown, the Isle of Wight Court House at Smithfield and Nansemond Court House.[55] From Nansemond, the coach followed the King's Highway to Edenton with a stage at Bennet's Creek.[56]

North Carolina

From Edenton there was just the one road south, which involved taking a ferry across Albemarle Sound, and detouring round the wide mouth of the Pimlico River before the road reached New Bern. Hugh Finlay, surveyor of the North American post roads, who travelled the 93 miles between Edenton and New Bern in 1774, said that the distance between Edenton and the opposite shore of the Albemarle Sound was 12 miles and that due to high winds the ferry was often unable to make the crossing for several days. The rest of the route was along a level firm road, except for the last 3 or 4 miles before the Neuse ferry opposite New Bern, where they had to plough through heavy sand. He said the ferry to New Bern was 'a mile over and the boat is very bad'.[57]

At New Bern Samuel Cornell allegedly became one of Sarah's victims. Cornell had established his mercantile business at New Bern in 1754, and within ten years he had become the wealthiest man in North Carolina. He owned two plantations, a rum distillery, several warehouses, a retail store and at least three trading vessels. He lived in a spacious town house in New Bern that was valued at £7,500 in 1779. In 1767 he lent the colony £8,000 to build the governor's residence – the imposing Tryon Palace constructed of brick and marble. Cornell was a loyalist during the War of Independence. According to *Notable American Women* Cornell introduced Sarah to the governor of North Carolina. In his *History of North Carolina*, Francois-Xavier Martin said:

> In the course of the winter [at the beginning of 1772], a female adventurer passed through this province and attracted great notice. She had assumed the name of Lady Susanna Carolina Matilda, sister to the Queen of Great Britain, and had travelled through the province of Virginia, from one gentleman's house to another, under these pretentions [...] She received the marked attention of governor Martin and his lady, whilst in Newburn; and proceeded thence to Wilmington, where she was also received with great marks of distinction.[58]

Josiah Martin was the last British governor of North Carolina. It was he who would have entertained Sarah at Tryon Palace.

Sarah's journey from New Bern to Wilmington involved crossing the Trent River by Orm's ferry and the New River by Snead's ferry.[59] It was not possible to travel the 93-mile journey in one day. Josiah Martin or another gentleman whom she graced with her presence might have given her letters of recommendation so she could be passed from house to house along the route. If not, she could have made the journey on

Robert Sage's Wilmington and New Bern stagecoach, which stopped overnight at Sage's tavern near Holly Ridge, Onslow County.[60] Sage's tavern was still there in 1791 when George Washington undertook his southern tour; he spent the night at Sage's tavern and described it as an 'indifferent house'.[61]

Sarah arrived at Wilmington sometime in June 1772. She gave her title there as Sophia Carolina Augusta, Princess of Brunswick and Marchioness of Waldergrave. The Wilmington paper, the *Cape Fear Mercury*, said that she was travelling to Charleston incognito 'as she had neither carriages, horses, nor attendants'.[62] A later report in the *Cape Fear Mercury* in July 1772 said that there were 'various reports circulating about the Lady who passed thro' here a few weeks ago [...] one from the South, where the Lady now is [...] makes her no less a Personage than the Sister of our Gracious Queen Charlotte'.[63]

Another report in the *Cape Fear Mercury* described Sarah as 'a Lady of the first distinction, being no less, it is said, than a German Princess'.[64] This reference to a German princess reflected Sarah's claim to be the queen's sister (Queen Charlotte had been born in Germany). But it was also a reminder to their readers of the notorious Mary Carleton, the so-called German princess, whose story was reprinted throughout the eighteenth century in the *Newgate Calendar* and other biographies of famous criminals that were sold in America.

Mary Carleton was born Mary Moders, the daughter of a Canterbury fiddler. She married a shoemaker in Canterbury, but as he was unable to support her extravagances, she left him and went to Dover, where she married a surgeon. She was charged with bigamy, but the case was dropped when she claimed that she thought her first husband was dead. Her next move was to travel to the continent, where she settled in Cologne. Here she encouraged a wealthy old man to fall in love with her. He presented her with several fine jewels, a gold chain and other valuables. At last Mary agreed to marry him, and he gave her a large sum of money to prepare everything necessary for the wedding. Shortly before the wedding was due to take place, Mary took the valuables, the money, and more money that she stole from her landlady's chest, and decamped to England.

In England Mary pretended to be a German princess. She lodged at the Exchange Tavern in the Poultry, kept by a Mr King. King alerted his father-in-law, Carleton, to the prize. They decked Carleton's son, John, in fine clothes and set him courting the German princess, and John and Mary married in April 1663. Shortly afterwards, Mr King received a letter saying that the woman was 'an absolute Cheat, hath marry'd several Men in our County of Kent, and then run away from them with what they had [...] she speaks several Languages fluently, and hath very high Breasts'. The Carletons, disappointed in their attempt to become rich by marrying a German princess, had her arrested, and Mary was sent to Newgate to await her trial for bigamy. Her fame was such that she was visited in Newgate by Samuel Pepys, among others. The Carletons bungled the trial and she was acquitted. In 1664 Mary cashed in on her fame by becoming an actress playing herself in a play about her exploits. For the next seven years she used her sexual attractions to gain lovers whom she then defrauded by using various ingenious methods.

In 1671 Mary was transported to Jamaica, but returned to England before the term of her transportation had expired. She married a wealthy apothecary at Westminster, whom she robbed of £300 and then left; she netted another £300 by stealing from her lodgings. Eventually her luck ran out and she was hanged at Tyburn in January 1673.[65]

It has been said that, while Mary was in Jamaica, she set herself up as a prostitute at Port Royal serving the rich pirates who made that place their headquarters. She was described as being 'as common as a barber's chair: no sooner was one out, but another was in'.[66] This description is an enjoyable simile, worth quoting, but the story of her becoming a prostitute seems a later invention. I can find no contemporary account in any of the pamphlets and broadsides that were published immediately after her execution to support the story that Mary worked as a prostitute in Port Royal.

Charleston

Sarah arrived at Charleston on 7 July 1772 having 'travelled over-land from Philadelphia'.[67] It is not clear whether Sarah had actually travelled as far north as Philadelphia at that stage, or whether she had said she travelled from the important city to give credence to her royal pretensions.

As Sarah had 'travelled over-land' to Charleston, she would have endured the 175-mile journey from Wilmington. Hugh Finlay, who travelled the same road some eighteen months after Sarah, described it as:

Certainly the most tedious and disagreeable of any in the Continent of North America, it is through a poor, sandy, barren, gloomy country without accommodation for travellers. Death is painted in the countenances of those you meet, that indeed happens but seldom on the road. Neither man nor beast can stand a long journey tho' so bad a country where there's much fatigue and no refreshment.[68]

Finlay said that the taverns were 'inconceivably bad' and that the stretch of road known as Lynch's Causeway near the Santee River was:

A most shocking piece of road [...] a mile and a quarter through a swamp [...] it is a tract of boggy land, the road thro' it is made of logs of wood laid crossways and cover'd over with the mud of the bog; after rain it is a mere puddle. The horses sunk between the logs up to the belly.[69]

He described another section of the route as '14 miles thro' the woods in a very crooked path'. He also complained of 'bad bridges'.[70] In 1785 George Washington wrote to Sir Edward Newenham that 'between this State [Virginia] and Charleston (So. Carolina) no Stages are as yet established'.[71]

Despite the poor road communications with the rest of America, Charleston was a seaport capital with a population of 10,000, and was the economic, political and social focus of the entire Carolinas.

In 1773 Joseph Quincy of Massachusetts described Charleston thus:

The town makes a beautiful appearance as you come up to it and in many respects a magnificent one. I can only say in general that in grandeur and splendour of buildings, decorations, equipages, numbers, commerce, shipping and indeed everything, it far surpasses all I ever saw or ever expect to see in America.[72]

The newspaper account of Sarah's arrival at Charleston said that on her way through Virginia she 'was kindly and respectfully treated by many *discerning* people, to whom she made large and golden promises, which no doubt will be complied with in due time'. The report added that she had:

> Furnished abundant Employment for the naturally Curious and Inquisitive, as well as the Ill-natured. Among other Suggestions to prejudice the Lady, one is, that she is the Daughter of the Pretender, by the celebrated Jenny Cameron, and that her Tour through America is made to solicit Interest in Behalf of her unhappy Father.[73]

It appears that Sarah used Charleston as a base for her exploits until November 1772. On 17 December 1772 the Charleston newspaper, the *South Carolina Gazette*, remarked:

> The mysterious History of the FEMALE TRAVELLER, who arrived here in July last, and departed some few Weeks ago, after engrossing a good Deal of public Conversation, we hear, is in Part developed, and has reduced her illustrious Descent very low – *The* KNOWING ONES *are sometimes taken in.*

The reference to the 'knowing ones' being taken in, indicates that, even if the writer of the *South Carolina Gazette* was not persuaded, Sarah had managed to convince some people while she was based in Charleston that she was a person of high rank and influence, if not royalty itself. This is supported by the report of her return to Charleston in February 1773:

Last Thursday Night the extraordinary FEMALE
TRAVELLER, who lately excited so much Curiosity here,
and in the Northern Colonies, returned to this Town, by
Land, from North-Carolina, and is at Lodgings in King-
Street. – 'Tis affirmed, she is no longer *unknown.*[74]

King Street, where the report said Sarah had taken lodgings,
was the most prestigious street in Charleston, lined with fine
buildings. This shows that she was not short of cash when
she returned from her travels. While Joseph Quincy was in
Charleston in 1773, he dined at the home of Miles Brewton,
a merchant and plantation owner, at 27 King Street. He said
the house contained 'the greatest hall I ever beheld', gilded
wallpaper and 'the most elegant pictures, excessive grand and
costly looking glasses'.[75]

According to the report in *Rivington's New York Gazetteer*
for 13 May 1773, Sarah:

> Travelled from one gentleman's house to another under
> these pretensions [that she was the Queen's sister], and
> made astonishing impressions in many places, affect-
> ing the mode of royalty so inimitably, that many had the
> honour to kiss her hand [...] she had levied heavy con-
> tributions upon some persons of the highest rank in the
> Southern colonies.

Even where she did not levy heavy contributions in return for
exercising powers of patronage on their behalf, she was likely
to have been the beneficiary of southern hospitality.

The wealthy plantation owners of the Carolinas, like the
Tidewater aristocracy of the eastern counties of Virginia,
formed an interconnected network of elite families who

imitated the lifestyle of landed English gentry. They built large, brick mansion houses on their plantations, which they filled with luxury items, including imported carpets, silver plate, books and other possessions that would identify them as a people of status and wealth. They consciously cultivated what they saw as traditional English upper-class social values of politeness, liberality and sociability.

Speaking of the Carolinas, Hugh Finlay said:

> To travel with comfort in this part of the world, a stranger shou'd be furnished with letters of recommendation to the Gentlemen and Planters living on the road, but [...] this method of travelling wou'd be attended with inconvenience for the hospitable Americans will kill you with kindness, and detain you from pursuing your journey.[76]

Although Sarah appeared to have stretched credulity much further than she did in England by pretending to be the queen's sister, to some extent things were easier for her in America, especially in Virginia and the Carolinas, given the fabled southern hospitality. She was safely removed from the English networks of gentry and aristocracy, who were familiar with royalty, and therefore would have been able to debunk her stories. All she needed to do was to convince just one person that she was the queen's sister and, provided that person was well regarded and trusted to be of sound judgement, others within the same network would accept that person's word and pass on the information that the queen's sister was in America and that the first person in the chain had met her. After that there would be a snowball effect with the news of the queen's sister's arrival spreading around Virginia and the Carolinas from one trusted person to another. Plantation owners and their wives would then have been vying with each other to entertain Sarah in great style, and she would have been passed from plantation to plantation as she journeyed south.

If the story of Sarah's capture in *Rivington's New York Gazetteer* is true, it is likely that the newspaper accounts of her travels came to the attention of William Duvall or his agent Michael Dalton, and her fame led to her capture.

There is a fanciful modern story that Sarah was holding court at a plantation house outside Charleston when Michael Dalton arrived and surprised the whole company by announcing that Sarah was an escaped convict and escorting her off the premises at gunpoint.[77]

6

AMERICA: THE NORTH

If Michael Dalton did capture Sarah, she was soon free again. On 6 September 1773 the *Boston Post-Boy* reported that in the afternoon of Tuesday, 31 August 1773 a lady calling herself the Marchioness De Wal de Grave arrived in New York, a distance of some 750 miles from Charleston, and that:

> She is said to be the same described, in most of the public papers, under the name of Sarah Wilson, alias Lady Carolina Matilda, in character of a lady of quality, with alliances of the most exalted kind; still she insists upon the verity of these pretensions, and makes the same impressions on many who converse with her, as she has very remarkably done in the southern provinces.[1]

If Sarah was returned to William Duvall, it is possible that he decided that, having got her back, she was more trouble than she was worth. She was unlikely to have been a very diligent servant. It is more likely that Sarah managed to buy her freedom with some of the proceeds of her activities in the southern colonies, either by paying William Duvall at Bush Creek or, even more likely, by paying Michael Dalton on Duvall's behalf at Charleston and then sailing from Charleston along the coastal route to New York.

In law, servitude was not a condition of transportation. The sentence was simply one of banishment for a specified number of years. In practice, servitude was a condition for most convicts, as they did not have the money to buy their freedom. But if, as it seems, Sarah bought off the remaining period of her servitude, her punishment was then only banishment. There is no indication in the September 1773 report, nor in any of the subsequent news stories about her, to indicate that she was a wanted fugitive.

New York

Sarah stayed in New York for three months until late November 1773. At the time New York was the second largest city in America after Philadelphia, with a population of about 22,000. It was a major port, and, with a significant international and intercolonial trade, it was an important economic, political, administrative and cultural centre for the region. New York's residents included a group of very prosperous merchants who lived in substantial brick-built mansions in Bowling Green and other exclusive parts of the city. Such was the wealth of some of the merchants that a mere sixty-two families owned the eighty-five private coaches, chariots and phaetons that were in the city in the early 1770s.[2] The shops that were set up to cater for their tastes were full of fashionable clothes and accessories, and other imported luxury items.

The moneyed classes patronised theatres and musical recitals. They attended formal dancing assemblies, masquerades and intimate card parties that, as in London and Bath, were a feature of upper-class life at a time when the wealthy were beginning to be concerned with being seen to be refined, as well as rich.

New York's numerous opportunities and amenities attracted some of the more educated and ambitious people to the city. And it was stories about the wealth of some of its citizens that no doubt induced Sarah to try her luck there.

After Sarah left New York the newspapers closely followed her movements as she travelled from town to town. On 29 November 1773 the *Newport Mercury* reported that 'last Tuesday arrived here, from New-York, the lady who has passed through several of the southern colonies under the name and character of CAROLINA MATILDA, Marchioness de WALDEGRAVE, &c.' She had travelled from New York to Newport, Rhode Island, on one of the many packet boats that sailed along the coast between those two destinations. The *New-Hampshire Gazette* said that if she had travelled overland through Connecticut:

> We should certainly have known who and what she was, as it is generally the Custom at all the Public Houses there to ask a Stranger, what is his Name, and his Business, where he came from, where he is going, &c, &c, before they'll even give his Horse Oats.[3]

The Boston Tea Party

The next report of Sarah's travels was in the *Providence Gazette*, which reported that 'since our last, a Lady who has visited several Parts of America, under the Name and Characters of CAROLINA MATILDA, Marchioness of WALDEGRAVE, Princess of CRONENBURG, &c. passed through this Town from New-York on her way to Boston'.[4]

If Sarah travelled from Newport to Providence by road, that would have been a 35-mile journey – and a tedious one for such a relatively short distance, as it involved taking three separate ferries.[5] Alternatively, she could have sailed to Providence on one of the packet boats or stage boats that plied between Newport and Providence.[6] Whichever way she travelled, the journey would have lasted all day, so she would have had to stay at Providence at least for one night.

Early in the morning of Tuesday, 7 December 1773 Sarah left Providence by stagecoach; she arrived in Boston that evening after a journey of around 50 miles. The *Boston Evening-Post* reported:

> Tuesday Evening arrived in Town, incog. her Serene Highness the Princess of Cronenburgh, on a Tour through the Northern Parts of the Continent. This is supposed to be the same Lady who has passed thro' several of the Southern Colonies under the Name and Character of Carolina Matilda, Marchioness de Waldegrave, &c.[7]

There is no record of why Sarah went to Boston or who she met. We don't know whether she stayed at an inn, or rented rooms, or whether she was someone's house guest. All we know is that she spent just over a month in Boston at one of the most exciting times in its history and left on 11 January 1774.

Before Sarah arrived in Boston she would have heard that the town had been in a state of agitation since the beginning of November about the threat to impose the Tea Act.[8] The British Parliament passed the Tea Act in May 1773. It had three main aims:

To support the near-bankrupt East India Company;
To undercut the price of tea that was smuggled into America; and
To reassert the government's right to levy the so-called Townsend duty of threepence a pound on imported tea.

The act allowed the East India Company to reclaim the duties on importing tea to Britain that was destined for America. It also granted the company the right to ship its tea directly to North America without having to sell its tea to middlemen at the London Tea Auction. The effect of those changes was that, even with the Townsend duty, the company's tea in America would be cheaper than tea that was legally imported by other merchants and even cheaper than tea that was smuggled. The act, therefore, threatened to put legitimate tea importers out of business as well as the smugglers, and would have given the East India Company a virtual monopoly of the North American tea trade.

The company appointed factors, known as consignees, in Boston, New York, Philadelphia and Charleston to receive the tea on consignment. The consignees could then sell the tea on commission. In September and October 1773 ships containing East India Company tea set sail from England bound for those four ports. At the same time active opposition to the

Tea Act was beginning to grow in America. The newspapers were full of reports of angry meetings of people who were determined to prevent the tea from being landed.

The merchants were opposed to the act as they stood to lose their business. They also feared that if the government could in effect grant to a favoured company a monopoly on tea, it could create monopolies in the future on other goods. The imposition of the Townsend duties rekindled the 'no taxation without representation' argument: if the tea were unloaded and the duties paid, this would be seen as reaffirming parliament's ability to tax the colonies. Moreover, those duties were used to pay the salaries of some colonial governors and other officials. This was seen as a way of keeping those local officials dependent on the British government, rather than allowing them to be accountable to the colonists. In New York, Philadelphia and Charleston, protesters were able to persuade or force the consignees to resign, and the tea ships were allowed to return the tea to England unloaded.

A report from Philadelphia said that the consignees in that town 'wisely and virtuously determined to have nothing to do with so pernicious a Business, while the Teas are subject to a Parliamentary Duty, for the Purpose of raising a Revenue in America'.[9]

In Boston, things were different. The consignees in Boston – Richard Clark and Son, Benjamin Faneuil and Thomas and Elisha Hutchinson, the sons of Thomas Hutchinson, the Governor of Massachusetts – refused to resign. A week before Sarah arrived in Boston, the ship *Dartmouth*, with 112 chests of East India Company tea on board, had reached Boston after an eight-week voyage. On 29 November, as soon as the news of the ship's arrival broke, copies of the following notice were posted up all over Boston:

Friends! Brethren! Countrymen!

THAT worst of Plagues, the detested TEA shipped for
this Port by the East-India Company, is now arrived in this
Harbour; the Hour of Destruction or manly Opposition
to the Machinations of Tyranny stares you in the Face;
every Friend to his Country, to himself and Posterity, is
now called upon to meet at FANEUIL-HALL at NINE
o'clock THIS DAY (at which Time the Bells will ring) to
make a united and successful Resistance to this last, worst
and most destructive Measure of Administration.[10]

When the meeting began, Faneuil Hall was full to overflowing
and there were large queues outside, so the meeting voted to
adjourn to the Old South Meeting House, the largest building
in town. It was said that the meeting was attended by 'upwards
of 5000 Persons'.[11] The meeting resolved that the tea should
be sent back without any duty being paid and that a permanent watch of twenty-five men should be posted to prevent it
from being unloaded. While the meeting was taking place, a
messenger arrived with a letter from the consignees that they
would not be sending the tea back to England. The meeting
also received a proclamation from Governor Hutchinson calling it unlawful and ordering it to disperse, which the meeting
voted to ignore.[12]

Feelings in the town against the Tea Act were so strong
that those consignees who had not already left Boston took
refuge at Fort William on Castle Island, where British troops
were stationed. Governor Hutchinson later fled to his country
house at Milton, 10 miles away. Tensions increased still further when two more ships loaded with East India tea arrived
at Boston – the *Eleanor* on 2 December and the *Beaver* on

8 December – and when it became known that Governor Hutchinson had ordered Admiral Montagu not to allow any vessel to leave Boston Harbour without a pass.[13]

Since the beginning of December thousands of citizens in Boston and neighbouring towns met almost daily to try to decide what action to take if negotiations failed. The owners and the ship's captains found themselves caught in the middle of a standoff between two implacable parties. On the one side there were those who attended the meetings; they wanted the ships to return the tea to England without payment of the Townsend duties and had posted an armed guard at Griffin's Wharf to prevent the tea from coming ashore. On the other side stood Governor Hutchinson, who had refused permission for the ships to leave without the tea being unloaded and the duties paid, and had ordered a naval blockade of the harbour to prevent the ships from leaving with the tea still on board.

The law required customs officials to seize the ships' cargo if the duties were not paid within twenty days of arrival. The twenty day period for the *Dartmouth* was due to expire at midnight on 16 December; with the deadline fast approaching a notice was distributed throughout Boston and neighbouring towns calling for people to attend a meeting at the Old South Meeting House on the morning of 14 December. Francis Rotch, son of the owner of the *Dartmouth* and the *Beaver*, and the captains of those two ships, were asked to attend. The meeting voted that Francis Rotch, accompanied by a committee from the meeting, should apply to the collector of customs for a pass for the ships to leave the harbour with their cargo of tea. He returned to the meeting with the news that the collector had told him he could not issue a pass without consulting the controller of customs, which the collector undertook to do. The meeting was adjourned to 16 December.[14]

On 16 December, the last day of the *Dartmouth*'s deadline, thousands of people gathered in the streets, at Griffin's Wharf, at the Green Dragon Tavern and at the Old South Meeting House, to await events.[15] At ten o'clock between 5,000 and 7,000 people gathered at the Old South Meeting House for the reconvened meeting. As well as political leaders, wealthy merchants and professional people like Samuel Adams, John Hancock and Dr Joseph Warren, the town meetings included 'the whole body of people – women, apprentices, African Americans and servants.'[16]

Francis Rotch told the meeting that the controller of customs had refused to clear the *Dartmouth* for departure with dutiable articles on board without the duty being paid. The meeting then voted that he and a deputation from the meeting should go to Governor Hutchinson's house at Milton to request a pass for the *Dartmouth*. It was six o'clock and dark when Francis Rotch returned from his 20-mile round trip with the news that Hutchinson had refused to issue a pass. The meeting concluded that they had done all they could to return the tea 'safe and untouch'd to the proprietors', but had been prevented by:

The Consignees of the Tea and their Coadjutors, who have plainly manifested their inclination of throwing the community into the most violent commotions, rather than relinquish and give up the profits of a commission or contract [...] and no one being able to point out any thing further that was in the power of this Body to do [...] it was moved and Voted that this Meeting be immediately dissolved.[17]

Shortly before the meeting ended, a number of people had arrived and stood by the door, all disguised to protect their identities. Some were dressed as Mohawk Indians. When it became clear that all attempts at negotiation were at an end, the newcomers gave what was described as 'the War-Whoop', which was answered by a few in the hall. They led the way to Griffin's Wharf followed by a crowd from the meeting and others spilling out from houses and taverns.

Some 150 men boarded the three ships, broke up the 342 chests of tea the ships were carrying and threw their contents into the sea. Great care was taken not to damage the ships or any other goods. When someone managed to break a small padlock belonging to one of the captains, a replacement was purchased and sent to the captain.[18]

This action was organised and carried out by a group calling themselves the 'Sons of Liberty', who were opposed to taxation by the British. They used to meet under the Liberty Tree, a large elm in Hanover Square, and in the Green Dragon Tavern in Union Street in Boston's North End. George Hewes, one of those who took part in the raid, described how they set to work, 'first cutting and splitting the chests with our tomahawks, so as thoroughly to expose them to the effects of the water. In about three hours from the time we went on board, we had thus broken and thrown overboard every tea chest to be found in the ship.'[19]

Another description of the Tea Party explained that the participants on each ship organised themselves into three divisions: one to raise the chests to the deck; another to break open the chests; and the third to throw the contents overboard.[20]

Around 2,000 people stood on the waterfront watching the Sons of Liberty throwing the tea into the harbour. It is possible that Sarah was one of the spectators. She may even have attended some of the town meetings. If so, it would have been interesting to know who she was with. We do know that later on, she was acquainted with people who were active supporters of the American Revolution, and that when she was in Boston in 1777 she might have been living in the same household as one of those who took part in the Tea Party.

During her stay in Boston Sarah must have attracted some attention, for on Thursday, 13 January 1774 the Boston paper, the *Massachusetts Spy*, announced that:

> Tuesday last the Princess Carolina Matilda, alias, the Princess of Cronenburgh, alias, the Marchioness de Waldegrave, who has travelled *incog.* through all the Southern Provinces, and has resided in this metropolis for about a month past, sat [*sic*] out for Portsmouth, New-Hampshire. She is certainly the most surprising genius of the *female* sex that was ever *obliged* to visit America.

The reference to being 'obliged to visit America' shows that the journalist might have known, or at least suspected, that Sarah had been transported.

Further Travels in the North

The newspapers reported that Sarah arrived at Portsmouth on 13 January after a two-day journey in the stagecoach from Boston.[21] Compared with England, stagecoach travel in America was still in its infancy. There were stage lines connecting the major towns in the northern colonies, but due to the state of the roads, coach travel was much slower than in England. Jonathan and Nicholas Brown announced in 1772 that their stagecoach would 'compleat the whole Distance from New York to Boston in the Course of one Week' – a distance of some 215 miles, which indicates that the coaches were travelling little more than 30 miles a day, and that was on a well-established road.[22] John Quincy, president of Harvard, described his journey from Boston to New York in 1794 as follows:

> The journey to New York took up a week. The carriages were old and shackling and much of the harness was made of ropes. One pair of horses carried the stage eighteen miles. We generally reached our resting place for the night if no accidents intervened at 10 o'clock and after a frugal supper, went to bed with a notice that we should be called at three in the morning, which generally proved to be half-past two, and then whether it snowed or rained, the traveller must rise and make ready, by the help of a horn lantern and a farthing candle and proceed on the way over bad roads, sometimes getting out to help the coachman out of a quagmire or rut, and arrived at New York after a week's hard travelling.[23]

Bartholomew Stavers started the regular stagecoach service between Boston and Portsmouth in 1761 'for the encouragement of trade between these two places.'[24] Hugh Finlay said in 1773 that its arrival times at Portsmouth were very irregular and depended on the state of the roads. He also said that there were many stages on the route. The stages were at the roadside taverns which provided alcohol, basic food and lodging for travellers.

The road from Boston to Portsmouth crossed many rivers – the larger rivers by ferries and the smaller rivers and streams by bridges. Most bridges were of primitive construction where two poles were laid across the river with logs or planks placed across the poles. As late as 1838 a person travelling through Vermont remarked that his coach came to many bridges on which the planks had come loose and, 'the driver with great humour and alacrity set to work himself to place the planks across again in their proper places.'[25]

The *Essex Gazette* (Salem, Mass.) in a report datelined 'Portsmouth, January 21' said:

> In the last Gazette, it was mentioned, that the LADY who is said to be the Duchess or Princess of Cronenburgh, came to this Town. Her Title, we hear, is the *Duchess of Browtonsburgh*; or should she pass by the Title of the *Fair Stranger*, as it has been mentioned in some of the Southern Papers, perhaps it might be as agreeable. Indeed, her Arrival, and travelling through the Continent, *incog.* has occasioned much Employment to *busy Curiosity*. It is confidently said, she is a Person of the very first Distinction in Europe.[26]

This is the first reference to the use of the Browtonsburgh or Brotenburg title, a name Sarah appears to have invented.

On 24 March 1774 the *Boston News-Letter* reported: 'We hear from Newcastle, New-Hampshire, that her Serene Highness Caroline Augusta Harriot, Princess hereditary of Browtonsburg, Dutchess of Browtonsburg and Wormsgrove, Marchioness of Waldegrave, &c. has lately taken up her Residence in that Town.'

Newcastle was a very small town just outside Portsmouth. It was situated entirely on an island and populated mainly by fishermen and others who made their living from the sea. It is not known where or with whom Sarah was staying in Newcastle. It may be no coincidence that Sarah arrived at a time when there was a schism in the Congregational Church in Newcastle. Benjamin Randall, who later founded the Free Will Baptist denomination, was a member of the Congregational Church but found that 'men of intemperate and corrupt habits were allowed to come to communion each month without reproof [...] along with people with [...] no pretence to piety', which the minister, Rev. Stephen Chase, appeared to be doing nothing about. In the Spring of 1774 Randall started his own meetings. This led to antagonism between him and Stephen Chase. Randall left the Congregational Church to create a breakaway church in Newcastle and took some of the more pious members of the congregation with him.[27] This sounds the kind of thing Sarah was likely to have been mixed up in.

I can find no further trace of Sarah until January 1775, when she arrived at the home of Rev. Manasseh Cutler, the minister of the Congregational Church at Ipswich Hamlet, now Hamilton, Massachusetts. Ipswich Hamlet was renamed Hamilton at the instigation of Rev. Cutler in honour of Alexander Hamilton, one of the founding fathers of the United States.

Rev. Cutler wrote in his journal:

Jan. 25. Wed. A lady came to our house, who had made a great noise in the country, and has been the occasion of various conjectures. She calls herself Caroline Augusta Harriet, Duchess of Brownstonburges. Says she has resided in the Court of England for several years; that she eloped from the Palace of St. James. She appears to be a person of an extraordinary education, and well acquainted with things at Court, but is generally supposed to be an imposter.[28]

It is likely that Sarah arrived on the Boston–Newburyport stagecoach that passed through Ipswich twice a week in both directions.[29] She stayed with the reverend for three nights. The next entry in Rev. Cutler's Journal read: '*Jan. 28. Sat.* Our extraordinary visitor has left us. I conveyed her to town in a chaise.'[30] It is not known whether the town he meant was Salem, which was 12 miles from Ipswich, or Boston, which was 28 miles away.

It is not clear where Sarah went next. In July 1775 the *Newport Mercury* reported that 'Her Serene Highness CAROLINA AUGUSTA HARRIOT, Princess Hereditary of Browtonburgh, Marchioness of Waldegrave, &c.' had arrived in Newport in late June/early July from 'the eastward', and that on 12 July she had sailed for New York.[31]

In September 1775 the *New-York Gazette* reported that 'since our last arrived from the Eastward, on her way to the Southward, her Serene Highness CAROLINA AUGUSTA HARRIOT, Princess Hereditary of Browtonburgh, Marchioness of Waldegrave, &c.'[32]

This is the last newspaper report of Sarah's movements that is readily available. It is possible she continued to wander all over North America for some years in the hope of repeating her earlier success in finding suitable targets she could persuade that she had great powers of patronage and could confer some lucrative appointment in return for cash. However, against the background of the outbreak of the War of Independence and the notoriety the newspaper reports had given her, it is unlikely that she would have had any great success. The newspaper reports may have worked in her favour for a short while by turning her into a celebrity – a celebrity to whom people were willing to open their doors and offer hospitality. She may have received some short-term comfort as a house guest of those, such as Rev. Manasseh Cutler, who were curious about her story and were prepared to entertain her for a few days. But with the war engrossing people's attention, such opportunities were likely to have become less and less frequent.

While still maintaining the pretence of being a member of European royalty, Sarah recognised the prevailing revolutionary spirit and the strong biblical tradition in that part of America in which she found herself, and decided to play along with it. It seems that, as was the case with the Friths in Cheshire, she decided to play the religious card and, in view of the spirit of the age, her next set of contacts and benefactors were not only religious, but were also involved in the revolutionary cause. Manasseh Cutler became a chaplain in the revolutionary army during the War of Independence.

Cambridge, Massachusetts

We do get some fleeting glimpses of Sarah's life after she stopped appearing in the newspapers. In September 1776 she was at Cambridge, Massachusetts, almost certainly as a guest of Mary Stedman, the wife of Captain Ebenezer Stedman.

Cambridge was founded by the group of Puritans who set sail from England in 1630 with the aim of building their community around a purer, more biblical church.

Ebenezer Stedman's ancestors arrived in Cambridge not long after the original settlers and were involved in the running of the town meeting house from an early stage.[33] In 1756 Ebenezer Stedman subscribed £17 8s towards the building of a new meeting house; a plan of it shows that he had two family pews. During the siege of Boston, when Cambridge served as the headquarters of the Continental Army, George Washington worshipped at the meeting house.[34]

Ebenezer Stedman played a minor role in the American Revolution. He had been elected as a selectman, responsible with other selectmen for the day-to-day running of the town of Cambridge. He was one of the five overseers of the poor.[35] He was also the captain of the local militia. After the Massachusetts Committee of Safety was formed in Autumn 1774 under the chairmanship of John Hancock, the committee used to hold its meetings, together with the Massachusetts Committee of Supplies, at Ebenezer Stedman's house. The Committee of Safety was responsible for calling out the militia whenever it judged the safety of the people required it.

At the meeting of the two committees at Ebenezer Stedman's house on 8 November 1774, they voted 'to procure all the arms and ammunition they can, at the neighbouring provinces on the continent'. There seemed to have been little doubt in the minds of the committee members that the outcome of events would be war between the American patriots and the British. At further meetings at Stedman's house on 3 and 13 February 1775, the committees voted to purchase all the powder they could and move certain field pieces and mortars to the town of Concord. On 7 and 14 March, the committees met again at Stedman's house and voted £500 to be given to Dr Joseph Warren and Dr Benjamin Church to buy 'such articles for the provincial chests of medicine, as cannot be got on credit', and voted that watches should be kept constantly at places where the magazines were kept.[36]

When Paul Revere undertook his famous rides to Lexington on the night of 18 April 1775 to warn local leaders that the British were marching there to arrest John Hancock and Samuel Adams and to destroy the stockpile of arms at Concord, he stopped at every town along the route to warn the local militia commanders that the British were coming. Ebenezer Stedman was awakened at an early hour. Stedman then spread the word by sending an express rider to warn the militia leaders in Woburn, 10 miles away. Major Loammi Baldwin of Woburn noted in his diary on 19 April 1775: 'This morning a little before break of day, we were alarmed by Mr Stedman's express from Cambridge.' It is thought that Revere rode through Cambridge on his way to Lexington and that Stedman received the news directly from Revere. [37]

Ebenezer and Mary's son William was 11 years old when Sarah was at Cambridge. In 1803 William was elected to the House of Representatives and was one of the first members of the American Antiquarian Society after it was founded in 1812. Some time between October 1813 and October 1814, he donated 'Three Letters from a person calling herself the Princess Brotensburg' to the manuscripts collection of the Antiquarian Society.[38] Those documents came from his parents' home. They included a page of verse dated 'September ye 26th Anno Domini, 1776. Cambridge'. Here is an extract:

Thou God who over all presides,
Who rules ye tempests & Commands the Tides,
Deign from thy Heav'nly Throne, my Voice to hear,
And grant Propitious this my fervent Prayer.

Oh! In thy boundless Goodnys, Lend thy Aid:
To an unhappy Wandering Oppressed Maid;
Be calm my Sorrows, & my Grief Assuage,
Protect & Comfort Me, from Stage to Stage:
Untill a Period to my toils shall Come,
And then in Mercy, dost Conduct me Home.

Boston Again

Sarah appears to have spent most of 1777 in Boston. Boston stood on the Shawmut Peninsula, a land mass of less than 1,000 acres joined to the mainland by a swampy, mile-long, 50-yard-wide isthmus known as 'the Neck'. Violent waves pounded the Neck and sometimes destroyed the road during winter storms. The land lay so low that high tides often washed across the rough road, preventing carriages from travelling.

After the battles of Lexington and Concord in April 1775 the British army, under the command of General Gage, retreated to Boston where they were besieged by the militias from the surrounding Massachusetts communities. Those militias were later joined by militias from New Hampshire, Rhode Island and Connecticut. The siege of Boston lasted until March 1776.

During the first months of the siege there was a mass exodus of people fleeing the city along the Neck with whatever goods they could carry. As they left, they passed loyalist refugees fleeing in the opposite direction who were seeking the protection of the British troops. Despite the influx of loyalists, the civilian population, which stood at 15,000 in 1765, plummeted to less than 3,000.[39] This was a mix of Bostonians who remained to protect their property and the property of their friends who had left, and loyalist refugees from the countryside.

Among those who left Boston was a bookseller named Henry Knox and his wife, Lucy Flucker Knox. Lucy had been born into a life of privilege and luxury as the daughter of Thomas Flucker, a wealthy Boston merchant. Lucy's mother, Hannah, was the daughter of Brigadier General Samuel Waldo, who had accumulated a fortune in Boston. He also owned a huge tract of land in the Province of Maine. In 1770 Thomas Flucker was appointed by the British Crown as the secretary of the colony of Massachusetts.

Henry was from a much poorer background. He had to leave school at the age of 12 to earn his living when his father died, and he got a job as a bookseller's clerk. Fascinated by military topics, he read voraciously on the subject, with a special focus on artillery. He joined a local artillery company and in 1772 co-founded the Boston Grenadier Corps. He was also a member of the Sons of Liberty, although it is believed that he took no part in the Boston Tea Party.

In 1771 Henry opened his own bookshop, where he and Lucy met and fell in love. Lucy's parents opposed the union. They did not want a son-in-law 'in trade', and they especially did not want one who supported the revolutionary cause of those who had demonstrated against taxes and had thrown the tea into Boston Harbour. However, they eventually and reluctantly gave their consent to the marriage. The couple were married in 1774, when Lucy was 17 and Henry was 23. The final break between Lucy and her parents came at the onset of the war when she and Henry left Boston to support the revolutionary cause. Her parents remained in Boston until the evacuation of the loyalists in March 1776. They sailed to England and Lucy never saw them again.[40]

Once Henry had settled Lucy safely in Worcester, 40 miles from Boston, he returned to join the militia besieging the city. He directed cannon fire at the Battle of Bunker Hill and his skills as an artilleryman greatly impressed George Washington. Thereafter Henry accompanied Washington on most of his campaigns, becoming the chief artillery officer of the Continental Army and rising to the rank of general. After the war President Washington appointed him as the first United States Secretary for War.

During the siege of Boston, the militia surrounded the town on three sides, totally blocking all land access, but, due to the strength of the Royal Navy, the harbour and sea access remained under British control. The British were therefore able to continue to receive supplies and reinforcements by sea. As the siege wore on with no progress on either side, Washington ordered Henry Knox to lead an expedition to retrieve the cannon that had recently been captured from the fort of Ticonderoga in Essex County, New York.

Knox and his men arrived at Ticonderoga on 5 December 1775 and commenced hauling 60 tons of heavy artillery by ox-drawn sled some 300 miles to the Continental Army's headquarters at Cambridge. The journey was a technically challenging and complex operation. It involved crossing the frozen Hudson and Connecticut rivers and the snow-draped Berkshire Mountains. The cannon finally reached Cambridge on 27 January 1776.

Washington deployed some of the longer-range cannon on Dorchester Ridge overlooking Boston and its harbour. This broke the stalemate by causing the British to withdraw their fleet out of the cannons' range. It was impossible to get supplies in by sea as well as by land, so conditions in Boston rapidly deteriorated. Eventually, agreement was reached that the British would evacuate Boston if the Americans would let them leave peacefully. On 17 March 1776 the Americans watched from the heights as a fleet of some 120 ships containing the British troops and loyalist families sailed from the harbour.

Even in the early stages of the siege food was in short supply. On 23 July 1775 William Carter, a lieutenant in the 40th Regiment of Foot, was complaining that fresh provisions were scarce and 'vegetables, we have none.'[41] When meat was available, it was sold at prohibitive prices and was of dubious quality. One inhabitant remarked that animal carcases were 'offered for sale in the market, which formerly we would not have pick'd up in the street'. Bread quadrupled in price and milk remained unobtainable for months.[42]

Besides the threat of famine, numerous illnesses and diseases plagued the population, including diarrhoea, dysentery, food poisoning, malnutrition and typhoid. But the greatest terror was smallpox; an outbreak erupted in May 1775 and grew more prevalent as the siege dragged on.[43]

The winter of 1775–6 was particularly severe. William Carter, writing from Boston on 31 December 1775, said that 'the Cold is so intense that the ink freezes in the pen whilst I write'.[44] A fuel shortage meant that British soldiers were ordered to tear down buildings and fences to provide firewood. Cannonading and fire caused further damage. Towards the end of the siege discipline broke down completely. John Rowe, a Boston merchant, described in his diary entries for 11 to 16 March 1776 instances of loyalists and British soldiers breaking into houses, shops and warehouses and stealing as many goods as they could carry.[45]

It took years for Boston to recover after the siege. When people returned they found that many homes were unrecognisable and some had been completely demolished. The furniture of many houses had been carried off or broken in pieces.[46] Even as late as 1777 when Sarah was in Boston, smallpox was still rampant. Lucy Knox, who returned to Boston shortly after the siege ended, wrote to Henry on 3 April 1777 that the number of persons infected made it dangerous for her to move around.

In her next letter to Henry, dated 13 April 1777, Lucy added the following postscript:

> I send you a letter which the famous Duchess of Brotenbourgs Princes of Frankfort and cousin of the queen of great Britian [sic] begs your care of – she brought it to me unsealed that I might give her my opinion whether it would offend his excellency or not – it is a very artful affair – and may at least afford him some amusment, however – you will use your judgment – whether you would deliver it or not.[47]

It is not known whether Henry gave the letter to George Washington; he did not refer to the letter in his replies to Lucy. One can only speculate on what the self-styled cousin of the Queen of Great Britain wanted from George Washington in the middle of a war against the British. It shows, however, that, while she was in Boston, Sarah had developed sufficient intimacy with Lucy to be able to recognise that she and her husband had the potential to act as intermediaries between her and George Washington. From the playful tone of her postscript it appears that young Lucy was amused by the claims of the 'famous Duchess'. It also appears that Sarah had demoted herself from queen's sister to queen's cousin, probably in the interests of realism.

During Sarah's stay in Boston, there were at least two rumours of invasion. In late April 1777 there were claims that the British had sent an army of 13,000 to attack Boston.[48] In August there was another panic. Abigail Adams wrote to her husband John, the future President of the United States:

> We have never since the Evacuation of Boston been under apprehensions of an invasion from them eaquel to what we sufferd last week. All Boston was in confusion, packing up and carting out of Town, Household furniture, military stores, goods &c. Not less than a thousand Teams were imployd a fryday and Saturday – and to their shame be it told, not a small trunk would they carry under 8 dollors and many of them I am told askd a hundred dollors a load, for carting a Hogshead of Molasses 8 miles 30 dollors.[49]

Sarah was living in Boston at a time when people in the town were suffering from high prices and a scarcity of goods as well as having to contend with the aftermath of destruction and continued outbreaks of smallpox. The loss of trade with the British meant that goods only came from intermediaries in the Caribbean, making them more expensive. The war had disrupted agricultural production as farm workers left to join the army, thus raising the price of agricultural labour. The demands of the military added to the scarcity of goods and provisions. Provincial governments were paying for the war by printing money, stoking up inflation.

In March Abigail Adams reported that bread was being rationed to one loaf a day and that the meat on sale was 'miserabley poor, and so little of it that many people say they were as well supplied in the Seige'.[50] Lucy Knox told Henry that 'the price of every thing is so exorbitant indeed it is difficult to get the necessarys of life here at any price'.[51] In April Abigail Adams wrote:

> That a Scarcity prevails of every article not only of Luxery, but even the necessaries of life is a certain fact. Every thing bears an exorbitant price [...] Indian Corn at 5 shillings, Rye 11 and 12 shillings, but none scarcly to be had even at that price, Beaf 8 pence, veal 6 pence and 8 pence, Butter 1 & 6 pence; Mutton none, Lamb none, pork none, Sugar mean Sugar £4 per hundred, Molasses none, cotton wool none, Rum N.E. 8 shillings per Gallon, Coffe 2 & 6 per pound, Chocolate 3 shillings.[52]

The town's merchants were held to be responsible for hoarding supplies in order to artificially drive up prices. On 19 April 1777 someone calling himself Joyce Junior, named after the Cornet George Joyce who seized King Charles I from Parliament's custody in 1647 and handed him to the New Model Army, led a crowd of some 500 Bostonians. They seized five merchants who were considered to have been the worst offenders and put them in a cart. With drum and fife following, the crowd hauled the merchants out of town and took them to the gallows at Roxbury. In a symbolic hanging the crowd 'timpd up' the cart, dumped out the men, and told them never to return to Boston.[53]

Bostonians had a reputation for rioting. Between 1700 and 1764, there were just four riots in New York and six in Philadelphia, whereas Boston had twenty-eight. In 1710 there was a severe shortage of food, yet the merchants were hoarding grain and exporting it for greater profits. Andrew Belcher was one of the richest merchants in Boston. When one of his ships was resting at anchor in the harbour with its hold filled with grain, a group of men rowed out and broke the rudder.[54] Three years later Belcher was once again hoarding grain with the intention of exporting it for profit. The Boston minister Cotton Mather tried unsuccessfully to deflect the town's anger away from the merchants by telling his parishioners, 'Tis the Lord who has taken away from you what he had given to others'. However, the townsfolk chose to blame Andrew Belcher rather than God for the high price of bread, and 200 people rioted on the Boston Common. They attacked Belcher's ships, broke into his warehouses looking for corn, and shot the lieutenant-governor when he tried to intervene.[55]

There were further riots in Boston while Sarah was there. For several weeks in July 1777 crowds broke into merchants' stores, seized coffee and sugar and dealt them out in small quantities to townspeople. Towards the end of that month there was a 'Female Riot'. One merchant had a great store of coffee which he was refusing to sell at a reasonable price to the small shopkeepers so they could sell it to the poor at a price they could afford, and Abigail Adams reported:

A Number of Females some say a hundred, some say more assembled with a cart and trucks, marchd down to the Ware House and demanded the keys, which he refused to deliver, upon which one of them seazd him by his Neck and tossd him into the cart. Upon his finding no Quarter he deliverd the keys, when they tipd up the cart and dischargd him, then opend the Warehouse, Hoisted out the Coffe themselves, put it into the trucks and drove off. It was reported that he had a Spanking among them.[56]

There was another female riot in July at Copp's Hill in the North End of Boston.[57] In September a crowd seized five 'monopolizers and extortioners' and carted them out of town.[58]

On 3 October 1777 Sarah sent a letter to Mary Stedman, giving her address as North End, Boston. North End was Boston's oldest neighbourhood and had been long established by the time Sarah lived there; it was a busy, noisy place of docks and shipyards and small manufactories, peopled by mariners, craftsmen and waterfront labourers, along with wealthy merchants. Wharves, warehouses, churches and other public buildings dominated the district. A place of great contrasts, the great brick-built mansions of wealthy ship owners and merchants stood close to the craftsmen and labourers' wooden houses that stood weathered by wind and sea spray.

Despite the numbers who had left Boston, never to return, North End in 1777 was a crowded place. It was populated by those who had remained during the siege, by returning Bostonians who had not made a new life for themselves elsewhere and were settling back into their damaged homes, and by refugees from outside Boston who had been displaced by the war.

It is not clear who Sarah was staying with while she was at North End. The religious culture of the area was strongly Puritan. At the top of North Square stood the church where Increase Mather and his son, Cotton Mather, ministered to the Puritan Congregationalists of Boston. In 1769 Boston hosted ten Congregational [Puritan] Meeting Houses, three Church of England churches, one French, one Anabaptist, one Irish and one Quakers' Meeting House.[59] From the tone of her letters, it seems that Sarah was acting the part of a devoutly religious princess in order to impress a Puritan host.

Certainly the following letter Sarah wrote to Mary Stedman is playing to her knowledge that the Stedmans were a deeply religious family:

From a Certain Princess
To the Worthy Mrs Mary Stedman

My Dear Friend

We humbly hope, that these few Lines will Come safe & find you, and your Consort, Capt Stedman, & the whole of your Family in the Sweet Shades of good health, & happiness, Heartly wishing at the same Time, that both you & yours, May be in the Royal Ark of Almighty Love & Mercy.

We beg Leave to inform you that We propose to leave Boston! in a Very Shorte Time, for the Southward, if the Blessed God, be willing by Reason of having had the Happiness of Seeing The Honble William Langborne; Esqr of Virginia; a Gentleman who know us, on our first arrival on the Continent & Lady S. Langborne his Mamma, was our sincere Friend, tho' now No More on the Shore of Time, And our dear friends in that quarter, have Requested Mr Langborne, to find us out & to preswade us to Return to them again, & they will Endeavour to Make us as Comfortable & happy, as We can wish in a Strange Land; Lady Anne C. Moore as sent Me Word, if I'll Return, she will send her Coach & Six, to Meet Me, in the Jerseys, & that Her Ladyship's Arms, will be Reddy to Receive Me With ye Warm Love, &c.

I now beg Leave to inform you that I was Extreemly [sorry] I had not the pleasure of Seeing you when you was so kind, to Call on us, Miss Furbur, was very sorry that you did not Lite and have Tea, and that found her in her disable by Reason of our Friend Mr Grant, being Extreemly Ill! & still Remain so, that he Is not Expected to Live: – Miss Furbur presents her Love to you & shall be proud to waite on you, any Time you Come to Boston.

Be pleased to Give my sincere Love to the Whole of your Family & Except ye same yourself; Tell Mr B I hope he often as Meditated, on what I sayd to when going to Boston if he has not I implore he will [missing bottom of the page]

Hoping that the Lord Almighty Three in One May be yr Guardian through Time & your Portion & Bliss! Through a Boundless Eternity.

Dominis Vobiscum

Adieu

Brotonburgh

N.B.

We Request ye favour of seeing some of you next week, & for you To apoint the Day & we will Take Care not to be out, We pray you will Bring or send Mrs Houseman's Life to Me & send Me a Line or Two, by Return of ye Gentleman, Mr Chalendar, who is Bearer of this a Worthy young Man, & one of Mr Grant's Family who serv'd his Time with Him, – I flatter Myself you will Receive him kindly, & send me a Line by Hime. &c.

North End,
Boston
October ye 3d Anno Domini

Miss Furbur was almost certainly the Miss Elizabeth Furbur who died in 1790 and is buried in Copp's Hill Burying Ground in North End, Boston. Her gravestone reads:

In Memory of Miss Elizabeth Furbur,
Daught[er] of Mr Richard and Mrs Abigail Furbur,
who Died May 10th 1790. Aged 41 Years.
Christ the Redeemer is my Deliverer from Chaos & the
Power of Death
Jesus amid the Conflagration will shine forth as a
Conqueror for me
over Sin Destruction & the King of Terrors.

Mrs Abigail Furbur died on 11 July 1750, a year after Elizabeth was born, and Richard died not long after, on 15 February 1753. Both are buried at Copp's Hill. There are no records to show who adopted Elizabeth, nor who paid for her gravestone and the inscription.

Mr Grant was probably Samuel Grant (1705–84) who lived in Union Street, North End. He was one of the wealthiest upholsterers in Boston. In 1742 he became a deacon at the congregational New North Church, but, according to a history of the church, 'in November 1776, Capt. Samuel Barrett and Capt. John Simpkins were chosen deacons. This was done at the desire of Messrs Grant and John Barrett, whose age and infirmities rendered them incapable of performing their duties.'[60]

Despite his infirmities, Samuel Grant did not die until 1784. His son, Moses, lived with his father in Union Street. Moses was a member of the North End Caucus, an informal political organisation, many of whose members were also members of the Sons of Liberty, including Samuel Adams and Paul

Revere. One of their meeting places was the Green Dragon Tavern where it is said they planned the Boston Tea Party. Moses Grant took part in the Tea Party; his place was in the second division, whose task was to smash open the chests.[61] Some time after Samuel's death, Moses moved to Court Street and joined the Brattle Street Church, another Congregational church, where he was appointed deacon in 1793.[62]

Clearly, the Grants and the Stedmans had similar political and religious views. As Cambridge was only 8 miles by road from Boston, or 4 miles by crossing the Charles River, it is likely that both families were part of the same circle, or at least were acquainted with each other. It is therefore reasonable to assume that the Mr Grant whom Sarah mentioned in her letter to Mary Stedman who was 'extreemly ill' in 1777 was Samuel Grant, whose age and infirmities prevented him from continuing his duties as a deacon in 1776, even though Sarah's report of his imminent death was premature. It is possible that Miss Furbur was part of the Grant household and that when she died in 1790, it was Moses Grant who paid for her stone and chose the inscription. It might even be that Sarah was also part of that household during 1777. It is also possible that she became acquainted with the Grants in the month she was in Boston back in 1773 when the Tea Party took place. It was probably through Samuel and Moses Grant that Sarah got to know Lucy and Henry Knox.

Mrs Houseman's Life was the commonly used title of *The Power and Pleasure of the Divine Life; exemplify'd in the late Mrs Houseman of Kidderminster*. The book was first published in 1744 by Richard Pearsall, a dissenting minister. Mrs Hannah Houseman was his eldest sister. She was an early influence on his religious life. The book was republished in Boston in 1755. According to the mawkishly, and lengthily, entitled,

Faith Triumphant exemplified in the Death of Mrs T---, She died Monday the 29th of April 1771, of a Child-bed Fever, Eight Days after her Delivery of her Twelfth Child, aged Thirty-Seven, which was written by her widower, John Trotter, another dissenting minister, the reading of *Mrs Houseman's Life* was the means of Mrs Trotter 'first being awakened'.

It is doubtful whether Sarah was telling the truth when she said she had recently met William Langborne. Langborne joined the 6th Virginia Regiment of the revolutionary army on 27 April 1777. Although he moved north with his regiment, he would not have travelled as far north as Boston. Even if they had met, Langborne was hardly in a position to have been able to entertain Sarah at his home in Virginia. He and his regiment were involved in the Philadelphia Campaign and fought at the American defeats in the Battles of Brandywine on 11 September 1777 and Germantown on 4 October 1777. Shortly after those battles, Langborne was appointed as an aide to the Marquis de Lafayette, based in New Jersey.[63]

Despite her apparent intention of leaving Boston in 'a Very Shorte Time', Sarah was still in Boston on 23 October when she wrote the following letter to Mary Stedman:

From the Princess of Brotenburgh, &c.

To The worthy Mrs Steedman
Dear Madam

Be assured, that We, do most sincerely wish, that these few Lines, will Come safe & find you, & yours In the sweet Shades of good Health! & Happiness! Under the Most Gracious Care & Protection, of the Almighty Three In One.

We, also, do most Humbly hope, that your Consort, Good Mr Steedman, is by this Time Restor'd to His former Health: – For We, was Extreemly Sorry, & Concern'd, too See Him, so Very Weak & Low.

Be pleased, to Take the Commission, of the Two Letters, which the (oppressed Princess!) as sent you (the One) is for your Good Consort, (& Mrs Cockran;) We know you will Send her's by a Carefull Person.

Pray assure yourself that our prayers, & good wishes, will attend you Whilst on the shore of Time & Through Boundless Eternity.

I Remain Madam,

With True Esteem, your sincere Wellwisher In our Most Sweet Lord Jehovah

Brotenburgh

(N.B.) Pray Remember My Love to your worthy Daughter Mrs Goodwin & to all Friends, Pray Let me Hear or See from you at all Times: Remember Me In the Winter.

North End,

Boston.

October ye 23rd Annoqui Domini 1777

Although these two letters seem excessively sanctimonious to modern eyes, they seem quite mild when compared with letters written by other people in religious circles at the time – see, for example, the letter from Martha Houlbrook, Elizabeth Frith's mother, in Appendix 2.

Alderman Hewitt said that when he challenged the veracity of Sarah's claims, 'she then assumed the countenance of a hypocritical Methodist, and said she trusted in her dear Lord Jehovah, and was not afraid of what man could do unto her.'[64] As well as illustrating one of Sarah's techniques,

Hewitt's statement also shows the hostile attitude that those in authority had towards Methodism. They regarded Methodists' enthusiasm with disdain and their preachers with suspicion, ready to abuse the trust of their female followers either financially – commenting that 'Women have robbed their Husbands to lend to the Lord through their Hands' – or sexually, as in the case of the Methodist preacher in Norwich who was accused of 'debauching one of his Female Followers'.[65] Some considered that that the Methodists' piety and enthusiasm were bad for their mental health. The newspapers claimed that Methodism had driven people to Bedlam and even suicide.[66] In 1767 *Berrow's Worcester Journal*, reporting that in Newcastle 'they have almost finished a new Mad-House', commented that it was 'remarkable that they have now no less than three Lunatick Hospitals there; whereas before the Introduction of Methodism they had not one'.[67]

Sarah was able to adopt an act of religious enthusiasm where she considered that it would suit a particular audience, although it misfired in Alderman Hewitt's case. The letters that Hewitt found addressed to Sarah from members of the Frith family with their frequent references to the blessings of God and other religious expressions show that they were passionately devout Christians. Sarah no doubt made a pretence of sharing their enthusiasm as well as acting the part of the Right Honourable Viscountess Lady Wilbrihammon.

There is no indication in Rev. Manasseh Cutler's journal that Sarah arrived unannounced when she came to stay at his home for three nights in 1775. It seems likely that she had been recommended to him by a kindred spirit. She might even have been passed from parsonage to parsonage in the north in the same way as she was passed from plantation house to plantation house when she was in the south.

There is a curious story in the *Boston Post-Boy* (see Appendix 3) of a woman who charmed her way into a group of Methodists in North Yorkshire and persuaded them that she was a noblewoman with great powers of patronage. She seems very similar to Sarah, and might even be her if the writer made a mistake with the date of the report.

Berwick, Maine

Those letters are the last trace I have of Sarah during her lifetime. It is not clear how long she remained in Boston, or where she travelled after that. At some stage before 1780 she appears to have been adopted by John and Lydia Costelloe or Costilloe, a wealthy couple in Berwick, Maine. Lydia's father, Colonel Thomas Wallingford, who died in 1771, was a great landowner and one of the richest men in New Hampshire. In around 1760 Lydia married Samuel Lord, of Berwick; he drowned along with two others when his boat overturned in the Salmon Falls River during a thunderstorm on 17 May 1773.[68] His body was not found until 30 May after it had floated over a mile downstream. When it was returned to his home, Lydia reportedly ordered it to be left outside until it dried. She is quoted as saying, 'It will get my floor dirty. Leave it on the porch.'[69] Lydia married John Costelloe the following year.

Sarah died in 1780. This is how the newspapers reported her death:

Berwick, Feb. 26, 1780.
Departed this life on Wednesday morning last, at the house of Mr John Costelloe (of this town) a strange

lady, who called herself the Dutchess of Cronenburg: But is supposed to be one Sarah Wilson, a convict, who about nine years past travelled through the State of South-Carolina, imposing upon the public, under the name of Lady Carolina Matilda, and called herself own sister to the Queen of Great-Britain. The generosity of Mr Costelloe in taking in this distressed person, after she was forsaken by every one, is really worthy of being noticed: As also the tender treatment she received from Mr Costelloe's Lady; who notwithstanding her being convinced, in her own mind, of her being an imposter, with an easy grace peculiar to herself addressed her by the title she assumed; and during her sickness gave her that attendance a lady of that character might have expected. And although Mr Costelloe was not at home at the time, the most decent preparations were made for her funeral; which was this day attended with the greatest solemnity, where Mrs Costelloe appeared as chief mourner.[70]

John Costelloe was one of the Berwick volunteers who chose to serve for either a three-month or a six-month stint in the revolutionary army in Captain Pray's company in 1780, which probably explains his absence.

There is no record of the nature of the illness that led to Sarah's death. The newspapers had described her as being slender with a pale complexion, which indicates that she was far from robust. She might have even been quite frail. It could be that the years of wandering across England and America in all weathers had finally caught up with her.

It appears that Lydia arranged Sarah's funeral, but there is no record of where she is buried. There are two contenders: Old Fields Burial Ground in Berwick, or Salmon Falls Old Town Cemetery across the river at Rollinsford, New Hampshire. Lydia's first husband, Samuel Lord, was descended from Nathan Lord who emigrated from Rye in East Sussex as a child and became proprietor of 77 acres of land at Old Fields, which is now in South Berwick. Members of the Lord family continued to live at Old Fields and were buried in the Old Fields Burial Ground.[71]

However, despite living in Berwick, Lydia married John Costelloe at the First Parish Church at Dover, New Hampshire[72] and buried her son Isaac Lord in 1771, and husband Samuel in 1773, in Salmon Falls Old Town Cemetery.[73]

About a fortnight after the reports of Sarah's death, the following notice was placed in the newspapers, almost certainly by John Costelloe himself:

Wednesday, the 23d of Feb. last, departed this life, in the twenty ninth year of her age, at the house of Mr John Costilloe, in Berwick, her serene highness Caroline Augusta Harriot, the Dutchess of Brotensburgh, Marchioness of Waldegrave, &c. &c. &c. not Sarah Wilson, as the malicious vulgar have been pleased to call her. This lady left the Court of Britain in the latter part of the year 1768, and arrived in Virginia in 1769, where she was well known, and kindly received by a noble Lord, then Governor of that place, and many other persons of distinction, that knew her to be no counterfeit – She was rendered truly unhappy by her being given in marriage to the King of Sweden's eldest son, Charles Frederick Adolphus Johannes, Duke of Brotensburgh, and High Marquis of Waldegrave and la Franceford, Baron of Mausgrave, High Admiral of the Golden Phoenix, &c.

&c. &c. She was first cousin to Charlotte, Queen of England, and daughter to the Empress Dowager of Upper Saxony and Palatine. She was a lady of superior sense, of distinguished abilities, of undissembled piety, and peculiar distress, which rendered her worthy the esteem of all, particularly the humane and tender hearted.

> When the last trumpet breaths the rending sound,
> And wakes the sleeping nations under ground,
> Then shall you in the rank of saints appear,
> And in your hand a golden sceptre bear.[74]

Although Lydia Costelloe was convinced that Sarah was an imposter, it seems that Sarah had managed to persuade John Costelloe that her stories were true. Sarah had carried on reinventing herself to the last.

WHO WAS SARAH?

So, who was Sarah Wilson?

For once Sarah was telling the truth about her identity at the Devizes quarter sessions in October 1767. She said her name was Sarah Boxall, her maiden name was Wilson, and that she had married a farmer named Boxall in Frensham some two years earlier. That much we already knew, although the marriage to Thomas Boxall was invalid. She also said that her own relations were living in London.[1] There is no reason to doubt that Sarah was telling the truth about this as well. It seems certain that she came from London, and she might still have had relatives there or at least had connections with whom she spent her days when she was supposed to be arranging for her inheritance and Thomas Boxall's commission. She was familiar with London's geography – witness her disappearing act in Lincoln's Inn Fields. John Hewitt said that Sarah was a 'menial servant in the kitchen of George-Lewis Scott'.[2] Scott lived in Leicester Square.

When Sarah appeared at the Westminster sessions in January 1768, her address was given as 'late of the Parish of

Saint James within the Liberty of Westminster'.[3] The parish of St James was centred round the church of St James, Piccadilly. To the north its boundary was with St Marylebone running along Oxford Street. To the east it had a boundary with St Anne, Soho, running along Berwick Street and Rupert Street. To the south there was a boundary with St Martin-in-the-Fields, roughly along Pall Mall. In the west there was a somewhat more irregular boundary with the parish of St George Hanover Square, which partly followed Conduit Street, Old Bond Street and Dover Street. Somewhere in the parish of St James, Westminster, probably towards the east of the parish, was where Sarah had her base – a hidey-hole to which she returned from time to time when she tired of her adventures in the country.

The parish of St James contained extremes of wealth and poverty. While the west was characterised by newly built fashionable squares where aristocrats and gentry had their town houses, the east was a maze of narrow streets, a place of poverty and vice, teeming with disreputable tenements, mean courts, low alehouses and dark alleys. It was one of the poorest parts of the city. Between 1718 and 1775 there were only twelve years where the records showed the addresses of the women and, out of the 147 parishes within the London Bills of Mortality, St James had the fifth highest population of women who were sentenced to be transported at the Old Bailey.[4]

The newspaper account of the Frensham adventure said Sarah was aged about 25. However, if the version in the court records is correct, a year after leaving Frensham she managed to convince Mrs Davenport or Mrs Davenport's niece that she was a teenager who had run away from boarding school. The newspaper reports in 1766 and 1767 said she was aged about 20.[5] In 1766 she told John Hewitt that she was 'about

20 years of age' and Hewitt did not suggest she was lying.[6] It is possible, therefore, that she was the Sarah Wilson who was born on 16 July 1745 and baptised on 9 August 1745 at the Bridewell Hospital Chapel, the daughter of William and Sarah Wilson, of whom nothing is known.

The second notice of her death gave her age as 29 in 1780. This is clearly wrong, but suggests that, in telling her stories, Sarah had knocked five years off her age.

We know nothing about Sarah's life before she turned up in Frensham, although the newspaper report in January 1765 said that, from the description given, she was thought to be the same woman who 'for near two years past obtained money, by imposing on the compassion and credulity of different persons in town and country'.[7] This indicates that Sarah started her impostures, wandering around the country, living on her wits, possibly as early as the beginning of 1763 when she was aged about 17 or 18. The references to 'imposing on the credulity and compassion' also indicates that Sarah had already achieved some notoriety, at least to the extent that the writer seemed to have been aware of Sarah's techniques: that she imposed on the credulity of those at one level of society who believed she had great powers of patronage; and imposed on the compassion of those at a higher level who believed that she was a fellow aristocrat who had fallen on hard times (or those who probably gave her money just to get rid of her).

It is not surprising that we have no details of her deceptions in the 'near two years' leading up to her arrival in Frensham, or in the subsequent gaps between the stories on both sides of the Atlantic that did get reported. Her victims were probably too ashamed to risk public humiliation by publicising their gullibility. However, in the light of what we do know about her, a novelist or a scriptwriter could have fun filling in those gaps, imagining what she got up to during the unrecorded periods, and conjuring up the likely conversations between Sarah and those she encountered on her travels.

Sarah certainly had a very full and varied life. From 1763 to 1780 she travelled around England and America, seldom staying long in one place. Her temporary homes and places she visited ranged from prison and the *Thornton* convict ship to stately homes and the grand plantation houses of Virginia and the Carolinas. She may have stood on the wharf at Boston harbour and watched the Sons of Liberty empty the chests of tea into the sea on the night of the Boston Tea Party. She was interrogated by the famous London magistrate, Sir John Fielding. Other people she met ranged from aristocrats such as the Earl of Denbigh at one extreme to characters from the Georgian underworld at the other. The teenage pickpockets, the highwaymen like William Dunk and his gang, and the prostitutes, such as poor Charlotte Lyons who died in the workhouse aged only 20, were people with whom she would have forged a common bond as a survival mechanism during her long weeks in prison and on board ship.

Sarah spent the last ten or so years of her life wandering round the Thirteen Colonies at a critical period in American history. During her travels she would have heard many differing views about the deepening rift between Britain and America. On stagecoaches, in roadside taverns and in drawing rooms, patriots and loyalists would have been arguing their cause and, no doubt, asking the queen's sister for her views. She would have had to make an assessment about what her questioners would have wanted to hear. She met and conversed with loyalists like Samuel Cornell and Governor Josiah Martin, as well as those who actively supported the rebellion against British rule like Lucy Knox, the Stedmans and Rev. Cutler.

New Lives of Boundless Possibilities

During Sarah's lifetime around 60 per cent of men and 40 per cent of women could sign the marriage register.[8] Statistics based on the number of people who could sign their names underestimate the number of people who could read. Most people learned to read before they could write. The main objective of those who advocated popular education was to teach children how to read the scriptures, and many were taught to read only. For most people there was no need to be able to write in order to earn a living. But once people learned to read, that ability was maintained and developed by the expansion of the written word in everyday life, such as in chapbooks and other cheap literature, tradesmen's flyers, other advertising material, and newspapers.[9] Walls and shop windows were plastered with printed material. Discarded printed material was used as wrapping paper and toilet paper, extending the printed word to those who couldn't afford to purchase it.[10]

It seems likely that Sarah spent her childhood in London, which had the highest levels of literacy in the country. As early as the 1720s some two-thirds of all women in London were literate.[11] Of the fifty-five marriages that took place in St James's church, Westminster, in November and December 1764, forty-five of the brides signed their names (82 per cent). Only ten marked their name with an X. In three cases the bride was better educated than the bridegroom: she signed her name while he could only mark his with an X. By contrast, of the thirteen marriages that took place at St Mary's Frensham during 1764 and 1765, only Sarah and four other brides signed their names; the other eight marked their name with an X. If we take Sarah's marriage out of the equation, only 33 per cent of the Frensham brides could sign their names.

The high degree of female literacy in London was largely due to the abundance of charity schools that existed in the city, many of which taught girls as well as boys. Some of the schools taught girls to read only, with the rest of their education devoted to needlework and domestic skills that would equip them for a life of domestic service. Other schools taught the girls writing as well.

The schools in London that taught girls included:

St James Westminster charity school, for 80 girls;
A school belonging to Castle Baynard ward, for 30 boys and 20 girls;
Christ's Hospital, which had two mistresses teaching around 50 girls;
Blackfriars School, which clothed and instructed 40 boys and 30 girls in reading, writing and accounts;
Christ's Church charity school, for 30 boys and 20 girls;
Archbishop Tenison's school, for 30 boys and 14 girls;
A school in St Mary le Strand where 40 girls were taught to read, knit and sew;
Greycoat Hospital, for 70 boys and 40 girls, who were 'put out apprentices';
St Paul's Covent Garden charity school, for 20 girls, who were 'cloathed, taught to work, read and write, and have £3 given to put them out to do all manner of household work';
St Dunstan's Parish charity school, for 40 girls, who were 'educated, cloathed, and put out to service';
Two charity schools founded by Sir John Cass – one for 50 boys and 40 girls and the other for 40 boys and 3 girls;
Raine's school for 50 poor boys and 50 poor girls; and

Southwark, which had a charity school for 60 girls and another for 20 girls, and also a free school for 50 girls.[12]

In many cases the intention was that boys as well as girls should be taught nothing more than what would turn them into useful and dutiful servants and pious and respectful members of the community.[13] In a Charity School sermon in 1755, the Bishop of Norwich said:

> There must be drudges of labour [...] as well as coun-sellors to direct, and rulers to preside [...] These poor children are born to be daily labourers, for the most part to earn their bread by the sweat of their brows. It is evident then that if such children are by charity brought up in a manner that is only proper to qualify them for a rank to which they ought not to aspire, such a child would be injurious to the community.[14]

But even just being taught to read could open new worlds of the imagination, and confirm the bishop's fears that such children could get ideas above their station and be discontented with their place in society. An example of this was Mary Carleton, the German princess. She:

> Took much pleasure in reading, especially Love Books, and those that treated of Knight Errantry [...] she proceeded to *Amadis de Gaul*, and reading of his fair Lady the Princess *Oriana*, she sometimes fancied her self to be some such Princess [...] or that in time she should be dignified with some Illustrious Title [...] The meanness of her quality did not suit with her spirit [...] she was discontented and was resolved to seek her fortune.[15]

Both Mary Carleton and Sarah were escapologists. They needed to escape from their allotted roles in life: in Mary Carleton's case from the life of a wife of a Canterbury shoemaker; and in Sarah's case from being a 'menial servant in the kitchen of George-Lewis Scott'. In order to do so, they created a series of new identities for themselves that they could vary according to their perceptions of their audiences. By escaping from their 'real lives' they could create new lives for themselves of boundless possibilities, even to the extent of becoming princesses.

Sarah's Letters

Despite her nomadic existence, Sarah was a habitual correspondent. She exchanged letters with the Frith household while she was staying with Robert Hudson. In her letters to Lucy Knox and Mary Stedman she enclosed other letters for them to pass to third parties. Ignoring the childish flourishes at the beginning of her letters to Mary Stedman, Sarah's handwriting in the main body of her letters is mature and symptomatic of someone who was well used to writing.

The study of handwriting as a means of analysing a person's character is known as graphology. Although graphology is generally regarded as a pseudoscience, Sarah's letters have such an eccentric appearance that it is tempting to see what graphology supposedly tells us about her character.

The most striking feature is the ornate lettering at the top and bottom of the letters. According to graphology theory, this shows that the writer is unconventional, imaginative and creative and wishes to be recognised as such. It is also supposed to indicate someone with a lack of objectivity who is concerned with image, is vain, likes being the centre of attention and has a desire to be something that they are not. Such a person may also have a love of luxury as well as having vulgar taste.

The large handwriting indicates ambition, self-confidence, the need to be acknowledged, a general desire to live a rich life on a large scale, neglect of realities, and a tendency to be stagey and to be a poseur. It could also mean a lack of consideration of others, a lack of ability to be subordinate, a lack of modesty and possible megalomania.

Similarly, the large capitals at the beginning of words are a sign of showing off, a call for attention, an exaggeration of the writer's self-importance, arrogance, pride, vanity and delusions of greatness, as well as an indication of dishonesty. Sarah's royal 'We' is larger than the other words in the sentences. Again, this points towards an inflated sense of self-importance.

Sarah's writing slopes to the right. This is a sign that the writer is an extrovert, always looking for new people and new things. It points to someone with a longing for success and recognition in the social sphere, someone who is spontaneous and headstrong, but who lacks discipline and common sense. It could also be a sign of ruthlessness.

The wide left margin is a sign that the writer is interested in moving on, away from the past. It also points to someone who is sociable. The narrow right margin means impatience and a desire to get on with things.

Sarah's upper strokes on the letters *b, f, h, l* and *t*, and her lower strokes on the letters *f, g, p* and *y*, are extended by a considerable distance away from the centre of the letters. The extended upper strokes are a sign of someone who has unrealistic expectations of what they can achieve. The extended lower strokes indicate that the writer is focused on instinctual needs and material considerations. The long *y* is said to show that the person loves to explore and travel. The loops in the strokes are a sign of dreams and imagination.

In the main text of her letters, Sarah writes in a straight line. The baseline neither slants uphill nor downhill. This is a sign of determination, a person who goes straight to her goals without being distracted. Her letters *m* and *n* have rounded tops. These are known as arcades and are the sign of a covering, protective nature, diplomatic courtesy, a screening of one's thoughts and a calm and calculating attitude. It can also indicate a tendency towards lying and hypocrisy. Similarly, the closed letter *o* is a sign of secretiveness.

The high-flying dots over the letter *i* are a sign of imagination, high-flying thought and a lack of realism. The cross near the top of the lower case *t* is also a sign of high-flying dreams and neglect of realities. The *t* cross extending quite some distance to the right indicates enthusiasm, determination and quick thinking.

The hooks at the beginning of the capital letters and at the end strokes are a sign of avarice, selfishness or tenacity.

The large signature means that the person wants to make an impact and needs to gain people's attention. The signature with loops and angular letters is the sign of someone with a listening appearance who shows interest in others, but who is using the information for their own advantage.

All this seems to confirm what we know about Sarah's character.

'The Greatest Impostress of the Present Age'

Like most people who could read and write, Sarah was probably an avid newspaper reader. By the middle of the eighteenth century the newspaper was one of the most easily accessible forms of literature. Copies of newspapers on both sides of the Atlantic could be found in coffee houses and inns, taverns and alehouses. It seems that Sarah was using the material in newspapers to find new identities for herself.

The name Wilbraham cropped up in the newspapers from time to time. Thomas Wilbraham was a Fellow of the Royal College of Physicians; Wilbraham Bootle was MP for Chester; Randle Wilbraham of Rode Hall, Cheshire was MP for Newton. The Wilbraham family were prominent landowners in Cheshire. Sarah probably chose to adopt the name Wilbraham because it sounded vaguely aristocratic, redolent of wealth. She also called herself Lady Wilmington. Lord Wilmington was a short-lived prime minister from 1742 until his death in July the following year. When Sarah chose that name in England she would have had no idea that in a few years' time she would be visiting Wilmington, North Carolina.

In America Sarah adopted names that sounded royal or aristocratic, which she could have also taken from the newspapers. American newspapers copied items from the London press about the English court and high society. They reported, for example, that Earl Waldegrave had been appointed as the king's Master of the Horse.[16] Lady Waldegrave, who had a clandestine marriage to the king's brother, the Duke of Gloucester, also made frequent appearances in the American press.[17]

The royal family provided a handy supply of names from which Sarah could pick and mix. Queen Charlotte was formerly Sophia Charlotte of Mecklenburg-Strelitz. King George and Queen Charlotte's first daughter, born in 1766, was called Charlotte Augusta Matilda. Their second, born in 1768, was called Augusta Sophia. All these were names Sarah used.

The king's sister, Caroline Matilda, might have been another inspiration. In 1766, when she was 15 years old, Caroline was married to mad King Christian of Denmark. Caroline was not allowed to take her English ladies-in-waiting with her and she left England in tears. Christian took an instant dislike to his new wife and spent his time chasing whores and young men. He liked to play leapfrog over the backs of visiting dignitaries when they bowed to him. Diplomats complained that, when they were discussing affairs of state with him, without warning he would slap them violently across the face.

In 1770 Queen Caroline began an affair with Johann Frederick Struensee, the King's physician. In July 1771 she gave birth to a daughter, Princess Louise Auguste, who, because of the resemblance, was known as 'la petite Struensee'. In January 1772 King Christian's horrible stepmother managed to bully the king into signing the orders for the arrest of Caroline and Struensee. Struensee was sentenced to a terrible death: first his right hand was chopped off, then his body was broken on the wheel and he was finally beheaded. Caroline was imprisoned in Cronenburg Castle and later exiled to Celle in Hanover, where she died in 1775 aged 25. From April 1772, the American papers were full of news of the affair and Caroline's incarceration at Cronenburg.[18]

The 1771 advertisement said that Sarah made the public believe she was the king's sister. This might have been a mistake, as the later reports referred to her claims to be the queen's sister. Or it might have been that she *did* start out to

claim that she was the king's sister, but changed her mind as
she could no longer keep up that pretence once the newspapers became full of stories about the real Caroline Matilda.
The queen's actual sisters were Christiane, Karoline and
Sophie Louise.

While newspapers might have helped Sarah to create her
identity and provide snippets of court gossip she could use
to impress people with her apparent inside knowledge of the
doings of royalty and the court, the newspapers' description
of her distinctive appearance contributed to her downfall.
Reports of her arrest in Devizes came to the attention of the
authorities in London who were looking for the person who
defrauded Mrs Davenport. In America after 1773, wherever
she moved, the newspapers followed her. The more people
knew about Sarah, her appearance and her methods, the less
likely it was that she would be able to extort money from
them by pretending to have great powers of patronage. With
that route cut off, the newspapers turned out to be helpful once again. Sarah turned her fame to her advantage by
reinventing herself as a celebrity, relying on people's curiosity about her. Was she genuine, or was she was an imposter?
The only way you could find out was to get to know her by
inviting her to stay for a while as a house guest and probably
present her with a small gift of cash. Afterwards you could
dine out for months with stories about the time the queen's
sister/the famous Marchioness of Waldegrave/the notorious
Sarah Wilson came to stay.

In England, the newspaper accounts of Sarah's adventures
fed into a general anxiety about the unreliability of identities
and fears of social disintegration. People knew each other
in small face-to-face communities, but increasing mobility
meant that people could move around the country constantly

reinventing themselves. Seeing people's real social origins behind their masks of self-presentation became more and more difficult. In the absence of rigid dress codes or any rules restricting their purchase, clothes alone were no longer a reliable indicator of class identity. Despite this, a person's outward appearance, when it was combined with upper-class manners and the ability to tell a convincing story, was generally regarded as a reliable signifier of status.

William Duvall's advertisement said that Sarah made 'a common practice of […] marking her cloaths with a crown and a B'. This pseudo-official mark on her clothes helped to make her claim to be Sophia (or Susanna) Carolina Augusta, Princess of Brunswick or Brotenburgh, more convincing. Her fine clothes, her collection of jewels and the queen's picture combined with her authentic self-presentation were enough to be able to convince people, especially some of the more socially pretentious plantation owners in the south, that she was the person she claimed to be.

In mid-eighteenth-century England a person's identity and life chances were largely determined by inheritance. If you were born poor, you remained poor. There were very few ways that a poor woman was able to rise above the status she was born in, and most of those involved some form of falsehood. In Sarah's case, she decided to rise above her allotted status by becoming an imposter and inventing a series of new identities for herself.

Sarah had the problem that the social classes were quite distinct from each other. There was a general reliability of social signifiers – of dress, demeanour, accent and choice of words – so it was possible to recognise the class of a new acquaintance within seconds. Sarah had to learn how to ape the behaviours of the upper classes in order to carry off her impostures.

If, as is likely, she came from the rough east end of the parish of St James, it would not have taken her long to stroll to the wealthy west end of the parish where she could observe how the aristocratic ladies moved and spoke. Once she was able to mimic their mannerisms, she could escape from the constraints of her own life and create the identity she wanted. She wanted to be a noblewoman, and to have that confirmed by people's acceptance of that status. And in America, where she could get away with this more easily, she wanted to be a princess, and to be treated as such.

George-Lewis Scott, Sarah's erstwhile employer, lived in a substantial town house on the north side of Leicester Square, next door to Saville House where the Duke of York lived.[19] Scott was a mathematician, a Commissioner of Excise, a member of the Board of Longitude and, most importantly, a royal tutor.[20] The advertisement in the *Salisbury Journal* for the lost publication *A Plain Narrative of Facts* said that it contained Sarah's 'whole History, from her first Elopement from the Hon. Mrs. Sc-t's, till her Discovery and Commitment to Devizes Bridewell'.[21] It is likely that 'Mrs Sc-t' was Mrs Scott.

While she was a servant at George-Lewis Scott's house, living next door to the Duke of York, Sarah probably exchanged gossip with the duke's servants. She might have picked up other stories from her employer. Fanny Burney said that Scott was 'very sociable and facetious too'. At a party in 1769 he entertained her with 'droll anecdotes and stories among the Great and about the Court'.[22] Deploying apparently inside information about the goings on at court certainly helped Sarah to authenticate her persona. It also would have made her hosts feel honoured to be the recipients of privileged information.

When she was staying with Rev. Manasseh Cutler at Ipswich Hamlet, Massachusetts, in January 1775, he noted that Sarah appeared to be 'a person of an extraordinary education, and well acquainted with things at Court'. It is not known how much of her apparent acquaintance with the court was due to facts that Sarah remembered from her time in George-Lewis Scott's household, or facts she had picked up from the newspapers, or whether they were interesting stories that she had made up herself.

Sarah was able to convince people that she was who she said she was, and that she had great power of influence and patronage, not only because of her ability to lie convincingly and consistently, but also because of her victims' predisposition to believe her stories, having been reassured by her dress and behaviour. Some of her adventures in England showed that, even when she was not equipped with a set of upper-class clothing, her superb acting ability alone was sufficient to make people believe that she was the daughter of a nobleman.

Once Sarah's targets had managed to convince themselves by her accent or clothes that she appeared to be the person she was claiming to be, a form of imposter blindness set in. They were blinded to the suspicion that Sarah might be an imposter. They believed what she was telling them, no matter how preposterous her stories might have seemed. In fact, the more preposterous her claims, the more believable they were. They were unable to envisage that Sarah would be so reckless as to risk the consequences of such a perilous course of action if those wild claims were untrue.

Once afflicted by imposter blindness, her targets would stick to their belief that Sarah was the real deal, despite any evidence to the contrary. When this happened, the imposture became a collaboration between Sarah and the targets.

The victims became complicit in the imposture because they wanted to believe that the young lady sitting in front of them really was the Countess of Wilbraham with great powers of patronage or that she was the queen's sister honouring them with her presence. They wanted to believe her because of the benefits she offered. She made her victims feel good about themselves and appealed to their vanity and greed.

Sarah was the supreme opportunist, ready to take advantage of any situation that presented itself, assessing the people she encountered as to whether they were hoping to avail themselves of the 'prestigious appointments that lay in her gift'. She had a remarkable understanding of human nature and a capacity for adapting and embroidering her story to suit different audiences. Yet she was totally lacking in empathy or conscience. She could win the trust of her victims and befriend them, often over long periods, even to the extent of marrying one, and then abandon them. She left poor Thomas Boxall and his father penniless and humiliated. She must also have had quite a thick skin, being used to rejection. Although we know of some of the occasions where her performances were successful, there must have been countless occasions when doors were slammed in her face.

In America, she made life interesting for a hospitable and gullible people who thought that they were actually entertaining a member of the British royal family, or at least a significant member of the aristocracy. With her apparent familiarity with court life and the gossip of upper-class English society, Sarah was a welcome guest, being wined and dined, having the occasional use of a carriage, gifts of money and letters of introduction to the next plantation house.

Sarah was able to turn up uninvited on the doorstep and convince people in England that she was an aristocrat, and convince people in America that she was the queen's sister. She was adept in picking up details of potential victims, fabricating new identities, and applying careful name dropping as a prop to her performances. She was a performer who needed an audience. By bringing her fictional self to life by convincing others of its reality she became her own work of art. As soon as she adopted her false identity her life became exciting and challenging. The exhilaration of seeing others accept her as the person she wanted to be, for having the status which she could otherwise never obtain, was its own reward. Any material gain in terms of money, clothes and food and drink was a bonus.

Lord Denbigh wondered whether Sarah was disordered in her senses.[23] It is difficult to know to what extent her act had taken over her life, whether she actually began to believe that she was of noble birth, and eventually that she was a princess. In order to successfully play the part, Sarah must have had a strong sense of self-belief in her creation. Other people's acceptance of her false identities would have reinforced that self-belief. After a while she might have stopped pretending to be the person she wanted to be, and actually became that person in her own mind. Lydia Costelloe humoured Sarah by playing along with her fantasies, even though she knew that Sarah was an imposter. Sarah certainly had a natural authority that enabled her to imperiously command and control Richard Frith's household.

Sarah moved around England and America travelling light with no baggage, real or metaphorical, to remind herself, or suggest to others, who the real Sarah Wilson was. She broke away from the limitations of the life she was born to lead. Taking control of her own destiny, she reinvented herself as the person she wanted to be. She ventured out into the world as the heroine of her own story, whether the young heiress taking to the road to escape the prospect of a loveless marriage or a princess from the old world beyond the seas.

Sarah carried on reinventing herself to the last. According to what is likely to have been John Costelloe's account of her death, Sarah said she left England in 1768 having been rendered unhappy by being given in marriage to the King of Sweden's eldest son, Charles Frederick Adolphus Johannes. This was a relatively safe story to tell, as the Swedish royal family seldom featured in the American press. However, the King of Sweden's eldest son was called Gustav (he later became King Gustav III); Charles was the second son and Frederick Adolphus the third. Sarah was also supposed to have claimed that her mother was the Empress Dowager of Upper Saxony and Palatine. This might have been a reference to Maria Antonia Walpurgis, Dowager Electress of Saxony. She had seven surviving children, none of whom was Sarah Wilson.

Alderman Hewitt had years of experience dealing with all kinds of criminals. Yet when he was writing in 1778 about only those few adventures in England that he knew about (he did not appear to know about the Frensham incident nor the episode in London for which she was transported), he called Sarah 'the greatest impostress of the present age'. Although she was totally dishonest, Sarah was a creative, highly intelligent and engaging character who invented a remarkable series of different lives for herself on both sides of the Atlantic. I only wish we knew more about her.

FRENSHAM AND HEADLEY PARISH RECORDS

Frensham, St Mary

Baptism: Thomas, son of Robert Boxall, 19 March 1720.
Marriage: Thos Boxall and Flora Spreakley, 6 November 1746.
Baptism: Thomas, son of Thos Boxall, 25 September 1747.
Marriage:

'Banns of Marriage between Thomas Boxall & Sarah Charlotte Lewsearn Willsbrowson, both of this parish were regularly publish'd on three several Sundays in this Church pursuant to a late act of parliam[t] relating thereunto by Richd Bridger, Curate, Dec. 17th 1764.'
'Thomas Boxall & Sarah Charlotte Lewsearn Willsbrowson, both of this parish were married in this Church, By Banns, this seventeenth Day of December 1764 by Richd Bridger, Curate.'
'This Marriage was Solemniz'd between us
Thomas Boxall
Sarah Charloter Lewsearn Willsbrowson

In the presence of
The mark of X Thomas Boxall the Father
Austin Crafter.'

Burial: Ann, daughter of Thomas Boxall of Witmore, 2 April 1779.
Burial: Flora, wife of Thomas Boxall of Chirt, 14 November 1779.
Marriage: Thomas Boxall and Ann Over, both of this parish, 20 December 1779.
Baptism: Thomas son of Thomas Boxall at Witmore, 13 October 1780.
Burial: Thomas Boxall aged 76, 30 May 1824.

Headley, All Saints

'Banns of Marriage between Thomas Boxall of the Parish of Frensham and Anne Over of this Parish were published in this Church, & no Impediment alledged, on these three several Sundays, viz. Nov. 17, 24 and Dec. 1 1776.' They did not follow through with the marriage at that stage.
Baptism: 'Anne, a natural Child, born in the Parish of Frensham Dr of Thomas Boxall & Anne Over of the said Parish of Frensham, March 19 1779.'

APPENDIX 2

LETTER TO SARAH FROM ELIZABETH FRITH'S MOTHER

Liverpool, April 15, 1766

Honoured Madam

I was not a little surprized and rejoiced to have the favour of a line from under your hand, especially from a Lady so highly favoured of the Almighty. Madam, when I read the contents of your loving letter, my heart was filled with gratitude and thanks, to think of the glorious appearing of the great God and our Saviour Jesus Christ, to meditate on the love of a divine Redeemer, and the blessed hope of everlasting life, which awaits us, and which by the purchase of Christ's blood being shed for us, we shall shortly be put in possession of, is matter of great rejoicing to think that when this earthly house of our tabernacle is dissolved, we shall have a building of God, a house not made with hands, eternal in the heavens: Therefore my loving sister, as I make bold to call you, continue ye in my love, as Christ exhorts his disciples, and run with patience the race that is set before you, looking unto Jesus, who for the joy that was set before him endured the cross, despised the shame, and is set down on the right hand of the Majesty on high. Set your affections on things above, for on the earth is no lasting, no real abiding satisfaction; for man is born unto trouble as the sparks fly upward, as the holy scriptures do declare, and our experience confirms, as the holy apostle advises us, wherefore comfort one another with these words so I would comfort myself and others, that our light afflictions, which are but momentary, shall work for us a far more exceeding and eternal weight of glory, so comforting the expression, that one would hardly think our suffering in this life worth our notice; the exalted happiness it brings to our mind, is far above all temporal felicity, whilst we look not at things temporal but at things eternal, to think of shortly being welcomed into the everlasting kingdom of light, and love, and glory, with Come ye blessed children of my Father into the joy of your Lord. And now, honoured Madam, may the Almighty, who has the keeping of all hearts in his hand, keep your hearts and minds in the knowledge and love of Jesus Christ our Lord, who at his glorious appearance shall change our vile bodies, and to fashion them like unto his glorious body, according to the mighty working whereby he is able to subdue all things unto himself. Pray acquaint my son and daughter, and daughter Martha that we are all in a very good state of health at present, hoping these few lines will find you in the same. I rejoice to hear of your being well inclined, and I intreat you to press forward for the prize of your high calling of God in Christ. I hope by this reacheth you my daughter Elizabeth is safely delivered. I hope my daughter Suzannah is very well in health, and I would be very glad to hear from them. So no more at present, but our love to you all; and my blessing to my children.

From your friend and well-wisher till death
MARTHA HOULBROOK
Tuesday 11 o'clock

P.S. Pray do me the favour of sending me a line from you at all opportunities.

For
The Honourable Lady Wilbrihamman,
At Mrs Elizabeth Frith's, at Crowton,
In Cheshire,
Near Middlewich.
With Care.

APPENDIX 3

WAS THIS SARAH?

The following item appeared in the Massachusetts paper, the *Boston Post-Boy*, on 13 February 1769. Unlike most items datelined London in the American press, this does not appear to have been copied from an English newspaper – indeed, I cannot find this story in any of the English papers. It appears, therefore, that it was sent to the *Boston Post-Boy* by a private correspondent.

There are similarities between the techniques employed by the woman in the article and those employed by Sarah: the semblance of piety as required to suit the intended audience; discovering the opinions of her intended dupes which she could then use to her advantage; letting slip that she was from the nobility; offering places in government; and providing assurances that she would soon be in possession of great wealth. However, if it was Sarah, this action must have taken place before October 1768, as she was in America then. Also, it is unlikely that Sarah would have hung around once people started doubting her story. Nonetheless, this is an intriguing account.

Extract of a letter from Ruth [Reeth] (in Swale-dale, near Richmond, Yorkshire)
October 12, 1768.

About three weeks past a woman made her appearance here dressed in a meanish habit, and took her lodgings according to the figure she had cut; she appeared very religious and serious, constantly attending the meetings of the Methodists, by which Means she soon attracted the attention of some of their Chiefs, who discoursed with her not only upon religious topics, but also political ones. After she had discovered the enmity they had to a celebrated patriot, and affection for Lord Bute, she told them, as a secret, that her name was Lassels [Lascelles], and that she was nearly related to the above-mentioned Nobleman, that she had traversed the greatest part of England in that disguise, only (she said) that she might discover who were well affected to that worthy Nobleman, but she there intended to put an end to her peregrinations, and to that end had appointed her coach to be there, which she expected every day; and indeed she was rather glad than sorry that it was not come, as she had the more time to spend with such affectionate friends, to prepare herself to act in her proper sphere, and to equip those her votaries with genteel apparel. She told them that she would be careful to provide places under the Government, for them: Mr W----m, who had behaved with great respect to her, was to have a place worth £300 &c. &c. And Mr H-----y, a place worth £100 &c. &c. &c. Upon the strength of this all the shops in the town were employed to furnish them with every thing they wanted, and not only so, but drapery and millinery goods were sent for in abundance from Richmond; the lady herself gave orders for goods to a great amount, which were to be paid for when her coach came which she assured them would be soon; but sometime having passed without the appearance of any such thing, the people of the town began to tire of expecting the coach, and supplying her with goods, therefore sent to let her know that if she did not give some authentic proof she was the person she pretended to be, they would make use of methods not at all to her satisfaction which she was not able to do, a constable and guard were appointed to conduct her out of town, with no other equipage than what she brought with her. Notwithstanding her being detected, she has made sad confusion in the town, and many great losers.

APPENDIX 4

THE AFTERMATH: MYTHS AND STORIES

After the reports of Sarah's death in 1780, her story disappeared from public memory until 1819 when there was a brief mention of her in a biography of Queen Charlotte, based on the May 1773 story in *Rivington's New York Gazetteer*.[1] This received a wider circulation when it was repeated in the *Percy Anecdotes* in 1820.[2] In 1829 Francois Martin repeated the story in his *History of North Carolina*, adding the further information about her visit to Governor Martin at Tryon Palace and her move to Wilmington.[3]

The next reference was in 1837 when William Dunlap added to the lists of obvious untruths attached to Sarah's history by writing an 'original tale', *Tom Bell and the Princess Susannah Carolina Matilda*, for the *New-York Mirror*.[4] According to Dunlap, Sarah perpetrated her frauds in the southern colonies with the aid of an accomplice, the famous Tom Bell, and that, just as she was about to be captured by Michael Dalton, Tom Bell ran off with her jewels and the money they had obtained. Dunlap repeated this story later that year in *A History of New York for Schools*.[5]

Dunlap's story was a total fabrication; Tom Bell's activities had ended long before Sarah came on the scene. The real Tom Bell was born in Boston in 1713, and his adventures featured in around 100 newspaper reports published between 1738 and 1755.[6] Tom Bell's main method was to assume the name of a prominent family in another part of America, approach a wealthy resident with a tale of distress and borrow money and depart. He also obtained money by forging letters of credit. Impersonating a New Jersey clergyman in 1741 allowed him to steal goods and horses. By the 1750s his growing notoriety made it difficult for him to continue his activities. He claimed to have gone straight and issued proposals for a memoir, *The Travels and Adventures of the famous Tom Bell*. This did not attract many subscribers, no doubt because people thought it was yet another of his frauds, so the book was never published.[7]

Dunlap seems to have been unwilling to accept that Sarah acted alone. His story assumes that a mere woman was incapable of successfully carrying off her frauds without the help of a male accomplice, an assumption that recalls the argument that Shakespeare was incapable of writing his plays because of his class origins. There is no evidence that Sarah had an accomplice. Certainly in America it appears she had no friends and she acted, and travelled, alone. The newspapers expressed surprise that she travelled without attendants, or incognito. The contemporary definition of incognito was 'unknown, without attendance [meaning attendants], or marks of distinction.'[8]

In England it appears that Sarah had family or acquaintances in London. It also appears that she knew some of the underworld characters in order to get the forged letters from noblemen that Alderman Hewitt found on her and the pretend £100 bill she showed Mrs Davenport's niece. While in or around London, she may have enlisted the support of others, such as the man in livery at St Albans she called her second coachman. However it is not clear whether these were accomplices or dupes. Alderman Hewitt assumed the latter when he described Sarah as 'acting alone, and without assistants, except such as she by her own artifice procured and deceived.'[9]

In 1855 Dr John Doran published *Lives of the Queens of England of the House of Hanover*. He repeated the story that Sarah had stolen the queen's jewels, but added an embellishment that the queen got to hear that Sarah was pretending to be her sister and found that amusing:

Queen Charlotte would have thought nothing more of her, had her majesty not heard, with some surprise, that her sister, Susannah Caroline Matilda, was keeping her court in the plantations. Never was surprise more genuine than the Queen's; it was exceeded only by her hilarity, when it was discovered that the Princess Susannah was simply Sarah Wilson, at large. That somewhat clever girl, having stolen a queen's jewels, thought nothing, after escaping from the penal service to which she was condemned, of passing herself off as a Queen's sister. The Americans were not so acute as their descendants; so in love were some of them with the greatness they affected to despise, that they paid royal honours to the clever impostor.[10]

Alice Morse Earle retold Sarah's story in *Colonial Dames and Good Wives*, published in 1895. She said Sarah had:

In her enforced home a most extraordinary and romantic career of successful fraud [...] She travelled through the South from plantation to plantation, with plentiful promises of future English offices and court favours to all who assisted her progress; and liberal sums of money were placed at her disposal, to be repaid by Queen Charlotte; and she seems to have been universally welcomed and feasted.[11]

New myths about Sarah seem to have been invented in the twentieth century to add to the tale about the stolen jewels. The strange thing about these stories is that they are not half as interesting as the reality. One story is that Sarah was born in a Staffordshire village in 1754, the daughter of a bailiff. This would have meant that she was only 10 years old when she married Thomas Boxall. Another story is that Michael Dalton captured her at gunpoint while she was holding court at a plantation house outside Charleston and returned her to William Duvall where she remained for a further two years. This is despite Sarah's well-documented travels during those years. The story continues that at the end of the two years she gained her freedom again by swapping places with another girl called Sarah Wilson. She then married an army officer, Captain William Talbot of the 17th Light Dragoons, whom she set up in business with the money she had accrued during her impostures. They moved to New York, had a large family and lived happily ever after.[12]

There actually was a Captain William Talbot of the 17th Light Dragoons, but it is highly unlikely that he and Sarah would have met. William Henry Talbot came to America as a lieutenant in the 16th Light Dragoons, one of the first regiments sent to reinforce the American garrison. Their voyage to America took three months, during which the soldiers and their horses lived in foetid conditions. They landed at Halifax,

Nova Scotia in October 1776.[13] Shortly after disembarking, they took part in the Battle of the White Plains near New York.[14] In June 1778 Lieutenant Talbot was promoted to captain in the 17th Light Dragoons.[15] He took part in the Siege of Charleston and the Battle of Waxhaws, South Carolina, in 1780.[16] In 1781 the regiment was sent to New York where it remained throughout 1782.[17] Captain William Talbot died on 6 March 1782 and is buried at St Paul's Chapel Churchyard, 209 Broadway, New York.[18]

In 1845 Sarah featured in a short story, *The Richmond Hebe*, by Maria Jane McIntosh. This delightful piece of nonsense was published in the Christmas issue for that year of the *Ladies' National Magazine* (Philadelphia). The story was set in December 1771 at the 'handsome mansion' in Richmond, Virginia where a Colonel Elliott lived with his wife and his son, Randolph, 'a manly youth of twenty' and their daughter, Gertrude, the Richmond Hebe of the title. The family had two guests staying with them over Christmas. One was Herbert Grayson, Gertrude's 'betrothed lover'. The other was a lady who had recently arrived in Richmond. She was addressed as the Lady Augusta de Waldegrave, 'but it was well known that under this less imposing title she veiled the illustrious rank of princess'.

It was for Randolph's sake that Lady Augusta was invited into their home. Randolph was due to go to England the next year to finish his education. Lady Augusta, once she returned to England and was restored to the favour of the royal family, would be able to pull strings on Randolph's behalf to help secure his success in life.

As time went on, Randolph was becoming more and more besotted with Lady Augusta. Herbert and Gertrude were becoming increasingly concerned about the 'future suffering to Randolph from an unrequited and hopeless attachment to their noble visitor'.

Although all the Elliotts were won over by Lady Augusta's charms, 'her varied conversation, now animated and expressive, now gay and sparkling, and anon breathing a tender melancholy', Herbert was concerned she might be an imposter. He told Gertrude of his fears, but Gertrude, like the rest of her family, dismissed his concerns. She was convinced that Lady Augusta was the real princess she claimed to be.

To everyone's surprise, Herbert, who had hitherto been somewhat cold towards Lady Augusta, started to court her. He escorted her to the local ball instead of Gertrude, and arrived to collect her in his coach with outriders, footmen and coachmen, all attired in showy livery.

One afternoon Herbert took Lady Augusta for a ride in the country. As they were leaving, he handed Gertrude a book, saying that it contained something about the subject on which they differed the other day, and if she took the trouble to read the article, she would see that he was right. Gertrude, however, was too upset to look at the book. It seemed that Herbert and Lady Augusta were becoming lovers. Colonel Elliott and Randolph were concerned about the effect this was having on Gertrude's happiness and were growing increasingly angry about the way Herbert appeared to be traducing her honour. One day as Randolph rushed past her, he whispered, 'Gertrude, you shall be avenged.'

With great difficulty, Gertrude managed to persuade her father and Randolph not to do anything rash. She said she would seek an interview with Herbert which would resolve the matter.

When Herbert was shown into Gertrude's room, she said, 'This interview, I feel assured, must be as embarrassing to you as it is painful to me, Mr Grayson, I will, therefore, make it as brief as possible. I have but a few words to say, I wish only to restore to you your freedom from every shadow of obligation imposed on your honour [...] At the same time permit me to return the presents which have lost their value to me. You will find them in this box.'

Herbert was shocked by this. He asked whether the past had been a delusion. He said that the caprice of woman could go no further than to sever such a tie so causelessly. Gertrude replied, 'I have desired, Mr Grayson, to part from you without even the appearance of reproach, and, therefore, I have forborne to speak of a cause which I have assured your own heart could not fail to present to you.'

'It presents none, Gertrude. How I have loved you I will not now say, but this much is due to myself – never were you dearer to me than when I entered that door today.'

'And yet for days past who would not have said that another possessed your heart and ruled your every action.'

'Whatever others may have thought, Gertrude, you, to whom I confided the motive of all which might have seemed singular in my demeanour, could not have doubted me for a moment.'

'I remember no such confidence.'

'Not in the letter which I gave you a few days since?'

'The letter which you gave me a few days since! I do not understand you. I have certainly received no letter from you.'

Herbert then realised what had happened. The book he had given Gertrude lay on the table. He picked it up, and a letter fell out. He handed the letter to Gertrude. He told her that he was convinced that Lady Augusta was an imposter and could see that Randolph 'was fast becoming her prey beyond redemption, and that she would not hesitate to advance herself, and ruin him by a marriage'. He therefore decided to lure her from her quarry by flaunting his wealth and presenting himself as a more advantageous match. He managed to persuade her that they would be in danger if they remained in Richmond, and, as a result, Lady Augusta sent him a note in which she said that, in view of the haste in which they must leave Richmond, and due to the unexpected delay of her remittance, she would need Herbert to advance her £100, which she would repay 'a hundred fold [...] to prove how devotedly I am thine own Augusta'.

Herbert then showed Gertrude the advertisement from William Duvall of Bush Creek. He said he had met Lady Augusta that very morning and gave her the £100 and a copy of the advertisement and advised her to leave Richmond immediately as more of those papers were around: 'Had I not believed that a public exposure of her here would be unpleasant to your father and distressing to Randolph, I would not have aided her escape.'

Needless to say, they all lived happily ever after. Herbert won from Gertrude a promise to marry him, a promise to which Colonel Elliott, when informed of Herbert's claims on his gratitude, readily confirmed, and 'the sight of Lady Augusta's, alias Sarah Wilson's note, and of the advertisement, cured Randolph of every wound, save that inflicted on his pride, and even this was forgotten in his sister's happiness'.

The story ends: 'Should any reader feel any interest in the subsequent fate of our fair aspirant to royal honours, Sarah Wilson, we can only say that the scenes enacted by her in Richmond were repeated, though under other names, in various cities'.[19]

Although this is a work of fiction, there are elements that ring true. Accounts suggest that Sarah was an engaging conversationalist and good company. The reason Herbert gave for not reporting Sarah to the authorities reflects what was likely to have happened in real life, both in England and in America. We do not know how many people she fooled and who decided to write off their losses rather than expose themselves to the ridicule as the gullible dupes of a clever woman. But what we do know is that Sarah was able to obtain sufficient funds to be able to afford to travel all over England and most of the thirteen colonies. Those stories about her that made it into the newspapers are likely to be just the tiny tip of a very large iceberg.

NOTES

Prelude

1   *Morning Chronicle*, 3 October 1786.

2   *Public Advertiser*, 9 April 1787.

3   E.A. Judges (1901), *Some West Surrey Villages*, p. 104.

4   William Cobbett, *Rural Rides*, entry for 10 November 1822.

5   The parish of Frensham was far more extensive than it is now: it stretched along the Hampshire border from just south of Farnham to the Sussex border taking in Rowledge, Churt, Pitfield, Hindhead and Shottermill as well as the village of Frensham itself. The newspaper account said that farmer Boxall lived 'near Hadleigh in Hants'. Hadleigh was an alternative spelling of Headley, the parish on Frensham's western border.

6   *Devon and Exeter Gazette*, 11 November 1898.

7   *General Evening Post*, 3 July 1766.

8   *Devon and Exeter Gazette*, 11 November 1898.

9   *London Chronicle*, 10 January 1765.

10 *General Evening Post*, 3 July 1766.

11 *St James's Chronicle*, 17 October 1767; *London Evening-Post*, 20 October 1767; *Salisbury Journal*, 26 October 1767.

Chapter 1

1   Charlotte Charke (1755), *A Narrative of the Life of Mrs Charlotte Charke*, p. 235.

2 Ibid., p. 262.

3 *Gentleman's Magazine*, December 1767, p. 573.

4 Arthur Young (1770), *A Six Months Tour through the North of England*, vol. 4, pp. 573–86.

5 Alderman J.Hewitt (undated, possibly 1778), *Memoirs of the Celebrated Lady Viscountess Wilbrihammon, alias Mollineux, alias Irving, Countess of Normandy, and Baroness Wilmington, the greatest Impostress of the present Age*, p. 3.

6 *The Times*, 9 May 1787.

7 *The Times*, 2 April 1789.

8 *Derby Mercury*, 12 November 1773.

9 *Ipswich Journal*, 5 November 1774; John Russell (1853), *Memorials and Correspondence of Charles James Fox*, vol. 1, pp.92–3; Alice Drayton Greenwood (1916), *Hugh Walpole's World*, pp. 211–12.

10 *Derby Mercury*, 12 November 1773.

11 *London Chronicle*, 9 November 1773; *Middlesex Journal*, 11 November 1773; *Derby Mercury*, 19 November 1773.

12 *London Chronicle*, 29 October 1774.

13 *London Evening-Post*, 29 November 1774; *Hampshire Chronicle*, 5 December 1774.

14 T.S. Willan (1970), *An Eighteenth-Century Shopkeeper: Abraham Dent of Kirkby Stephen*, p. 2; *London Evening-Post*, 4 March 1762 and 19 April 1766.

15 James Woodforde, *The Diary of a Country Parson*, 23 May 1765 and 2 January 1775.

16 James Raven (2014), *Publishing Business in Eighteenth Century England*, p. 20.

17 Charles Jenner (1772), *Town Eclogues*, p. 27.

18 Pierre-Jean Grosley (1772), *A Tour to London*, vol. 1, pp. 47–8.

19 *London Evening-Post*, 4 March 1762; *Gazetteer*, 29 March 1766.

20 *Public Advertiser*, 11 February 1764.

21 Jonas Hanway (1754), *A Letter to Mr John Spranger*, pp. 37–8.

22 *Lloyd's Evening Post*, 5 October 1764.

23 *London Evening-Post*, 15 July 1762.

24 *Gazetteer*, 23 May 1766.

25 *Public Advertiser*, 6 July 1765.

26 *St James's Chronicle*, 15 March 1764.

27 Pierre-Jean Grosley (1772), *A Tour to London*, vol.1, p. 36.

28 *Public Advertiser*, 5 August 1765.

29 *Morning Chronicle*, 9 February 1778.

30 *Lloyd's Evening Post*, 13 June 1764.

31 *Public Advertiser*, 1 and 16 January and 22 April 1765;
   Gazetteer, 8 May 1765; *London Evening-Post*, 25 May 1765;
   Gazetteer, 29 May 1765; *London Evening-Post*, 11 June and
   4 July 1765; *Gazetteer*, 23 July 1765; *Lloyd's Evening Post*,
   9 and 21 August 1765; *Gazetteer*, 4 September 1765; *St James's
   Chronicle*, 10 September 1765; and *Gazetteer*, 31 October 1765.

32 Jerry White (2012), *London in the Eighteenth Century*, p. 225.

33 *Baldwin's New Complete Guide* (1768), p. 205.

34 Alderman J. Hewitt, *Memoirs of the Celebrated Lady Viscountess
   Wilbrihammon* (n.d.), pp. 16-18.

35 *Public Advertiser, Gazetteer and New Daily Advertiser*, and
   St James's Chronicle, 16 January 1768; *Lloyd's Evening Post*,
   18 January 1768; *Stamford Mercury*, 21 January 1768; *Ipswich
   Journal*, 23 January 1768; *Gentleman's Magazine*, January 1768,
   p. 44.

36 *Public Advertiser*, 6 April 1764; *London Evening-Post*,
   19 April 1766.

37 *London Evening-Post*, 4 November 1766.

38 Lord Derby and his son, Lord Strange, lived in Lancashire.

39 Alderman J. Hewitt, *Memoirs of the Celebrated Lady Viscountess
   Wilbrihammon* (n.d.), pp. v–vi.

40 Coaches that advertised their services at 3*d* per mile included
   the London, Stamford, Doncaster and York Flying Post-Coaches
   (*Public Advertiser*, 2 May 1764); the London and Southampton
   Flying Post-Coaches (*London Evening-Post*, 25 August 1764);
   the Bristol and Bath Post-Coaches (*St James's Chronicle*,
   14 February 1765); the Newcastle, York and London Fly
   (*Newcastle Chronicle*, 28 September 1765) and the Ipswich and
   Colchester Post-Coaches (*General Evening Post*, 1 July 1766).

41 Cheshire wills and probate, 1770.

42 John Murray (1870), *Handbook for Shropshire, Cheshire and
   Lancashire*, p. 103.

43 *London Evening-Post*, 17 July 1766.

44 John Hoyle (1770), *Dictionarium Musica*, p. 40.

45 Thicknesse (née Ford), Ann, in *Oxford Dictionary of National Biography*.

46 Charles Burney (1771), *The Present State of Music*, p. 6.

47 *Public Advertiser*, 27 November 1762.

48 *Gazetteer*, 18 November 1763; *Public Advertiser*, 7 December 1763.

49 *Gazetteer*, 8 December 1762.

50 *Whitehall Evening Post*, 1 November 1760.

51 Abraham Rees (1819), *Cyclopaedia*, vol. 17, entry for 'Guitarra'.

52 Ibid.

53 *Gazetteer*, 2 October 1764.

54 *Public Advertiser*, 14 August 1764.

55 John Hawkins (1776), *A General History of the Science and Practice of Music*, vol. 4, p. 113.

56 Alderman J. Hewitt, *Memoirs of the Celebrated Lady Viscountess Wilbrihammon* (n.d.), p. 6.

57 The bishop's transcription of baptisms shows Sarah Charlotta Irvin, Daughter of Richard Frith of Crowton, but the *London Evening-Post* for 17 July 1766 gives the baby's name as Sarah Charlotte Wilbraham Irving Frith.

58 *London Evening-Post* for 17 July 1766; Alderman J. Hewitt, *Memoirs of the Celebrated Lady Viscountess Wilbrihammon* (n.d.), pp. 1–4.

59 Alderman J. Hewitt, *Memoirs of the Celebrated Lady Viscountess Wilbrihammon* (n.d.), pp. i–ii.

60 *London Evening-Post*, 9 January 1766.

61 David Mountfield (1976), *The Coaching Age*, p. 55.

62 Woodforde's *Diary*, 20 May 1774.

63 Alderman J. Hewitt, *Memoirs of the Celebrated Lady Viscountess Wilbrihammon* (n.d.), pp. ii–vi and 7–8.

64 *General Evening Post*, 3 July 1766; *London Evening-Post*, 3 July 1766.

65 Alderman J. Hewitt, *Memoirs of the Celebrated Lady Viscountess Wilbrihammon* (n.d.), p. 18.

66 *London Evening-Post*, 30 October 1766; *Newcastle Chronicle*, 1 November 1766.

67 Alderman J. Hewitt, *Memoirs of the Celebrated Lady Viscountess Wilbrihammon* (n.d.), pp. 18–19.

68 *St James's Chronicle*, 17 October 1767.

69 C. Bruyn Andrews, ed. (1936), *The Torrington Diaries: Containing the Tours through England and Wales of the Hon. John Byng*, vol. 3, p. 119.

70 *St James's Chronicle*, 10 September 1767; *London Evening-Post*, 12 September 1767.

71 John Howard (1777), *The State of Prisons in England and Wales*, p. 364.

72 *Hampshire Chronicle*, 10 December 1787.

73 *St James's Chronicle*, 17 October 1767; *London Evening-Post*, 20 October 1767; *Salisbury Journal*, 26 October 1767.

74 Audrey Eccles (2012), *Vagrancy in Law and Practice under the Old Poor Law*, pp. 13–14.

75 *Salisbury Journal*, 12, 19 and 26 October 1767.

76 *Notes and Queries*, 5 July 1851 p. 8; 'Wilts Notes and Queries' in the *Wiltshire Archaeological and Natural History Magazine*, 1854, p. 213.

Chapter 2

1 London Metropolitan Archives (LMA), MJ/SR/3197.

2 LMA, WJ/CC/B/223/92.

3 Edward Walford (1878), 'The city of Westminster: Introduction', *Old and New London*, vol. 4, pp. 1–13.

4 William Smith MD (1776) *State of the Gaols in London, Westminster and of Southwark*, pp. 24–6.

5 Ibid., pp. 9–10.

6 Jacob Ilive (1757), *Reasons offered for the reformation of the House of Correction, Clerkenwell*, p. 22.

7 *Journals of the House of Commons*, vol. 37, p. 308.

8 John Howard (1777), *The State of Prisons in England and Wales*, p.193. Barrack beds were crude bunk beds, similar to industrial shelving.

9 Jonas Hanway (1772), *Observations on the Causes of the Dissoluteness which reigns among the lower Classes of People*, p. 22.

10 Old Bailey Proceedings, 14 July 1756, trial of Sarah Griffith, p. 239.

11 Ronald Paulson (1992) *Hogarth: The 'Modern Moral Subject'*, p. 246.

12 *Daily Journal*, 18 September 1730.

13 LMA, WJ/CC/B/223 and MJ/SP/1767/11.

14 LMA, WJ/CC/B/223, MJ/SP/1767/11 and 12, and MJ/SP/1769/01.

15 LMA, WJ/CC/B/223.

16 Jacob Ilive (1757), *Reasons offered for the reformation of the House of Correction, Clerkenwell,* pp. 22–3.

17 Proc. Old Bailey, 9 December 1767.

18 LMA, WJ/CC/B/223.

19 City of Westminster Coroner's Reports, 24 December 1767.

20 *Reports on the Laws which concern the Relief and Settlement of the Poor etc* (1776), pp. 289–92.

21 Proc. Old Bailey, 15 July 1767.

22 LMA, WJ/CC/B/223; Westminster workhouse records.

23 City of Westminster Coroner's Reports, 4 January 1768.

24 John Howard (1791), *An Account of the Principal Lazarettos in Europe, etc.,* p. 129.

25 LMA, WJ/CC/B/223.

26 Minute Books of the Court of Governors of Bridewell, 26 November 1766.

27 LMA, WJ/CC/B/223.

28 Proc. Old Bailey, 2 May 1764 and 15 July 1767.

29 *Lloyd's Evening Post,* 29 March 1765.

30 LMA, WJ/CC/B/223; Proc. Old Bailey, 15 July 1767.

31 Proc. Old Bailey, 9 December 1767.

32 LMA, WJ/CC/B/223; Proc. Old Bailey, 9 December 1767.

33 LMA, WJ/CC/B/223.

34 Ibid.

35 *Public Advertiser,* 7 February 1768; *St James's Chronicle,* 8 March 1768.

36 *Whitehall Evening Post,* 3 June 1769; Proc. Old Bailey, 28 June 1769.

37 *Lloyd's Evening Post,* 26 July 1769.

38 *Lloyd's Evening Post,* 28 July 1769.

39 Proc. Old Bailey, 13 April 1768.

40 LMA, WJ/CC/B/223; MJ/SR/3197.

41 Proc. Old Bailey, 14 January 1768.

42 LMA, WJ/CC/B/223; *Gazetteer,* 22 December 1767.

43 LMA, WJ/CC/B/223 and MJ/SR/3197.

44 LMA, WJ/CC/B/223.

45 *Public Advertiser,* 4 January 1768; *Salisbury Journal,* 11 January 1768.

46 LMA, WJ/CC/B/223.

47 Proc. Old Bailey, 24 February 1768.

48 Proc. Old Bailey, 19 October 1768 and 7 December 1768.

49 LMA, MJ/SR/3197.

50 Proc. Old Bailey, 7 December 1768.

51 *Maryland Gazette*, 21 July 1768.

52 LMA, MJ/SR/3197.

53 Proc. Old Bailey, 6 July 1763, 14 September 1763 and
    22 October 1766.

54 *Public Advertiser*, 11 January 1768; *St James's Chronicle*,
    12 January 1768.

55 John Howard (1777), *The State of Prisons in England and Wales*,
    pp. 170, 174, 185 and 193.

56 *Gazetteer*, 13 January 1764.

57 Arthur Griffiths (1884), *Chronicles of Newgate*, p. 457.

58 Arthur Griffiths (n.d.), *The History and Romance of Crime*, vol. 2,
    p. 26.

59 John Howard (1777), *The State of Prisons in England and Wales*,
    pp. 13 and 151–2.

60 Samuel Denne (1771), *A Letter to Sir Robert Ladbroke*, pp. 14 and 81.

61 Batty Langley (1724), *An Accurate Description of Newgate*,
    pp. 40–1.

62 Ibid., pp. 42–5.

63 *Public Advertiser*, 7 April 1768.

Chapter 3

1 A. Roger Ekirch (1987), *Bound for America: The Transportation
   of British Convicts to the Colonies, 1718–1775*, p. 27.

2 Articles of Agreement with John Stewart, National Archive,
   7 April 1763.

3 Kenneth Morgan, 'Convict Runaways in Maryland, 1745–1775',
   Journal of American Studies, August 1989, p. 253.

4 Alexander Cluny (1769), *The American Traveller*, pp. 83–4.

5 Willow Mary Meyer (2011), *Beyond the Seas: Eighteenth-Century
   Convict Transportation and the Widening Net of Penal Solutions*.

6 *Gentleman's Magazine*, June 1764.

7 *London Chronicle*, 6 April 1758.

8 James Boswell (1791), *The Life of Samuel Johnson*, entry for 11 April 1773.

9 Jonas Hanway (1766), *An Earnest Appeal*, pp. 135–6.

10 *General Evening Post*, 29 March 1755.

11 Peter Wilson Coldham (2002), *More Convicts in Bondage, 1614–1775*, p. 211.

12 *Stamford Mercury*, 3 April 1746.

13 George Ollyffe (1731), *An Essay humbly offer'd for an Act of Parliament to prevent Capital Crimes*, pp. 11–12.

14 *Pennsylvania Gazette*, 9 May 1751.

15 *London Chronicle*, 12 May 1759.

16 *Maryland Gazette*, 30 July 1767.

17 *Maryland Gazette*, 20 August 1767.

Chapter 4

1 George Barrington (1802), *An Account of a Voyage to New South Wales*, p. 74.

2 *Public Advertiser*, 5 April 1768.

3 *Public Advertiser*, 6 April 1768.

4 *Public Advertiser*, 27 January 1767.

5 John Heneage Jesse (ed.) (1882), *George Selwyn and his Contemporaries*, vol. 2, p. 389.

6 *Public Advertiser*, 7 April 1768.

7 There is a list of some of the convicts who were transported on the *Thornton* in April 1768 in Peter Wilson Coldham (1997), *The King's Passengers to Maryland and Virginia*, pp. 202–3.

8 LMA, MJ/SP/1768/02.

9 *St James's Chronicle*, 16 April 1768.

10 *Lloyd's Evening Post*, 18 April 1768.

11 Proc. Old Bailey, 24 February 1768.

12 *Maryland Gazette*, 21 July 1768.

13 Proc. Old Bailey, 24 February 1768.

14 Ibid.

15 Proc. Old Bailey, 14 January and 24 February 1768.

16 Proc. Old Bailey, 12 December 1764, 19 February 1766, 24 February 1768 and 30 May 1770; Ordinary of Newgate's Account, 4 June 1770.

17 Proc. Old Bailey, 24 February 1768.

18 *Maryland Gazette*, 21 July 1768.

19 Proc. Old Bailey, 24 February 1768.

20 *Maryland Gazette*, 20 July 1769.

21 *Ipswich Journal*, 12 March 1768.

22 *Oxford Journal*, 29 August 1767.

23 *Maryland Gazette*, 13 July 1769 and 8 August 1771.

24 Peter Wilson Coldham (2002), *More Convicts in Bondage, 1614–1775*, pp. 208 and 210.

25 *Journals of the House of Commons*, vol. 37, p. 311.

26 Sir Stephen Theodore Janssen (1767), *A Letter to the Right Honourable The Lord-Mayor, etc.*, p. 62.

27 *Virginia Gazette*, 21 April 1775.

28 *Gottlieb Mittelberger's Journey to Pennsylvania in the Year 1750* (1898), pp. 20–1.

29 It is estimated that over 30 per cent of the sailors on the *Bounty* had contracted venereal disease. It is likely that it was they who infected the Tahitian women with the pox.

30 *Virginia Gazette*, 26 May 1774.

31 Gwenda Morgan and Peter Rushton (2004), *Eighteenth-Century Criminal Transportation*, pp. 60–1.

32 Edith M. Ziegler (2014), *Harlots, Hussies and Poor Unfortunate Women*, p. 61.

33 Kenneth Morgan, 'The Organisation of the Convict Trade to Maryland', *William and Mary Quarterly*, April 1985, pp. 220–1.

34 Gail Collins (2004), *America's Women: 400 Years of Dolls, Drudges, Helpmates and Heroines*, pp. 7–8.

35 *Gottlieb Mittelberger's Journey*, p. 24.

36 *Leeds Intelligencer*, 3 May 1768; *Gentleman's Magazine*, May 1768.

37 *Maryland Gazette*, 30 June 1768.

38 Ibid.

Chapter 5

1 William Eddis (1792), *Letters from America*, p. 3.

2 Ibid., pp. 6–7.

3 Ibid., pp. 69–70.

4 *Maryland Gazette*, 30 June 1768.
5 James Revel (n.d.), *The Poor Unhappy Felon's Sorrowful Account*, p. 4.
6 Kenneth Morgan, 'The Organisation of the Convict Trade to Maryland', *William and Mary Quarterly*, April 1985, p. 219.
7 W. Green (n.d.), *The Sufferings of William Green, being a Sorrowful Account of His Seven Years Transportation*, p. 9.
8 Peter W. Coldham (2010), *Settlers of Maryland*, p. 204.
9 A. Roger Ekirch, 'Exiles in the Promised Land', *Maryland Historical Magazine*, Summer 1987, p. 101.
10 See, for example, *Boston Post-Boy*, 17 May 1773; *Philadelphia Chronicle*, 17 May 1773; *Pennsylvania Gazette*, 19 May 1773; *Massachusetts Spy*, 20 May 1773; *Connecticut Journal*, 21 May 1773; *New-Hampshire Gazette*, 28 May 1773; *Newport Mercury*, 31 May 1773.
11 See, for example, *London Evening-Post*, 22 June 1773, *London Chronicle*, 22 June 1773, *Shrewsbury Chronicle*, 26 June 1773; *Reading Mercury*, 28 June 1773; *London Magazine*, June 1773, p. 311; *Oxford Magazine*, June 1773, pp. 253–4; *Annual Register for the Year 1773*, pp. 113–14.
12 Alderman J. Hewitt, *Memoirs of the Celebrated Lady Viscountess Wilbrihammon* (n.d.), p. 19.
13 *Gazetteer*, 17 September 1768.
14 *Old Bailey Proceedings Online*, 10 April 1771.
15 Treasury Bond with Christopher Read, Mariner. Dated 22 June 1771; *Westminster Journal*, 20 July 1771.
16 LMA, WJ/CC/B/223/116.
17 *Mills and Hicks British and American Register for 1774*, p. 12.
18 *Maryland Gazette*, 28 May 1752.
19 *Maryland Gazette*, 14 September 1769.
20 *Maryland Gazette*, 4 May 1758.
21 *Maryland Gazette*, 6 October 1774.
22 *Maryland Gazette*, 21 January 1762.
23 *Maryland Gazette*, 22 November 1764.
24 *Pennsylvania Gazette*, 31 August 1749.
25 *Maryland Gazette*, 19 January 1764.
26 *Virginia Gazette*, 4 February 1773.
27 *Maryland Gazette*, 2 July 1747.

28 *Maryland Gazette*, 8 November 1764.

29 *Pennsylvania Gazette*, 3 March 1753.

30 *Maryland Gazette*, 22 October 1772.

31 *Virginia Gazette*, 5 August 1747.

32 *Pennsylvania Gazette*, 18 June 1767.

33 *Virginia Gazette*, 9 May 1745.

34 *Maryland Gazette*, 2 May 1754 and 16 January 1764.

35 *Maryland Gazette*, 28 May 1752.

36 *Maryland Gazette*, 4 May 1758.

37 *Pennsylvania Gazette*, 30 October 1740.

38 *Maryland Gazette*, 11 April 1771.

39 *Maryland Gazette*, 19 March 1767.

40 *Pennsylvania Gazette*, 29 June 1758.

41 Minute Books of the Court of Governors of Bridewell, 25 February 1762.

42 Proc. Old Bailey, 14 September 1763.

43 *Maryland Gazette*, 21 June 1764 and 21 July 1768.

44 Maryland laws, An Act relating to Servants and Slaves, 1715.

45 William W. Hening (1823), *Statutes of Virginia*, vol.2, pp. 116-7 and vol.3, pp. 456-8.

46 William Burke (1770), *An Account of the European Settlements in America*, vol. 2, p. 211.

47 R. Brookes (1773), *General Gazetteer*.

48 William Eddis (1792), *Letters from America*, pp. 98–102.

49 John F.D. Smyth (1784), *A Tour in the United States of America*, vol. 2, p. 256.

50 *The North-American and West-Indian Gazetteer*, 1776.

51 Curtis Carroll Davis, 'The Curious Colonel Langborn', *The Virginia Magazine of History and Biography*, October 1956, pp. 403–4.

52 Edward T. James and others (1971), *Notable American Women 1607–1950: A Biographical Dictionary*, vol. 3, p. 628.

53 *South Carolina Gazette*, 1 August 1772.

54 Mary Newton Stannard (1917), *Colonial Virginia, its People and its Customs*, pp. 64–5.

55 Charles M. Andrews (1919), *Colonial Folkways: A Chronicle of American Life in the Reign of the Georges*, p. 221.

56 *Gaine's Universal Register, or, American and British Kalendar for the year 1775*, p. 165.

57 *Journal kept by Hugh Finlay, Surveyor of the Post Roads in the Continent of North America* (1867), pp. 85–6.

58 F.X. Martin (1829), *History of North Carolina*, vol. 2, p. 292.

59 *The North-American and the West-Indies Gazetteer*, 1776, p. xxiii.

60 Joseph P. Brown (1960), *The Commonwealth of Onslow*, p. 356.

61 George Washington diary entry, 23 April 1791.

62 *Cape Fear Mercury*, 1 July 1772, reprinted in the *Pennsylvania Packet*, 17 August 1772; *Boston News-Letter*, 27 August 1772; *Connecticut Journal*, 4 September 1772, *New Hampshire Gazette*, 11 September 1772, among others.

63 *Cape Fear Mercury*, 29 July 1772, reprinted in the *South Carolina Gazette*, 27 August 1772.

64 *Cape Fear Mercury*, 1 July 1772.

65 Anonymous (1673), *The Memoires of Mary Carleton, commonly called the German Princess*; Francis Kirkman (1673), *The Counterfeit Lady Unveiled*; Alexander Smith (1719), *A Compleat History of the Lives and Robberies of the most Notorious Highway-Men, etc.*, pp. 236–57; Carleton, Mary, in *Oxford Dictionary of National Biography*.

66 Clinton V. Black (1970), *Port Royal: A History and Guide*, p. 22; David Cordingly (1999), *Life among the Pirates*, p. 169.

67 Report datelined 'Charleston, July 30' in *Virginia Gazette*, 3 September 1772.

68 *Journal kept by Hugh Finlay, Surveyor of the Post Roads in the Continent of North America* (1867), p. 67.

69 Ibid., p. 63.

70 Ibid., pp. 63–4 and 66.

71 *The Writings of George Washington* (1931), vol. 28, p. 116.

72 Archibald Henderson (1923), *Washington's Southern Tour 1791*, p. 149.

73 *Virginia Gazette*, 3 September 1772.

74 *South Carolina Gazette*, 15 February 1773.

75 Walter J. Fraser (1989), *Charleston! Charleston!*, p. 129.

76 *Journal kept by Hugh Finlay, Surveyor of the Post Roads in the Continent of North America* (1867), p. 62.

77 Repeated in Sarah Burton (2000), *Imposters: Six Kinds of Liar*, pp. 49–50.

Chapter 6

1 *Boston Post-Boy*, 6 September 1773, reprinted in *Maryland Journal*, 9 September 1773; *Connecticut Gazette*, 17 September 1773; and *Providence Gazette*, 18 September 1773, among others.

2 Edward G. Burrows and Mike Wallace (1998), *Gotham: A History of New York City to 1898*, p. 193.

3 *New-Hampshire Gazette*, 14 January 1774.

4 *Providence Gazette*, 11 December 1773.

5 *Journal kept by Hugh Finlay, Surveyor of the Post Roads in the Continent of North America* (1867), p. 29.

6 Advertisement in *Providence Gazette*, 21 January 1775.

7 *Boston Evening-Post*, 13 December 1773.

8 *Massachusetts Spy*, 4 November 1773.

9 *Boston Gazette*, 8 November 1773.

10 *Boston Gazette*, 29 November 1773.

11 Broadside, *Committee of Correspondence for Boston*, 1 December 1773.

12 *Boston Gazette*, 6 December 1773.

13 Edward L. Pierce, ed. (1895), *The Diary of John Rowe*, p. 81.

14 Supplement to the *Boston Gazette*, 27 December 1773.

15 www.bostonteapartyship.com.

16 Ray Raphael (2001), *The American Revolution: A People's History*, p. 18.

17 Supplement to the *Boston Gazette*, 27 December 1773.

18 *Boston Gazette*, 20 December 1773.

19 Alfred E. Young (2001), *The Shoemaker and the Tea Party*, p. 44.

20 Samuel K. Lothrop (1842), *The Good Man: A Sermon Preached at the Church in Brattle Square*, p. 26.

21 *New-Hampshire Gazette*, 14 January 1774.

22 *Connecticut Courant*, 25 February 1772.

23 Seymour Dunbar (1915), *A History of Travel in America*, p. 187.

24 Allan Forbes and Ralph M. Eastman (1954), *Taverns and Stagecoaches of New England*, p. 28.

25 Oliver Wendall Holmes (1983), *Stagecoach East*, p. 55.

26 *Essex Gazette*, 25 January 1774.

27 Frederick L. Wiley (1915), *Life and Influence of the Rev. Benjamin Randall*, pp. 26–8.

28 *Life, Journals and Correspondence of Rev. Manasseh Cutler LL.D*
  (1888), pp. 47–8.
29 Joseph B. Fell (1834), *History of Ipswich, Essex and Hamilton*,
  p. 31.
30 *Life, Journals and Correspondence of Rev. Manasseh Cutler LL.D*
  (1888), p. 48.
31 *Newport Mercury*, 17 July 1775.
32 *New-York Gazette*, 4 September 1775.
33 Lucius R. Paige (1877), *History of Cambridge, Massachusetts*,
  pp. 259, 269, 270 and 661.
34 Ibid., pp. 292–3.
35 Ibid., pp. 220 and 465.
36 *The Journals of each Provincial Congress of Massachusetts in
  1774 and 1775* (1838), pp. 505–13.
37 David H. Fischer (1994), *Paul Revere's Ride*, p. 141.
38 *Communication from the President of the American Antiquarian
  Society, October 24th 1814*, p. 25.
39 Jacqueline Barbara Carr (2005), *After the Siege: A Social History
  of Boston, 1775–1800*, p. 323.
40 James Henry Stark (1907), *The Loyalists of Massachusetts and the
  Other Side of the American Revolution*, p. 403.
41 William Carter (1784), *A General Detail of the several
  Engagements ... of the Royal and American Armies during the
  Years 1775 and 1776*, p. 8.
42 Jacqueline Barbara Carr (2005), *After the Siege: A Social History
  of Boston, 1775–1800*, p. 25.
43 Ibid., p. 27.
44 William Carter (1784), *A General Detail of the several
  Engagements ... of the Royal and American Armies during the
  Years 1775 and 1776*, p. 18.
45 Edward L. Pierce, ed. (1895), *The Diary of John Rowe*, pp. 95–7.
46 Abigail Adams to John Adams, 14 April 1776, *Founding Families*,
  National Archives (USA).
47 Gilder Lehrman Institute, Henry Knox Papers HKP 3-154.
48 John Adams to James Bowdoin, 29 April 1777, *Founding
  Families*, National Archives (USA).
49 Abigail Adams to John Adams, 5 August 1777, *Founding
  Families*, National Archives (USA).

50 Abigail Adams to John Adams, 8 March 1777, *Founding Families*, National Archives (USA).

51 Gilder Lehrman Institute, Letter from Lucy Flucker Knox to Henry Knox, May 1777.

52 Abigail Adams to John Adams, 20 April 1777, *Founding Families*, National Archives (USA).

53 Abigail Adams to John Adams, 20 April 1777, *Founding Families*, National Archives (USA); Barbara Clark Smith, 'Food rioters and the American Revolution', *William and Mary Quarterly*, January 1994, p. 21.

54 Jack Tager (2001), *Boston Riots: Three Centuries of Social Violence*, p. 27.

55 Billy G. Smith (2004), *Down and Out in Early America*, p. 15; Howard Zinn (1995), *A People's History of the United States*, p. 51.

56 Abigail Adams to John Adams, 31 July 1777, *Founding Families*, National Archives (USA).

57 Fitch E. Oliver, ed. (1890), *The Diary of William Pynchon*, p. 34.

58 *Independent Chronicle* (Boston), 18 September 1777.

59 William Price (1769), *A New Plan of ye Great Town of BOSTON*, text of cartouche.

60 *Historical Notices of the New North Religious Society in the Town of Boston*, 1822, pp. 20 and 27.

61 Samuel K. Lothrop (1842), *The Good Man: A Sermon Preached at the Church in Brattle Square*, pp. 26–7.

62 *The Manifesto Church. Records of the Church in Brattle Square Boston* (1902), p. 44.

63 Curtis Carroll Davis, 'The Curious Colonel Langborn', *Virginia Magazine of History and Biography*, October 1956, p. 406.

64 Alderman J. Hewitt, *Memoirs of the Celebrated Lady Viscountess Wilbrihammon* (n.d.), p. iii.

65 *London Evening-Post*, 11 August 1739 and 1 December 1759.

66 *London Evening-Post*, 11 August 1739; *Gazetteer*, 26 April 1762; *Ipswich Journal*, 5 March 1774.

67 *Berrow's Worcester Journal*, 16 July 1767.

68 *New-Hampshire Gazette*, 21 May 1773; *Boston Evening-Post*, 24 May 1773; *Essex Gazette*, 25 May 1773; *Connecticut Journal*, 28 May 1773.

69 Lawrence P. Hall (1988), *Tales of Effingham*, p. 150.

70 *Independent Chronicle* (Boston), 16 March 1780; *Providence Gazette*, 18 March 1780; *Connecticut Gazette*, 29 March 1780.

71 C.C. Lord (1912), *A History of the Descendants of Nathan Lord*, pp. 25, 42.

72 *Collections of the Dover, N.H., Historical Society* (1894), p. 174.

73 J.E. Frost (Compiler) (1981), *Dover Misc. & Rollinsford (Cemetery Records)*, p. A23.

74 *Independent Chronicle*, 30 March 1780; *Providence Gazette*, 1 April 1780; *Pennsylvania Journal*, 12 April 1780; *New-Hampshire Gazette*, 15 April 1780; *Pennsylvania Evening Post*, 28 April 1780.

Chapter 7

1 *London Evening-Post*, 20 October 1767.

2 Alderman J. Hewitt, *Memoirs of the Celebrated Lady Viscountess Wilbrihammon* (n.d.), p. 19.

3 LMA, MJ/SR/3197.

4 Jennifer Lodine-Caffney (2006), *From Newgate to the New World: A Study of London's Transported Female Convicts 1718–1775*, p. 84.

5 *General Evening Post*, 3 July 1766; *London Evening-Post*, 30 October 1766; *London Evening-Post*, 12 September 1767.

6 Alderman J. Hewitt, *Memoirs of the Celebrated Lady Viscountess Wilbrihammon* (n.d.), p. iv.

7 *London Chronicle*, 10 January 1765; *St James's Chronicle*, 10 January 1765.

8 R.S. Schofield, 'Dimensions of Illiteracy, 1750-1850', *Explorations in Economic History*, 10(4), 1973, p. 444.

9 Victor E. Neuburg, 'Literacy in Eighteenth Century England: A Caveat', *Local Population Studies Magazine*, Spring 1970, p. 44.

10 Kevin Williams (2010), *Read all about it*, p. 79.

11 John Brewer (1997), *The Pleasures of the Imagination*, pp.167–8.

12 John Entick (1755), *A New and Accurate History and Survey of London, Westminster and Southwark*, vol. 4.

13 M.G. Jones (1938), *The Charity School Movement*, p. 74.

14 *Sermon preached by the Bishop of Norwich at the Anniversary Meeting of the Charity Schools in and about London and Westminster*, 1 May 1755.

15 Francis Kirkman (1673), *The Counterfeit Lady Unveiled*, pp. 10–12.
16 *Pennsylvania Gazette*, 5 April 1770.
17 See, for example, *Boston Post-Boy*, 11 June 1770; *New Hampshire Gazette*, 27 April 1772; *Massachusetts Spy*, 20 August 1772.
18 See, for example, *Pennsylvania Packet*, 13 April 1772; *New-York Journal*, 30 April 1772, *Boston Evening-Post*, 1 June 1772; *Connecticut Gazette*, 17 July 1772; *Virginia Gazette*, 5 November 1772.
19 Westminster Land Tax Book, St Anne's Soho, 1763.
20 Scott, George Lewis, in *Oxford Dictionary of National Biography*.
21 *Salisbury Journal*, 2 November 1767.
22 A.R. Ellis, ed. (1889), *The Early Diary of Fanny Burney*, vol. 1, p. 155.
23 Alderman J. Hewitt, *Memoirs of the Celebrated Lady Viscountess Wilbrihammon* (n.d.), p. i.

Appendix 4

1 John Watkins (1819), *Memoirs of Her Majesty Sophia Charlotte Queen of Great Britain*, pp. 223–4.
2 'Sholto and Reuben Percy' (1820), *The Percy Anecdotes*, vol. 4, p. 86.
3 F.X. Martin (1829), *History of North Carolina*, vol. 2, p. 292.
4 *New-York Mirror*, 7 January 1837.
5 William Dunlap (1837), *A History of New York for Schools*, vol. 1, pp. 78–88.
6 Steven C. Bullock, 'A Mumper among the Gentle', *William and Mary Quarterly*, April 1998, p. 233.
7 Brooks E. Kleber, 'Notorious Tom Bell', *The Pennsylvania Magazine of History and Biography*, October 1951, pp. 416–23; Bell, Thomas, in *Oxford Dictionary of National Biography*.
8 Benjamin Martin (1749), *A New English Dictionary*.
9 Alderman J. Hewitt, *Memoirs of the Celebrated Lady Viscountess Wilbrihammon* (n.d.), intro. 'To the Reader'.
10 Dr John Doran (1855), *Lives of the Queens of England of the House of Hanover*, vol. 2, p. 71.
11 Alice Morse Earle (1895), *Colonial Dames and Good Wives*, pp. 165–72.
12 Gerald Sparrow (1962), *The Great Imposters*, pp. 79–86; Egon Larsen (1966), *The Deceivers: Lives of the Great Imposters*,

pp. 52–7; Sarah Burton (2000), *Imposters: Six Kinds of Liar*, pp. 49–51; William Donaldson (2002), *Brewer's Rogues, Villains, Eccentrics*, p. 650.

13 www.qrlnymuseum.co.uk.

14 *London Gazette Extraordinary*, 30 December 1776.

15 *London Gazette*, 3 October 1778; *Kentish Gazette*, 7 October 1778.

16 Patrick O'Kelley (2004), *Nothing but Blood and Slaughter: The War in the Carolinas*, vol. 2, pp. 35–56; *Historical Record of the Seventeenth Regiment of Light Dragoons* (1841), p. 30.

17 *Historical Record* (1841), p. 37.

18 www.registers.trinitywallstreet.org.

19 Maria Jane McIntosh, 'The Richmond Hebe', *The Ladies' National Magazine* (Philadelphia), December 1845, pp. 184–92.

SELECT BIBLIOGRAPHY

Primary Sources

Brookes, Richard, *General Gazetteer*, 1773.

Burke, William, *An Account of the European Settlements in America*, 1770.

Charke, Charlotte, *A Narrative of the Life of Charlotte Charke*, 1755.

Cluny, Alexander, *The American Traveller*, 1769.

Cutler, William Parker and Cutler, Julia Perkins (eds), *Life, Journals and Correspondence of Rev. Manasseh Cutler LL.D*, 1888.

Eddis, William, *Letters from America*, 1792.

Finlay, Hugh, *Journal kept by Hugh Finlay, Surveyor of the Post Roads in the Continent of North America*, 1867.

Gaine's Universal Register, or, American and British Kalendar for the year 1775.

Green, William, *The Sufferings of William Green, being a Sorrowful Account of His Seven Years Transportation*, n.d. (*c*. 1774).

Hanway, Jonas, *Observations on the Causes of the Dissoluteness which reigns among the lower Classes of People*, 1772.

Hewitt, Alderman J., *Memoirs of the Celebrated Lady Viscountess Wilbrihammon, alias Mollineux, alias Irving, Countess of Normandy, and Baroness Wilmington, the greatest Impostress of the present Age*, n.d. (possibly 1778).

Howard, John, *The State of Prisons in England and Wales*, 1777.

Howard, John, *An Account of the Principal Lazarettos in Europe, etc.*, 1791.

Ilive, Jacob, *Reasons offered for the reformation of the House of Correction, Clerkenwell*, 1757.

Journals of each Provincial Congress of Massachusetts in 1774 and 1775, 1838.

Langley, Batty, *An Accurate Description of Newgate*, 1724.

Mills and Hicks British and American Register for 1774.

Mittelberger, Gottlieb, *Journey to Pennsylvania in the Year 1750*, 1756, trans. 1898.

North-American and West-Indian Gazetteer, 1776.

Ollyffe, George, *An Essay humbly offer'd for an Act of Parliament to prevent Capital Crimes*, 1731.

Revel, James, *The Poor Unhappy Felon's Sorrowful Account*, n.d. (*c.* 1780).

Smith, William, *The State of the Gaols in London, Westminster and Borough of Southwark*, 1776.

Smyth, John F.D., *A Tour in the United States of America*, 1784.

Young, Arthur, *A Six Months Tour through the North of England*, 1770.

Newspapers and Journals

English

Annual Register

Gazetteer

General Evening Post

Gentleman's Magazine

Ipswich Journal

Lloyd's Evening Post

London Chronicle

London Evening-Post

London Magazine

Newcastle Chronicle

Oxford Magazine

Public Advertiser

Reading Mercury

St James's Chronicle

Salisbury Journal

Shrewsbury Chronicle

Stamford Mercury

Select Bibliography

American

Boston Evening-Post
Boston Gazette
Boston News-Letter
Boston Post-Boy
Cape Fear Mercury
Connecticut Courant
Connecticut Gazette
Connecticut Journal
Essex Gazette
Independent Chronicle (Boston)
Maryland Gazette
Maryland Journal
Massachusetts Spy

New-Hampshire Gazette
Newport Mercury
New-York Gazette
Pennsylvania Evening Post
Pennsylvania Gazette
Pennsylvania Journal
Pennsylvania Packet
Philadelphia Chronicle
Providence Gazette
Rivington's New York Gazetteer
South Carolina Gazette
Virginia Gazette

Secondary sources

Andrews, Charles M., *Colonial Folkways: A Chronicle of American Life in the Reign of the Georges*, New Haven CT, 1919.

Beattie, J.M., 'Sir John Fielding and Public Justice: The Bow Street Magistrates' Court, 1754-1780', *Law and History Review*, Spring 2007.

Burton, Sarah, *Imposters: Six Kinds of Liar*, London, 2000.

Carr, Jacqueline Barbara, *After the Siege: A Social History of Boston, 1775–1800*, Boston, 2005.

Coldham, Peter Wilson, *The King's Passengers to Maryland and Virginia*, Westminster MD, 1997.

Coldham, Peter Wilson, *More Convicts in Bondage, 1614–1775*, Baltimore, 2002.

Coldham, Peter Wilson, *Settlers of Maryland*, Baltimore, 2010.

Collins, Gail, *America's Women: 400 Years of Dolls, Drudges, Helpmates and Heroines*, New York, 2004.

Donaldson, William, *Brewer's Rogues, Villains, Eccentrics*, London, 2002.

Doran, Dr John, *Lives of the Queens of England of the House of Hanover*, vol. 2, Boston, 1855.

Dunlap, William, *A History of New York for Schools*, New York, 1837.

Earle, Alice Morse, *Colonial Dames and Good Wives*, Boston, 1895.

Ekirch, A. Roger, *Bound for America: The Transportation of British Convicts to the Colonies, 1718–1775*, Oxford, 1987.

Ekirch, A. Roger, 'Exiles in the Promised Land', *Maryland Historical Magazine*, Summer 1987.

Fischer, David H., *Paul Revere's Ride*, New York, 1994.

Forbes, Allan and Eastman, Ralph M., *Taverns and Stagecoaches of New England*, Boston, 1954.

James, Edward T. and others, *Notable American Women 1607–1950: A Biographical Dictionary*, vol. 3, Cambridge MA, 1971.

Larsen, Egon, *The Deceivers: Lives of the Great Imposters*, New York, 1966.

Lodine-Caffney, Jennifer, *From Newgate to the New World: A Study of London's Transported Female Convicts 1718–1775*, Missoula MT, 2006.

Martin, Francois-Xavier, *History of North Carolina*, vol. 2, New Orleans, 1829.

Meyer, Willow Mary, *Beyond the Seas: Eighteenth-Century Convict Transportation and the Widening Net of Penal Solutions*, UC Berkeley Electronic Theses and Dissertations, 2011.

Morgan, Gwenda and Rushton, Peter, *Eighteenth-Century Criminal Transportation*, Basingstoke, 2004.

Morgan, Gwenda and Rushton, Peter, 'Fraud and Freedom: Gender, Identity and Narratives of Deception among the Female Convicts in Colonial America', *Journal for Eighteenth-Century Studies*, September 2011.

Morgan, Kenneth, 'The Organisation of the Convict Trade to Maryland', *William and Mary Quarterly*, April 1985.

Morgan, Kenneth, 'English and American Attitudes Towards Convict Transportation, 1718-1775', *History*, October 1987.

Morgan, Kenneth, 'Convict Runaways in Maryland, 1745–1775', *Journal of American Studies*, August 1989.

Oxford Dictionary of National Biography, Oxford, 2004.

Paige, Lucius R., *History of Cambridge, Massachusetts*, Boston, 1877.

Percy, Sholto and Percy, Reuben (John Byerley and Joseph Clinton Robertson), *The Percy Anecdotes*, vol. 4, London, 1820.

Raphael, Ray, *The American Revolution: A People's History*, London, 2001.

Sparrow, Gerald, *The Great Imposters*, London, 1962.

Stannard, Mary Newton, *Colonial Virginia, its People and its Customs*, Philadelphia, 1917.

Vaver, Anthony, *Bound With an Iron Chain*, Westborough MA, 2011.

Watkins, John, *Memoirs of Her Most Excellent Majesty Sophia Charlotte Queen of Great Britain*, London, 1819.

White, Jerry, *London in the Eighteenth Century*, London, 2012.

Ziegler, Edith, 'The Transported Convict Women of Colonial Maryland, 1718–1776', *Maryland Historical Magazine*, Spring 2002.

Ziegler, Edith M., *Harlots, Hussies and Poor Unfortunate Women*, Tuscaloosa AL, 2014.

INDEX

You may also enjoy …

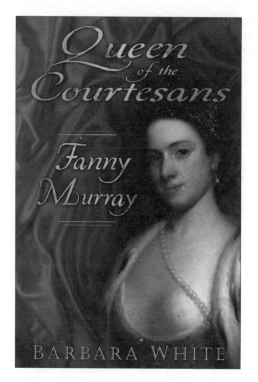

978 0 7524 6869 3

Queen of the Courtesans takes readers from the brothels of Covent Garden to sex romps at Medmenham Abbey to marital respectability in Edinburgh. Fanny Murray's triumph against almost insuperable odds is a remarkable story, as rich in the telling as it is enthralling.